BLOOD MATCH

BLOOD MATCH

The Divine Vampire Heirs, Book One

by

GINNA MORAN

Sunny Palms Press

ISBN 978-1-942073-21-5 (soft cover)

Cover design by Silver Starlight Designs
Cover images copyright Depositphotos

For Inquiries Contact:
Sunny Palms Press
9663 Santa Monica Blvd Suite 1158
Beverly Hills, CA 90210, USA
www.sunnypalmspress.com
www.GinnaMoran.com

For Malory and your beautiful, gothic, passionate soul.

1

Donor Life

"DON'T DO IT, JEWEL. YOU'LL never make it home by curfew." Ramona blocks our front door, crossing her arms like she could possibly stop me from exiting the apartment.

For one, she's a foot shorter than me, waif-thin, and wobbling on her feet from hunger. And two, if she doesn't let me go, we'll die—not just me and her, but our little cousins Dana and Fallon, too. I know it. She knows it. And today at five o' clock was the only time the Blood Match Center had available for me to come in for the month.

If I wait for the next opportunity to see if Dad returns, we risk Donor Life Corp realizing our situation, and they'll kick us out of our apartment. Without shelter, we won't last a week on Starlight Row and less if we venture outside the wrought iron gates of Dark Terrace Ranch, if they'd even allow us to leave.

It takes two people donating blood to barely maintain our living arrangements, not counting food and bare necessities, and without Dad, I'm alone. Ramona is a year too young to be a donor and Dana and Fallon four years away from their chance as well.

I can't care for my little sister and cousins on my own. Dad couldn't even without my help. We're hungry more often than not, and if it wasn't for Brayla, my best friend, sneaking me what she could from her own sparse pantry, I don't think I'd even be standing.

"I'll be fine, okay?" I say, dangling my silver bracelet out to her. "This protects me, and you know it. I've been out past curfew four times since my birthday and survived."

Ramona shifts on her feet, her glare turning into worry. "You only have so much good luck."

"It's really not so bad." My quivering voice gives away my lie. Because not only is it bad, it's damn scary. Terrifying. Once the sun goes down, the shadows created by daylight disappear, and the shadow vampires can walk freely in the streets, their favorite thing being curfew breakers. Even my donor bracelet barely kept Chomper Jonas away the last time I missed curfew. If it wasn't for Brayla and her preparedness of carrying blood in a thermos, I'm sure I'd have lost a chunk of my shoulder—because Jonas doesn't use his incisors to puncture. He rips and spits. I saw the damage he did to Brayla's cousin Connor at his final donation before they incinerated his remains.

Ramona huffs a breath. "Then why are you shaking? Come on, Jewel. Please stay. We'll manage."

I never knew how awful it was until my eighteenth birthday a few months ago. Before then, I didn't have the need to race home before curfew, because I'd already be home well before dark. And now it seems I get late appointments once a month. I think Donor Life Corp schedules appointments close to sunset to give the shadow dwellers something fun to do, so they don't try to rebel.

I shudder at the memory of Chomper Jonas and Connor, suppressing the sudden fear the best I can—fear I want to protect my sister and cousins from as long as possible. Unlike me, they never have to risk leaving the apartment after dark, and if everything works out at the Blood Match Center, they won't ever have to experience the fears I now battle daily with Dad gone.

The perk of signing up for a Blood Match is that the donor's family gets permanent residency in Haven Springs, the human-only community across the river. As for me? I have no idea. It all depends on the vampire I match with. The best I can hope for is not to land in the home of someone like Chomper Jonas—and if I do, I pray it all ends fast. No matter what, my sisters and cousins will never have to worry about surviving. They'll get to live well and make something of themselves without having to donate blood to survive.

"Dad's going to kill you himself if you do survive," Ramona quips when I don't respond to her and pull my bag on my shoulder. "He told us that it could take him two weeks or more since his night pass expired. He's going to freak out. You know he doesn't want you to do this. If he did, he'd have asked you the second you turned eighteen."

"I'm sorry, Ramona." I straighten my shoulders, keeping my face expressionless.

I kept telling myself the same thing about Dad until two weeks turned to three, and now a whole month has gone by, and our donations are due again at the end of the week since dad missed the last.

Dad and I knew the risk he'd have to take to travel to Moon Crest for a transfer out of The Boxes, the nickname of our tower of apartments, and to The Orchards, where we could have a small patch of land to grow our own food. But he was still willing to take it. Ramona is right. Dad didn't want me anywhere near a vampire's lair. He left to try his best to prevent me from signing up to be matched with a vampire, but now I wish I'd have gone behind his back like I had planned. He'd still be here to take care of our family. Now, we'll both be gone, but at least Ramona and my cousins will have a good life in my absence.

I wish it were different, but I don't know what else to do.

Ever since Mom and Aunt Dottie died last year from a flu virus that killed almost half the people in our small community, things have gotten tough. Donor Life Corp required more from the donors without the extra incentive. Without Mom and Aunt Dottie, Dad had to provide for us four girls and himself, which is impossible. A one-to-one ratio of donors and non-donors is the norm for a somewhat comfortable living. Two-to-one like Aunt Dottie and my cousins was pushing it, but four-to-one? If I hadn't turned eighteen when I had, who knows what would have happened to us. At least now, I still have a chance to take care of my family.

"Jewel."

Reaching out, I pull my sister into a hug, spinning her as I do so. Tears burst from her eyes, and she tries to lock me in place, but I shove her back. She stumbles, releasing a small cry. I hate that I had to resort to pushing her, but I know she won't let me leave otherwise. "Ramona, I really am sorry. I'll make it up to you. But you have to know that I'm not willing to put your lives at risk based on hope. I'm going to be fine. The pamphlet said if I get matched, I'll even get to visit you all. Now, please, go pick up Dana and Fallon from Mrs. Peppers and make sure you save me some dinner, okay?"

"Jewel, wait!" she screams, scrambling from the floor. If Ramona hadn't made such a big deal about going to the neighbors, I'd have sent her there too. I should've forced her. Her being here makes me doubt a decision I have to make. I can't back out now. She depends on me no matter how hard this is on the both of us.

I rush from the apartment, slamming the door to give me the chance to make it to the stairwell. Ramona cracks open the heavy door to the stairs but doesn't follow me inside. She knows there's no stopping me now, and if I'm late to my appointment, I'll have to risk sundown for nothing. Once a time is agreed upon, you can't change it. I only have this one opportunity to match as only serious applicants are accepted.

"I love you, Ramona-Babona," I say, blowing her a kiss.

She stifles a sob, blowing a kiss back to me. "Love you, Jewel-Babewel. Good luck, okay? You better match with someone decent."

"A girl can hope."

Flying down the stairs two at a time, I reach the lobby of our apartment tower and wave to the heavily armed security guard who never says a word to me, though he's been guarding the front entrance of our tower for the last three years. He nods his head in acknowledgment but turns his attention to the video screen recording the sidewalk with a clear view of the sun lowering in the sky. I hope the matching process doesn't take too long. Once twilight disappears, it'll be a real nightmare getting home. I hope Brayla remembers to meet me there so we can walk home together.

I smack my hand on the digital palm print pad by the door and wait for it to light up green. The door unlocks for me, and I push it open and close it straight away, giving it a shake to make sure the lock slides back in place. No need to give Security Steve, the nickname I gave the guard because I don't know his real name, any extra work.

Silence greets me on Starlight Row, the street nearly abandoned this late in the day. Old broken down cars rust along the roads as a historic reminder of a time before I was born, when humans could go anywhere they wanted. That was before the Blood Hunger Plague unleashed vampires on the world. Conspiracy theorists like my dad think that the plague was released to reduce the population size the way nature supposedly intended by natural selection and to re-order the food chain. Now, personal vehicles are off limits to humans. Not that anywhere in Dark Terrace Ranch is far to travel to. We have a few buses, but the buses only go outside the city, which I've never been. As the daughter of a maintenance man, who was supposed to follow part-time in my dad's footsteps before he disappeared, I never had a reason to leave. And now I never will.

Rushing along the empty road, I pass a broken statue with a missing placard that's been here as long as I can remember. The man once had a head according to the picture my dad keeps of my grandparents in front of it from before the plague.

No one knows the real origin of the Blood Hunger Plague, but whatever caused it ravaged the continent and started a new world order, led by Donor Life Corp, which set The Divide in place and separated the cities to stop a war that would have left humans locked away as a food supply. It also created the Blood Match Program, open to people between the ages of eighteen and twenty-two to match with a vampire to be an exclusive permanent resident in their lair—home. *Watch your thoughts, Jewel. You can't call it a lair.*

Growls sound from between two tall buildings that remain

shaded all day. I keep my eyes trained on the broken concrete to not look over at the shadow dwellers. They never leave the safety of the shade, but it doesn't make me feel any better, not with how fast the sun sinks into the horizon.

Cool air picks up the sweaty hair from my neck, yanking it hard enough to surprise me. I spin around, my heart racing, but the streets are empty this time of day. A loud gong rings through the air, signaling that I have twenty minutes to get to the Blood Match Center ten minutes away. I suppress the fear of being watched, because I'm sure dozens of vampires do, and hug my arms to my chest.

I pick up my pace, bolting from a speed walk to full on sprinting, and cut across the street to take the shortcut between another tower complex and what will officially be my old high school with the crumbling brick façade and broken windows I can't remember ever having glass.

It amazes me that it's still in operation, considering the staff is purely made of volunteers since Donor Life Corp provides the skills people need to be a contributing member of society through trade work and apprenticeships. I only attended because my parents always said that there's more to life than what your vein can bring you. Unfortunately, I won't ever truly know what that means. I hope Ramona will, and she can tell me.

"Jewel! Hurry your damn ass up!" Brayla yells, waving from the top step of the Blood Match Center. "You were supposed to meet me here ten minutes ago."

I glance up at the tower, the long hand sliding toward five. What the hell? It did not take me twenty minutes to get here. It should've taken less than ten at my pace. Pushing the confusion away, I race toward Brayla.

Sweat pours down my face, sticking my dark tresses to my cheeks. The gong of the clock tower rings again, counting down faster than I can run. I push myself to sprint hard, my heart pounding in my ears. I'm not going to make it. I'm going to ruin everything. I knew I should've snuck out of the apartment when Ramona was in the bathroom, but I was afraid I wouldn't get the chance to tell her goodbye just in case something happens on my way home. And now, I might not have had to say goodbye after all, because if I don't make it...

"I'm here!" I shout, rushing through the open door Brayla holds for me. "Jewel Jordan. My appointment is...right now."

The woman behind a long counter jerks her gaze from me to the clock on the wall. "You were supposed to check in five minutes ago."

My eyes widen. "What? My appointment notification said five. It's five. I'm not late."

"And the check-in time said four fifty-five. I'm sorry, Ms. Jordan, but those are the rules. If you'd like to petition for a re-evaluation, you can do so in thirty days, but I wouldn't count on it. There are currently only ten available matches. We take our program seriously and need only those truly committed." The woman turns her attention behind me. "Make that nine matches now."

What the hell? I should've been here already. I left The Boxes with time to spare, and I've always been early. But I'm still on time. I'm not late. Something's wrong.

I open my mouth to tell the woman so, but the giant screen on the wall lights up with the name Ricardo Suarez. A shadow casts over the shiny counter next to me, and I shift on my feet to meet the wide gaze of a cute boy with dark hair and eyes, a clean-shaven face, and smelling of something sweet. Maybe fruit. It's been a few years since I've had some, but I think it might be that.

"Congratulations, Mr. Suarez. You're an eighty-one percent match to Carolina Charleston of the Charleston Manor." Eighty-one percent is something to cheer about, considering they don't pair eighty and below, and this dude just got extremely lucky. The woman turns to me. "Please excuse us, Ms. Jordan. Like I said, if you want to petition, you can file the paperwork in thirty days."

"But I don't have thirty days," I argue. "And I was on time."

"You were not."

A cool hand grabs my shoulder, and I swing my arm back to elbow whoever dares try to stop me from groveling to keep my appointment. A young guy in a suit catches my elbow, tilting his head down to look at me with eyes as dark as a midnight sky.

My whole body tenses under his death grip, my heart crashing into my ribcage, threatening to spill out on the floor.

His eyes dart to my throat and then to my mouth before focusing on my aqua eyes. I open and close my mouth to form words, but fear steals my voice. I've never been this close to a vampire before—never been touched by one either—and here I am, trying to argue my case to get matched to one while my whole body and soul realizes that maybe it was good luck that I missed my check-in time. Because holy shit balls, this guy is just as intimidating, if not scarier, than Chomper Jonas, who only managed to get close enough to get blood thrown in his face.

"Jewel's really sorry," Brayla says, stepping in close to draw the young-looking vampire's attention to her and away from me. Tucking her blond hair behind her ear, she forces her mouth to smile. "She was looking forward to this amazing opportunity."

The vampire loosens his hold on my elbow, and I nod my head, practically jerking my whole body with the action. "I didn't mean to miss my check-in. I swear I left on time from my apartment, but I guess the shortcut I took was the long way. I swear my appointment was at five. I have the card—" I feel my pockets, realizing I forgot it in my jacket I left on the hook by the door. "At home. I can retrieve it." Man, that was a lot of word vomit. My knees shake for good measure, offering to drop to the ground to grovel at his feet.

The vampire doesn't say anything as he studies me, glancing from my sweating, warm face and to the rest of my body, drinking me in inch-by-inch like he can envision the blood still racing through my veins from my fear. Flicking his hand out faster than I can react, he grabs hold of my chin and closes the space between us to sniff the skin right below my ear.

I shiver, trying not to squirm at his closeness. Squeezing my eyes shut, I brace myself for him to tear into my neck to teach me what happens to humans who cause a scene in the lobby of the Blood Match Center.

"You're undernourished," he whispers into my ear, slowly pulling back. "But that can be fixed."

I blink, unsure of what to say.

"You'll need a good cleaning as well."

I crinkle my nose, about to open my mouth to tell him that he should try living on water restrictions that barely provide enough to drink, but he releases me, and I nearly spill to the floor as my knees do actually give out on me. If he didn't catch me, I'm sure I would've bruised my ass on the shiny tiles.

Snapping my eyes open, I meet his dark gaze. He rights me on my feet and smiles, revealing his sharp incisors in the process. If Brayla wasn't standing behind him with fear distorting her usual soft features, I might have smiled back. Because without the scowl, he looks normal...ish. Attractive. Like he should be wearing jeans and a T-shirt and not a suit with his unkempt hair that looks like he rolled out of bed.

Instead of giving into my urge to smile, I swallow and whisper, "Thank you. If you'll excuse me, I need to be going to make it home by curfew. I'll be sure to fill out the petition form in thirty days like I was told."

The vampire tilts his head to the side, giving me yet another once over like he's trying to decide if I get to leave or not. His gaze travels from my lips to my boobs, trailing down each button of my shirt and to my jeans and back up again. *Shit, he looks hungry.*

I puff air through my lips, frowning under his intense scrutiny that makes me double check to make sure I'm not naked. Lifting my donor bracelet, I dangle it in his face. "You have to let me leave, you know. If I can't apply for a match, then I need to get home. I have people counting on me."

"Jewel," Brayla hisses at me.

I flick my gaze to hers, breaking the guy's stare, annoyance rushing through me in the process. "What? They told me I can't do that damn application because I was late when I was *on time*, and now this guy's gonna make our journey home a friggin' race for our lives all because he looks like he wants me to get naked for him. So don't *Jewel* me. Ramona needs me, so do my cousins. You know how import—"

A cold hand slaps over my mouth, startling me. I never saw the vampire move, and now he holds me from behind, his icy fingers over my lips, and his other arm slung around my stomach to keep me in place. Brayla screams out and rushes forward, but she suddenly stops in her tracks, the color draining from her face.

The vampire hums against my throat, sniffing my neck again. "You don't have to wait thirty days, Ms.—"

"Just call me Jewel," I mumble into his hand until he shifts it.

"Jewel. I'll allow you to complete your application this evening."

I clear my throat, trying to keep my voice steady. "You will? Why?"

He hums again, his agreement vibrating on my skin. "Your first application intrigued a number of my clients, and I think I know what happened on your way here."

"What do you mean?"

"It's nothing to concern yourself over." He softly touches my cheek, his smooth voice doing all sorts of things to my insides. He's definitely not the average shadow dweller. "What matters is you're here."

"So I can try to match?"

"Under one condition."

I bob my head, jerking it up and down. I'm at the point that I'd agree to anything he asks if it gives me the chance to try to match. My family will die otherwise. I know it. I've seen it myself when the Smiths downstairs lost their mom and were kicked out. "Okay."

The vampire releases a small laugh. "You don't want to know what the condition is?"

I swallow and shrug. "I'm desperate. I'll do whatever. I don't care." I regret my admission immediately. I need to learn to keep my mouth shut.

The vampire turns me in his arms to meet his black eyes, his whole face lighting up at my words. I should be more scared, but his mouth curls up into a smile that makes me both nervous and excited. Because he's going to ignore protocol so I can save my family. And whatever he wants can't be worse than the fate I already face. Hell, I'd probably allow myself to be matched with Chomper Jonas if it meant Ramona, Dana, and Fallon get out of this cage of a city.

The vampire leans forward, trailing his lips above my jawline without touching me to stop at my earlobe, making me shiver. "If you don't match with someone, you'll have a blood debt to work off with me that'll pass to your family, whom after looking over your information, I saw will all be coming into age soon enough." Of course he looked me up in the database. I can't help wondering if he set me up. I know my appointment said five. I wouldn't have forgotten a check-in time.

But I know I can't do anything about it now.

"A blood debt?" I ask. "Are you serious? I already get practically nothing as it is, and you expect me to pass it on to my sister?"

"I wouldn't ravish you unless you wanted me to. I kind of pride myself on morals. I might make you quite happy, so there's that, too."

I blanch.

"There's always the petition," he adds. "Which will certainly be denied."

Brayla gasps. "Jewel, don't do it. We'll figure this out. I have my appointment in a week. I'll see if I can include you all as my heirs—"

"Your appointment will be canceled, Miss," the vampire

says, twisting to look behind him at Brayla.

"What?" we both say in unison.

"You can't do that," Brayla argues.

The vampire releases me, spinning to grab Brayla in the time it takes me to blink. He lifts her off her feet, sending panic through my heart. Her saucer brown eyes meet mine, and she mouths for me to run.

But I can't. My body won't move.

"Okay, asshole. I accept your damn condition." The words come so quietly from my mouth that I'm not even sure I said them, but the vampire releases Brayla, letting her fall to her knees, proving that I must have managed to get my voice to work.

The vampire smiles at me. His fangs extend longer than I thought possible, and he brings my finger to his mouth, poking me with his incisor before sucking on the tip of my finger. My stomach churns at the sight, making me woozy. All he does is smile wider. This is far worse than getting pricked with a needle at the donation center.

"Mmm," he says, pulling my hand away from his mouth to put pressure on the pinprick hole to staunch any more blood from dripping. "I think I'll apply to match with you to enhance my odds. I wasn't planning to do so for another year, but I think I'd love to guarantee that we end up together."

Oh, shit balls. This can't be happening. I knew that it would be bad, but it's worse. This vampire might be my future and the death of me, and there's no certainty that I'll get to help my family.

“Ms. Sybil, please prepare a testing room for Jewel Jordan,” the vampire says to the lady at the counter, still going over paperwork with the boy, who has clearly paid close attention to everything that went down behind him. He gives me a weak smile, and all I do is glare at the shiny floor.

“I’m gonna wait right here for you, Jewel,” Brayla calls from behind me as the vampire tugs me along by my hand, my feet in robot-mode to stay at his brisk pace. “Good luck!”

“There’s no luck in Blood Matching,” the vampire says to me, waving me ahead of him to enter the room where the lady from the counter stands with the door open.

“Says you,” I mutter. Because I’m not only going to need good luck, I’m going to need a miracle.

Chuckling, the vampire nudges me into the room. “I look forward to the results, Jewel. You’re going to be a lot of fun to be around.”

2

Rule Breaker, Hungry Eyes, and Smiles

THE TESTING ROOM CONSISTS OF a single computer stationed against the wall so whoever is in the room can watch as I answer each question. And there are a ton—five hundred and twenty-three mandatory, twenty bonus ones, and a box for a personal statement. Along with the test, I have to have a physical—which I'm dreading—and give a blood sample, which is just whatever. I thought this whole process was supposed to be me giving a drop of blood to run through a computer, but the matching process apparently wants to make sure we're compatible on all sorts of freaky ass levels, like I'm not only signing up to be a food source in a vampire lair but something more.

"Dude, you should update your pamphlets to mention all this crap," I say, swiveling in my chair to face the vampire, who leans against the wall with his arms crossed.

"*Dude*? Really? You have quite the exquisite vocabulary, Jewel," he says, raising his brows. He hasn't moved an inch from his place since I sat down. Who knew I needed to be supervised to answer a bunch of dumb questions. "Might I suggest you add that to your list of strengths? Some donor recipients appreciate the back-world vernacular, myself included. It's rather charming."

Sighing, I mutter, "So, major weakness—vocabulary." The last thing I need is to be charming. Charm means more unwanted attention, and after spending the last who knows how many minutes with this guy, I can't imagine the rest of my life.

He chuckles. "Come on, *babe*. I'm trying to help you find a good match like myself."

I glare. "But you shouldn't be helping me. This is *my* test."

"And it's taken you twice as long as anyone who has ever taken the exam. We're not testing your IQ."

Turning back to the screen and away from him, I pound my finger to the mouse, clicking a few boxes about my interests, which aren't many. I've never done most of the stuff listed—like swimming? If you count falling into an inch deep puddle as swimming, then I definitely didn't find it enjoyable. "Can you just let me finish? You're going to muddle my score or sway my match percentage with your encouragement."

He releases a strange noise from his throat, like a purr from one of the many stray cats around that try to lure you into petting them before scratching you for trying. "Would that be so bad? I know the other recipients in line. I'm far superior to more than half of them."

"You sure think highly of yourself," I mutter.

He chuckles again, his shadow suddenly shrinking on the wall in front of me. His cool fingers touch my shoulder as he brushes the loose hair from my neck. "Not me," he whispers. "You."

"Me?"

He leans over my shoulder to meet my eyes. "I wasn't kidding about wanting to ravish you."

Warmth drains from my face as he leans closer, his cold breath playing with the strands of my hair I can't seem to hide behind no matter how much of it I allow to fall in my face to create a veil between us.

Jerking upright, he abandons me at the computer, and I can't stop myself from twisting in my chair to catch him smiling at me from across the room. He rotates his finger in a circle, motioning me to swivel back around.

A buzzer sounds out a moment later, and the door swings inward. I twist in my seat at the sight of two other vampires entering the room. They know I saw them, and it takes me holding my breath to steel myself from what's to come. Three vampires and me in one room can't lead to anything good.

"You sneaky little bastard," a deep, melodious voice says. "You know the protocols. If you've entered yourself to be matched to this particular human, you can't be in here."

"Well, no one else was available, and Jewel was worried about making it home on time."

I glower at my screen. He's blaming me. Of course he is. He wants me to be disqualified so that I owe him a blood debt. This was all a ruse. He tricked me.

"You could have postponed her testing," the other masculine voice quips. "But you're a selfish prick, you asshole. You knew I wanted this particular match."

At least I'm not the only one who thinks he's an asshole.

"As did I," the melodious voice says. "She's perfect."

OhmyeffingG it's like I'm not even here. He mentioned something about certain clients being interested in me, but they sound about ready to brawl it out. Something I definitely want to be far, far away from.

"Tastes good, too," the rule breaker vampire says.

Queasiness tightens my stomach. They argue about me like I'm the extravagant main course at one of the fine dining establishments on top of Red Ridge, overlooking the entire city—a place exclusive to vampires—and I only know about because dad once had to repair a door there.

As I feared, fighting breaks out behind me, and something—no, someone—crashes into the wall, sending plaster dust through the air. I stiffen, bowing closer to the computer screen, praying that they continue to turn on each other instead of putting all their unwanted focus on me.

My heartbeat picks up pace, pounding in my ears as the

fighting persists. I wince as another body flies into the wall next to me. I tense, feeling the heavy stare drink me in while I refuse to look at the vampire. The edges of my vision darken. I inhale a gasp of breath to settle my nerves the best I can.

And then a hand touches my shoulder, startling me.

I scream out, jerking in my rolling chair so hard that it falls out from under me. Pain radiates through my back as I wheeze a breath, my lungs struggling to gasp the air I forced out of them. I blink the tears from my eyes, remaining utterly still on the floor. Three silhouettes hover over me as I'm on the verge of losing my shit out of fear and anger.

Rule Breaker clears his throat, shoving his elbow into the ribcage of the other super attractive, extremely tall vampire trying to grab me. They bare their teeth at each other, making my fear worse, and I close my eyes, praying they're quick to tear me apart.

"Babe, are you okay?" Rule Breaker asks, staring down at me without moving to help me from the floor. "You look like you're going to throw up."

I don't respond, turning my gaze on the other two vampires, standing slightly behind him but still flanking his sides. I take in their handsome features, the blond on the right with softer, more boyish qualities and the most startling green eyes I've ever seen basically boring into my soul as he drinks me in like he's dying of starvation, and I'm the only thing that'll keep him alive—which I hate.

The other vampire, taller than both Hungry Eyes and Rule

Breaker, flashes his fangs at me in a smile so perfect that I can't stop looking at his mouth. Smiles wets his lips, studying me as hard as the other two guys. The three of them make me tense up at the sudden reaction of my body betraying me, good goosebumps prickling over my skin. Damn it, all three vampires are gorgeous and sexy as hell, nothing like Chomper Jonas and the other shadow dwellers of Starlight Row.

And they all know it. It's written all over their faces, and they are loving every miserable second of silence that passes between us as I lie on the floor, my body basically begging one of them to lift me up.

They all try at once, leading to them throwing more punches at each other.

"Shit balls! This isn't worth it," I yell, finally getting my body to cooperate to let me roll over. I crawl back to the computer, scrambling up to cancel my test. Because I can't do this. My sheer will to survive in this moment outweighs the fear of what will happen to my family if I don't follow through with the Blood Match test. I'm not even sure I'm going to make it out of this room alive.

"Oh, no you don't, Ms. Jordan," Hungry Eyes says, scooping me off my feet, spinning me away from the computer.

"What the hell? This is my right. It says I can withdraw my application anytime during the initial test," I snap, swinging my arms out at the vampire's back. I'm not even worried about the consequences of hitting him. He will not strip me of one of the few rights I have as a human.

"Come on, Austin. Put her down. If you mess this up for me, I'll guarantee you'll never get a match," Smiles says, cracking his knuckles.

I swing at the empty air in front of me, thrown off balance by Austin, AKA Hungry Eyes, setting me down. The three vampires smirk at me as I orient myself, taking in each of them from my place standing in front of them instead of on the floor.

Hungry Eyes turns away from the others to look at me and says, "I'm sorry for my poor behavior, Ms. Jordan. Please reconsider withdrawing your application. I've been waiting for the opportunity to try to match with someone such as yourself."

Smiles nods his head, reaching out to touch my cheek. His cold fingers send a shiver through me, making all three of the vampires smile with their fangs. "Pretty please? How you appear on paper doesn't compete with who you are in front of me. I'm certain you're my perfect Blood Match, and if you agree, I will write a contract to ensure you will never feel—"

"You can't bribe or coerce her, Diego," Rule Breaker says, shoving the tall vampire away. "You do what you want, babe. You don't want to accidentally match with these bastards, you got me to fall back on. I'll even throw in a clause to protect your next of kin...you know, just in case you let me—"

Reaching up, I cut off his words with my hand. He nips at my palm before sliding his tongue across my skin, making me jerk my hand away. I groan at the thought of the blood debt. I had nearly forgotten about what happens to me if I don't match with another vampire. Rule Breaker wags his eyebrows at me, and the two other vampires look ready to tear him apart at any moment.

"Are you kidding me, Kingston?" Austin says, his eyes flashing silver.

I take an automatic step toward the computer.

"I knew you liked to fight dirty, but this is—"

Sucking in a deep breath, I steel myself for what's to come. The room falls deathly quiet, all the warmth radiating from me freezing as the three vampires close the distance to me, their cool skin sinking into my bones as they stand in my personal space they probably don't even consider to be my space to begin with.

I click the mouse a couple more times and skip the personal statement, opting to proceed with an oral interview instead. I pound the enter button with my finger, watching the cursor spin a few times before a box pops up and announces the questionnaire portion of my test is complete.

Turning around, I face the three vampires, all looking at me with indecipherable expressions crossing their faces—except Kingston, AKA Rule Breaker. He looks stupidly and adorably pouty.

I hug myself. "What now?"

Kingston's pouty mouth curves up into a smile, and he offers me his hand. "My favorite part."

I stand frozen. "The blood test?"

Diego, AKA Smiles, grins at me. "No, that's my favorite part."

I sigh. "I'm going to assume it's not the oral interview I've opted for."

Austin shakes his head. "That's when the results get narrowed down."

"Please don't tell me—"

"The physical exam," Kingston says, grinning at me.

"Effing holy shit balls," I mutter. "Don't think I won't fight you if you try anything funny."

Diego glances at Kingston and Austin. "Her vocabulary—"

"Is hilarious, right? She even called me dude," Kingston says, biting his lip. "I could listen to her all night."

I snap my mouth shut, resisting the urge to drop a ton of F-bombs because amusement plays on all three of their faces. What started as a joking way of speaking quickly turned natural, and I can't help myself sometimes, especially when I'm freaked the eff out or annoyed.

I wish Dad had forced me to watch some other genres apart from his seemingly never-ending supply of dumb comedies my grandpa managed to save. But I hated the romances and I had enough horror in my life. I couldn't stand the idea knowing that some superhero or a badass woman assassin wasn't going to save my day. So brain-numbing comedy was always mine and Ramona's go-to as a form of entertainment.

Watching TV at night had been our pastime for as long as I can remember until we couldn't afford the electricity it took to run the TV. Books are far and few, most remaining at my old high school for the volunteers to use to teach the few kids around, and board games aren't fun with so many missing pieces.

Lately, I've taken to singing, though Mrs. Peppers always warns that our noise will attract the shadow dwellers closer. If they breach our security, poor Security Steve could probably only stop them long enough to regret his job.

Kingston snaps his fingers in my face, drawing my attention to him. Shaking my head, I push away my thoughts about my childhood to save them for another time when I'll really need something to get me through the turn my life has taken to assure that my family makes it.

"Do you think falling out of her chair damaged her?" Diego asks the others like I'm not even standing in front of them.

I raise my hand and flip him off. "I'm fine."

"She's scared is all," Austin says. "Can't you tell? Her heart's racing, and she's sweating profusely."

Kingston smirks. "I rather like her being so worked up. It's sexy as hell."

Reaching out his hand, Austin touches my shoulder. He whips his hand away just as quickly, tucking it behind his back at one glare from me. For a moment, he looks to be more nervous than I am, but he hides it by opening the door and saying, "This way, Ms. Jordan. We haven't all night to wait for your physical exam."

I gulp. "Do I have to?"

Kingston touches my other shoulder. "No, you can just come home with—"

Diego shoves Kingston, pushing him from the room and into the hall. He's quick to twist around to face us, not even stumbling under the force of the tall vampire. They square off, chests puffing out, fangs showing, and then Austin slides his cool fingers through mine and pulls me away from the both of them.

"Dr. Prajapati will be with you shortly, Ms. Jordan," Austin says, guiding me to the last room in the hallway. "You have nothing to be afraid of, and I'll make sure Kingston and Diego don't barge in while you're changing. You have my word."

I bob my head, wondering if he could really follow through with keeping the other two vampires away, and I can't help but wonder what his ulterior motives are. Instead of flat out speaking what's on my mind, I enter the room and drop my gaze to the shiny floor. "Thank you, Austin," I say quietly. "And you can call me Jewel."

He motions behind me. "Your gown is on the bed, and you can pull the curtain."

"Good luck, babe!" Kingston calls from somewhere down the hallway.

"Thanks, dude," I mutter more to myself. "I friggin' need it."

A laugh sounds out from the hallway followed by a huff.

And then silence.

Turning to the thin paper gown neatly folded on the bed, I hug myself for a moment. "This is for Ramona, Dana, and Fallon," I say to myself. "They're counting on you, Jewel. Just suck it up."

And that's what I do. Because this is my life now, and I better get used to it.

3

More Than a Blood Slave

"I THINK I'M ALL DONE here. I'll send your tests to the lab and will get your results in a few minutes, which I'll pass along." Dr. Prajapati peels off the clear gloves I had no idea she was wearing and discards them in the biohazard trashcan. Strolling to the cupboard, she pulls out a box and hands it to me. "Take these with you but don't eat them all in one sitting or you'll get sick. I'm honestly surprised you can even stand."

I take the box without question, looking at the contents. According to the description, she just handed me a box of twenty-four protein bars. Twenty-freaking-four. These giant bars could last my family a week or more if I stretch them accordingly. "I do what I have to."

She offers me a small smile. "Well, I'm sure you'll get matched today, and things will turn around for you. It's not cheap for match recipients, so most take extremely good care of their donors."

That does nothing for my nerves. "Do you know about any of them—I mean the recipients?"

"I'm sorry, Ms. Jordan. I can't divulge that information." The doctor scoops up the vials from her rolling tray and sticks them in her coat pocket. "But I do hope you find your perfect match."

I clutch the box of protein bars. "Thank you."

She nods. "You're welcome. Now follow the arrows down the hallway, and you'll find the phlebotomy technician waiting for you. Eat one of the bars after, okay? I don't want to have to come back here if you faint." Without another word, she disappears, closing the curtain behind her.

Peering around, I realize my clothes aren't on the plastic chair where I left them after changing into the paper gown. Heat crawls up my neck, and I do the best to position the bed sheet around me to go after the doctor.

"What's up, babe?" Kingston says, appearing out of nowhere to my right.

I jump, dropping the sheet in the process.

Before it can even hit the floor, Kingston swipes it from the air and hands it back to me, taking a moment to briefly glance at me in the stupid paper gown.

"Did you steal my clothes?" I ask, stepping back into the room, half considering ripping the curtain from the rod to wrap around myself. "Because if you did, I'll—"

"Scream at me? Hit me? Undress me and take my clothes?" he asks, smirking as he throws out the what-ifs from his mind. Shrugging from his suit jacket, he holds it out to me. "I'll save you the trouble and do it for you."

"Seriously, Kingston?" Diego says, strolling up behind Rule Breaker. He snatches the suit jacket before Kingston can hand it to me and shoves it back to him. "Keep your damn clothes on."

I crinkle my nose. "What? No, please don't. I'm not walking around here like this." I don't care who ends up naked as long as it isn't me.

Kingston laughs. "You heard my babe. She wants my clothes off."

I blush. I can't help it. "I'm not your babe—"

"I'm so sorry, Jewel. It took me longer than expected to find a size that would fit you," Austin says, appearing in front of me.

I screech out, managing to keep the sheet up this time. I swear if they continue to materialize faster than I can blink, my heart might give out on me. I think the three vampires realize it too, because Diego snatches the bag from Austin and shoves him back, sending him into Kingston.

"Seriously, bro. You knew she was already jumpy." Diego turns to me and hands me the bag. "There's a shower in the bathroom if you want one before you dress."

I peer into the bag, spotting the white fabric of what I'm pretty sure is a dress—something I've never worn. "It's getting late. I'd rather just—"

"No one minds waiting," Kingston says, pressing his lips into a line, reminding me of what he told me earlier about needing to wash myself.

Heat floods my face, and I'm suddenly self-conscious instead of terrified with the way the three vampires trail their gazes over me from my head to my feet. A part of me says screw it to the idea of a shower, because that's basically prepping myself as dinner to them, but another part of me doesn't want to pass up the chance to take a real shower, probably with hot water even.

"Look what you did, Kingston," Austin says, glaring his green eyes in Rule Breaker's direction.

"I just said we don't mind waiting," he argues.

"You said it like she—"

I run a hand through my wild tresses. "I'll take an effing shower if you promise to tell Brayla that I'm almost done. She's probably worried from how long it's taking."

The three vampires glance from one another before Austin clears his throat and says, "Your friend was sent home. The building is closed for the night for this occasion, and only authorized personnel and recipients are allowed here tonight past eight."

"Eight!" I shriek, spinning around like I could see a clock.

"It's been three hours? Oh, God, my sister—"

"We assure you that your friend made it home safely and your next of kin have been informed that you'd be late," Kingston says. "Relax, babe. It's all good."

"Her name is Jewel," Diego says. "Stop trying to force a non-existent connection to her by using a pet name."

"A pet name?" I ask.

"I'm only showing her my affection. She started it," Kingston says. "Not my fault if you can't see how perfect she is for me."

Diego clenches his fist, and I take an automatic step back and into Austin's cool arms. I had no idea he was behind me, and he doesn't hold me long, just spins me around and nudges me toward the open door I can hear the sound of water coming from.

Silence falls over the room, and I peek over my shoulder to catch sight of the three vampires staring at me, their attention no longer focused on each other. I step into the tiled room, my heart sliding into my stomach when I realize that there's not an actual door to shut them out. A shoulder-high wall and a flimsy plastic curtain are all that blocks me from some of my possible Blood Matches. If I had their hearing, I bet I could listen to their stomachs growling.

"Can you turn around or something?" I ask, setting the bag on the small table. I grab the towel hanging on the wall and drape it over the barrier, now ultra-aware that the vampires might have turned their backs toward me, but all of them refuse to leave me to my shower. It's like none of them trust each other, but I trust none of them. "Maybe wait out in the hall?"

They disappear with my request, and I release a deep breath, summoning my nerves to shrug the gown off to throw into the wastebasket. Steam clouds the air in front of me, and I slowly dip my toe in the spraying water, surprised that Austin managed to set it to the perfect temperature.

I step in completely, and an unwanted moan escapes my lips at how amazing the steady stream feels against my skin. Pressing the dispenser on the wall, I fill my hand with a strange yet pleasant herbal smelling shampoo, and my head tingles with a cooling sensation. It reminds me of the mint tea my mom used to drink. It calms my nerves enough to brave putting the conditioner in my hair next, something I've never used before.

I tilt my head back, running my fingers through my now silky tresses. Going through all this might've been worth it for the shower alone. It gives me serious envy toward the humans lucky enough to experience this on a regular basis.

A chuckle sounds out from the hallway, reminding me that I'm not really alone. I try my best to ignore the fact that with a vampire's super hearing, I basically can't hide anything from them. And apparently whatever they can hear is enough to make Kingston say, "Sounds like you're enjoying the shower, babe."

Something thuds into the wall. "Ignore him. He won't be around you for much longer," Austin adds.

Diego clears his throat. "Neither will you."

I quickly wash the rest of my body and shut off the water despite my urge to stay in the hot stream until someone physically drags me out. The second the fog clears, so do my senses, and I hurry to dress.

I stare at myself for a moment in the hazy mirror, taking in the long, simple white dress. From the pamphlets, I knew that donors wear something like this for a match, but I haven't even been matched yet. The guy in the lobby earlier still wore his own clothes too. What the hell?

A low whistle comes from the hallway, and I turn my attention to Kingston, Diego, and Austin all staring at me. I can't tell if they like the way I look or if I'm making them hungry, either way, I don't really want to find out what thoughts lay behind all of their intense gazes. I just want to get this over with.

"You look hot," Diego says, sounding like Kingston.

Austin elbows him. "He means stunning."

"Liars," Kingston says, grinning at me. "They both think you look good enough to eat."

I pale.

"Shut up, asshole," Diego says. "Don't put your words in my mouth."

"Oh, I don't *think* Jewel looks good enough to eat, I know she does," Kingston says, smirking. "But she's also funny as hell. My dream match."

I swallow, heat blooming up my neck despite how warm my skin is from the shower. When I decided to apply for a

Blood Match, I had no idea what to really expect. According to the brochure, every match is different, and the only promise that could be made was that my next of kin would gain an amazing life. I've known one other person to get matched, and I never heard from him or his family again, which I had hoped was a good sign, the point being to never return to your old life.

"She obviously doesn't agree," Austin quips.

"I—" I snap my mouth shut the second they all give me their undivided attention.

"You what?" Kingston asks. "You can speak freely, babe. I'd love to know what's on your mind without prying it from your lips against your will."

I blink a few times. "You c-can d-do that?"

"Among other things."

"Like what?"

"Make you the happiest—"

"Enough, Kingston. I know what you're doing, and we're running out of night to play your games," Diego says. He holds out his hand to me. "Jewel, allow me to escort you to the blood lab."

"Talk about games," Austin mutters. "Careful, Jewel. Diego is both a sore winner and loser."

Their banter and digs at each other make my head spin. Without thinking much over it, I take Diego's proffered hand and stroll behind him, my bare feet slapping against the tiles louder than the three of them combined. If I didn't see their feet touching the floor, I'd think they were flying.

"You guys are quiet as hell," I say, lowering my voice.

Kingston glides ahead of us and walks backward to face me. "And your stealth skills need some work, babe. You're going to attract every vampire to you in the vicinity, and it's still not too late for another to put their name into the pool of recipients."

"You worried you're not a match for her?" Austin asks.

"He knows he's not. That's why he tried to pull that blood debt shit. But Jewel's too intelligent for that," Diego says.

"Way smarter than you too, Kingston. You're just a pretty face," Austin adds.

Kingston unfastens a few buttons on his dress shirt and pulls it open, revealing the most impressive muscular chest I've seen in real life. He looks just like one of the old time action movie stars, the ones that the back-world thought were perfect superheroes. "You forgot my body."

I can't take my eyes away from the sculpted muscles peeking out from the bottom of the V his open shirt creates. With a flick of his finger, Kingston pops another two buttons, giving me the full view of his abs. And my body reacts despite me tilting my chin to look up at the blinding lights in the ceiling. I smack my head against another hard chest, and strong arms wrap around me from behind, stopping me from falling forward. I can't seem to move an inch without touching a vampire, my body acting like a pinball bouncing precariously between all three of them until I drop to my knees.

"Haven't you guys ever heard of personal space?" I glance up, narrowing my eyes at them.

All three of them take an automatic step away from me, surprising me. I had expected them to react angrily, yell at me, and possibly bite me even. But these three act nothing like Chomper Jonas, who would have attacked the second I bumped into him. It freaks me out more than it should. I don't even know what's going on and why they're treating me like I'm more than a food source about to be permanently given to one of them or whoever else is on the list.

"I'm sorry, Jewel. I got carried away with myself," Austin says first.

"My apologies," Diego adds next.

Kingston adjusts his shirt, slowly buttoning the fabric together. "I'm not sorry, babe. You like what I have to offer and you know it."

Diego punches Kingston in the arm. "You can't bribe her."

"I'm not bribing her. I'm showing her the better option."

The three of them get into it again, and I slide past them and break out into a sprint like I've found myself outside after sundown. My breath heaves as I push my muscles to keep up with me, but they can't, and I stumble, tripping over the light fabric of my dress. The world spins, my scream ripping through the air. Two pairs of hands hook around my waist, one set pushing me up while the other pulls me, and I balance mid-air.

"Holy shit balls," I say, my body tensing, my stomach squished between two powerful vampires' hands attempting to break my fall.

Kingston grins at me from below. "I got ya, babe."

"Me too, beautiful," Diego says from his position standing next to me.

My stomach twists, dizziness from spinning in the air getting to me. I cover my mouth with my hand as my body reacts. Kingston's eyes widen, and he releases me to cover his face. Diego's hands dig into me at the sudden drop of Kingston's support, and I dry heave.

Shadows edge my vision, the dizziness refusing to ease up even though Diego sets me down. For blood drinkers, both Kingston and Diego seem terrified of the possibility of my other bodily fluids managing to touch them, and for the first time since I came into the Blood Match Center do I find myself in a safe distance from the vampires.

It's Austin who appears in front of me, touching my face. "Here, drink this. You look like you're going to faint."

Panic rises in my chest as I fight to stay conscious, my body refusing to give my mind another moment of its time, probably because I haven't eaten in over two days, possibly three. I can't remember right now. I was planning to eat with my family the moment I got home, but whoever is in charge of the Blood Match Center failed to mention the possibility of it taking hours.

Room temperature water coats my tongue, dribbling down my chin for a second until I automatically swallow. Austin touches my forehead with the back of his hand, his hypnotic green eyes searching my aqua ones like he can peek into my head.

"If she's sick, they'll disqualify her from matching," Diego says, standing above Austin.

Kingston pulls out a gleaming, clear screen tablet from his suit pocket. The small device fits in his hand, and I watch his expression turn from worry to confusion, though I can't see what he sees from my position on the ground. "She's not sick. The results already came in, and she's in passable health."

"Then what's wrong with her?" Diego asks.

Austin studies me a moment longer before setting the glass of water down only to bring something else to my mouth. The sweet scent of whatever he holds to my lips makes my stomach scream, shooting pain through the rest of me. My hands jerk up without permission, and I grab onto Austin's wrist, startling him. I rip the food from his fingers and shove the whole thing in my mouth, tasting something sugary and unlike anything I've ever tasted. It's so good. And I mean, incredible and worth risking my life to steal from a vamp, delicious.

"She's starving," Austin muses. "When was the last time you ate, Jewel? I thought Donor Life Corp rationed meals with the donations. Has someone been stealing from you?"

Diego pulls another protein bar from the box I nearly forgot about from the doctor that I had left in the shower. He unwraps it and hands it to me. "Maybe it was a clerical error."

I don't respond to him, shoving it into my mouth, regretting it immediately. What I just ate now threatens to come right back up. Both Diego and Kingston step back again, but Austin remains in front of me, shifting to the side to pull my hair from my face. When I don't puke my brains out, he offers me the water again.

"It's your next of kin, right?" Kingston asks me, taking a cautious step closer. "You're going without so they don't have to. You rated highly for compassion, nurturing, and empathy on your match test, so I can assume my thoughts are accurate."

Slowly, I nod without saying anything else. I'd prefer they didn't bring my family into this. It's bad enough I have to be under their complete scrutiny, especially because I get nothing out of it. They could use something like this against me.

"Two donors for six people should be adequate for survival. Not exactly the best of living, but she shouldn't be this undernourished," Austin says. "She's swimming in the smallest size gown available."

"I'll fix that," Kingston says, offering me another protein bar.

Austin smacks his hand. "You'll be cleaning up her vomit if you do that."

"That's what the staff is for. Let me take care of my babe, all right? You know as well as I do that I'm the most compatible. The next two tests are only a formality." Kingston grins at me. "And once we're officially matched, you'll be the best fed. You can take all the damn showers you want and more if you let me join you, and I'll make sure your kin is set, so you never have to worry about them."

I frown, his words swirling through my mind. "Why? I'm going to be your live-in blood supply."

"Well, sure, I do expect us to get to the point where you're comfortable with allowing me to—"

Diego elbows Rule Breaker, his anger hot enough that his cheeks bloom in color that makes him almost look human. "Stop talking to her like you've already been matched. You shouldn't even be here, Kingston."

"Diego's right. You had your chance and you blew it. You're supposed to wait until the both of us got our matches," Austin says. "It's only fair."

I tilt my head back, still not feeling so hot. "You guys put in a lot of effort for a friggin' blood slave, you know. God, you should just Rock-Paper-Scissors the decision and be done with it. Just tell me where the lab is and let's finish this. My family's probably worried sick, and all I want to do now is lie down and sleep in peace for one more night before one of you accidentally kills me."

Three pairs of beautiful eyes stare at me. Their blatant surprise was the last thing I was expecting. You'd think I've offended them when I spoke the truth. If I wasn't on the verge of ending up homeless on Starlight Row, the chances of me living a long life in a vampire lair drops by more than half of my life expectancy living in The Boxes, at least, according to my vampire relations teacher from my old high school.

"I thought she was literate," Diego says to Austin and Kingston.

"She is." Kingston frowns at me but still gives Diego his attention. "I could hear her reading the questions out loud under her breath. I know she understood them because she had a hell of a lot of commentaries, especially when it came to the..." His voice trails off as my expression morphs from confusion to horror.

I stare at him with wide eyes, knowing exactly which set of questions he stopped himself from referencing. A part of me dies on the inside that he heard my remarks at all. I was just so annoyed with the extensive questionnaire that covered everything from my family history, to my hobbies, things I like, things I lack in experience in...I couldn't believe how many questions in regards to sex and desire the test included down to types of positions I still can't even envision.

Heat claws up my neck in hot, invisible scratches, and nothing I can think to say will hide the fact that I've never even kissed a guy and there's no way I could know if I like to do things this or that way. And now I'm freaking out. Nothing in the pamphlet said anything about my body. This was supposed to be about my being a permanent food source.

Kingston looks me square in the eyes. "Don't worry, babe. Those answers will stay between us. Your results come in percentage form, so only I know that—"

"Shut up, please," I whisper, wringing my fingers together.

He touches my hand, a smile playing on his pouty lips I now can't stop looking at as he runs his tongue over them. Leaning close, he whispers, "No judgment here, Jewel. While others might disagree and prefer someone with experience, I enjoy the idea of teaching you a thing or ten."

OhmyeffingGod.

Fire engulfs my face, and I drop my gaze to Kingston's hand, still holding mine. I refuse to even look at Diego and Austin, afraid of seeing their reaction from the secret of mine Kingston revealed.

"What the hell did you say to her?" Diego asks, and I realize that Kingston's whispered words somehow did manage to stay between us.

"That's between my babe and me," Kingston quips, squeezing my fingers again.

I groan, inhaling deep breaths as I try to stop myself from flipping the shit out. As I look into Kingston's midnight eyes, the way he captures me in his gaze like he knows everything crossing my mind, I realize how stupid and naïve I've been about this whole thing. When the lives of my family are at stake, nothing should matter. I told myself I'd do what I had to, but now the deeper I get into the application and match process, the more I realize that I care about myself too.

Licking his lips again, still smirking at me, Kingston pushes to his feet and shockingly pulls both Diego and Austin to theirs. Austin scoops up the box of protein bars and the water, tucking them at his side like I might attempt to attack him for them—which I consider for a split second—before Kingston and Diego both offer out a hand to pull me to my feet. I take them both and fly a foot into the air, screeching at the movement, but my feet gently touch the cool tile. Diego holds my hand an extra moment longer than Kingston, who pulls out his tablet from his pocket again to tap on the screen.

"I think you need to read over these one more time, babe," Kingston says, handing me his computer device. "I have a feeling you were either too worried about your survival to care or something got lost in your packet about the Blood Match Program."

"What do you mean?" I ask, skimming my eyes over the first page, which I recognize from the pamphlet. "I read the whole thing at least ten times. My best friend and sister did, too. So did my dad. You take a test, if you match with a vampire above eighty percent, then you move in as a sustainable blood supply. Those matched don't have to supply as much blood and recipients no longer need donations from the general population. Since donors no longer reap the benefits provided by usual donations, their next of kin get permanent residency in Haven Springs..." My voice trails off as I continue to scroll, seeing a dozen more pages with even sample questions from the test I had taken.

Whatever pamphlet that ended up on the bulletin board of The Boxes was missing pages. I had no idea, because it hadn't changed once in the last year after Mom and Aunt Dottie died, and I hit the age requirement and finally took notice of the program I swore I'd never apply for.

"Holy shit balls," I say. "Why doesn't Donor Life Corp resend this information when someone schedules an appointment? None of this was on the paperwork. I mean—this is more than I had expected. I assumed I'd be a live-in donor, with a weekly phlebotomist and occasionally a bite or two—or just dead."

"Dead? I only know two vampires with enough money to go through Blood Matches like that," Austin says. "And lucky for you, neither applied to match with you."

I release a breath. "But still. This is a little much."

"I had no idea we were so repulsive," Kingston quips. "Especially with the way you looked like you'd be the one to ravish me first."

I suck in a sharp breath at the same time Austin elbows Kingston and says, "Don't talk to her like that."

Kingston shoves Austin right back. "You know what? You can back out, Jewel. I'll allow it."

"But the blood debt," I whisper.

"He won't be alive to follow through with it," Diego growls, glaring at Kingston.

I brace myself for the three vampires to start throwing punches again, but they all swivel their heads back to me. I realize they can hear my heart beating wildly in my chest as I think over the possibility of being not just a blood match but a companion, possibly a lover, as well as the head of their daylight household, assuring their safety by day as they promise me and my kin protection from the night.

I can imagine Ramona screaming at me to back out now, that accepting such a life would be basically flipping my parents off for raising me to think of myself as more than a servant or a vein to a vampire. If I agree, it goes against what so many humans want away from. It's more about keeping my integrity and not giving up my freedom to fight for equality vampires can't keep from humans forever.

But then my stomach heaves again, and I imagine a hundred worse fates for me and my sister, for my cousins, than ending up in the household of a vampire, especially if it's the household of one of these three.

"Can you guarantee that I get to see my family like the brochure said?" I ask.

The three of them nod.

I tuck my hair behind my ear, knowing that my next question will walk me right into one of Kingston's seemingly favored innuendoes. "And you're not going to tie me up or something, right?"

"Only if that's what you like," Kingston says as I predicted, grinning and running his cold finger to the never-ending warmth tinting my cheeks rose.

I roll my eyes. "I don't even know what I like."

Diego flicks Kingston's hand away. "I'm sure you'll find out."

I deadpan, trying to even my racing heart, knowing they can hear my body reacting to their remarks. I don't know how much more of the three of them I can handle. My cheeks can't take it. Instead of saying as much, I ask, "You'll also let me use a phlebotomist for providing blood, too? I know the pamphlet says that blood extraction is to be determined—"

"If you're matched with me, then yes," all three of them say in unison. They glare at each other before turning back to me.

"Though we can explore other options when you're comfortable," Austin says, keeping his hands hidden behind his back. He's less touchy-feely than the other two, and I wonder how he runs his household. If a vampire could ever be gentle or empathetic, I bet Austin would be.

"And if I'm not matched with any of you?" I ask.

"I wouldn't worry too much about that, babe," Kingston says. "The chance of getting another candidate is slim. Out of nine, you've only matched eighty percent or higher with five of us at this point."

"What? Five? That seems unusually high."

Austin shrugs. "It is, so how about we get it narrowed down to one?"

All I do is nod.

Diego slides his arm around my waist. "You're going to love being with me."

4

Blood Brothers

A PHONE RINGS ON THE desk next to the man in the black lab coat. Dark liquid stains the front of the fabric in a splash of shadows, and I don't have to ask him to know it's blood. Donor Life Corp probably insisted on dark garb to hide the fact that the blood drawing process can sometimes be messy if the donor isn't exactly willing. But I've never met someone with a blood debt, dragged in and drained as much as possible before getting thrust out without another thought.

The phlebotomist hits a button on the phone a moment after he answers and Kingston's face lights up at the sight of me lying back in the chair, a rubber band twisted around my arm, while I clutch a dumb realistic heart-shaped squeeze toy until the tech tells me to release it.

"Hey, babe. How ya feeling?" he asks, his eyes flicking across the screen.

I raise an eyebrow. "If you must know, I feel like utter shit. But thanks for asking."

His finger darts over the screen as he taps something I can't see. Humming in his throat, he hits one more button, his eyes narrowing. "No more blood from Ms. Jordan, Quinton."

"The paperwork says—"

"I don't give a flying fuck what the paperwork says. I said stop. She doesn't look so good."

"There won't be enough for adequate tasting if I stop, Mr. Divine. She's obligated to provide at minimum one hundred and twenty milliliters per recipient, and I have only extracted about four hundred and fifteen milliliters."

Almost two cups? Even Donor Life Corp doesn't allow me to donate that much in one sitting. Only Dad donates the max. And according to the outdated medical textbooks I used to read at my old high school, there was once a time I'd have been denied altogether. But Donor Life Corp only cares about one thing—keeping vampires fed to maintain order.

"But there are five of us, and she weighs—" Kingston taps his screen again, his eyes widening as he must realize what the safest limit for me is, and then the call drops.

Everything happens so fast that I don't even realize the

phlebotomist no longer messes with my vein when he crashes into the wall. Austin swiftly and painlessly removes the needle from my arm and presses a cotton ball over the blood still seeping from my vein. His chest heaves for a moment, sending fear through me. Jerking his head to meet my eyes, he blinks once, twice, three times and then he smiles and squeezes a drop of synthetic skin on my arm to stop the bleeding completely.

"Eat this," he says, his voice low. "Slowly."

Cool fingers gently pinch my chin to guide my head away from Austin so that I can meet Kingston's gaze. "I'm sorry, Jewel. There was a clerical error and you should've only had to give blood for three individuals and not five."

"Huh?" I ask, confused by what's happening. Does this mean it's down to the three of them and the mysterious two vampires I haven't met yet dropped out?

Austin holds something to my mouth again. "Too much was taken, Kingston. She needs a transfusion."

"It might muddle the results."

"I'm going to drain that—"

"Take those to the tasting room immediately, and you will not question our authority again, Mr. Santiago," Diego says before Kingston moves and I get the chance to ask about my other possible matches. Diego rights the wide-eyed phlebotomist on his feet, straightening the black lab coat for the man, and leans in to peer into his eyes. "I won't help you against the rash actions of my brother if you don't hurry."

"Brother?" I ask, turning my heavy gaze back to Kingston

for answers. "And three? You three are my final matches? What happened to...?" I squeeze my eyes shut, feeling woozy and worse than usual after a normal blood donation draw.

Austin holds a glass of orange liquid to my lips when I'm not quick enough to take a bite from the brown-colored, hard-looking rectangular bar he keeps trying to feed me. "You have to drink or eat, Jewel."

I shake my head. "I don't feel so good. I'll throw up if I do."

Kingston swears, his hands balling into fists. It takes Diego grabbing the back of his jacket to stop him from going after the scared tech, who clutches a few blood vials like they'll explode in his fingers at any second.

"Careful, Kingston," Diego warns. "You don't want to be disqualified again."

I blink through my hazy vision, my head lolling so much that my chin hits my clavicle. Austin touches my face again, his fingers no longer as cold as they were before. I don't even shiver.

"Ah, hell," he mutters. "Screw it."

"Austin, no," Kingston says from behind him. "Stop."

"Make me," he growls.

I pass out.

A strange beeping sound rings in my ears, tugging me from the recesses of my dark consciousness. I push away a freaky ass dream that wants to replay in my mind about lying on a table to feed a group of faceless vampires. I think my subconscious is sending me a warning, but unfortunately, I must ignore it.

Shifting in a lounge chair, I wiggle my toes, sensations returning to my body. Something cold touches my forehead, and I jerk up, startling at the sight of my reflection in the glass of a mirrored window across the room. My aqua eyes crinkle in the corners, something looking different about me, but I can't put my finger on it. All I know is that I feel slightly better than I did after the blood draw.

"Hey, beautiful," Diego says, sticking something to my wrist. "I'm hooking you up to a machine that measures your body's reactions for the next test. This is the final evaluation to compile your results to assess compatibility."

I arch forward to right myself, trailing my gaze over my reflection again instead of looking at Diego's mesmerizing gray eyes. "What about the blood? Did you manage to get enough?"

"Don't worry your beautiful face about that," he muses.

"Diego."

He chuckles. "If you must know, there was a compromise."

I finally give him my full attention.

"It wouldn't be the first time I had to share something with my brothers," he adds. "We can sometimes play nice."

"Is the tech dead?" I can't help asking. If the phlebotomist died because of my inability to provide blood for the stupid amount of vampire candidates who apparently all want to take me home, then I'm going to feel a world of guilt.

"Do you really think so little of us? I was once human, you

know. If I disregarded a human enough to kill without good reason, I wouldn't have applied to be matched with you, Jewel. Donations sustain a great life for me."

I ignore his question about my feelings toward him being a vampire. I honestly don't know. If it were Chomper Jonas, I'd be quick to say yes, that I do in fact think he's the scum of the earth. But he's not Chomper Jonas. I don't know who he is except that he seems nice enough and is hot as hell. "And the other stuff?" I ask, clearing my throat.

The corners of his mouth tick up in a smile as he picks up on my insinuation without me having to say exactly what I mean. Since I skimmed over the rest of the pamphlet, sex seems to be the first thing on my mind, and I'm freaking out a little. "There are many vampires who prefer to kill another than fall into their bed. Not to mention females aren't exactly plentiful if that's what a vampire is looking for. How your father managed to raise four females to almost adulthood is a feat in itself. The population ratio of males to females is ten to one since the flu outbreak and transfers in and out of Dark Terrace Ranch have been put on hold until the quarantine is withdrawn. Maybe in a year or two."

His words sink into me. I had no idea about the dwindling female population or the quarantine. Dad never mentioned either, but I know why he didn't mention the quarantine. I'd have signed up for a Blood Match immediately. My heart clenches as pain sweeps through me. He was willing to risk everything to save me from this fate, and now he's missing—and possibly dead—for no reason.

"What about my sisters? You said no transfers."

"There are exceptions, though I'm sure there will be a lot of disappointed people by their untouchable status."

I scowl at the thought of anyone getting anywhere near my family. "Let them be disappointed."

His words get under my skin, drawing my thoughts from Dad to Ramona and the women I interact with on a daily basis like Mrs. Peppers. Plenty of women live in The Boxes. Our floor alone has twenty other apartments with at least one woman in each. As for everywhere else, I haven't even noticed the apparently readily available guys. Thinking about how long the groceries were going to last took precedence over dating. And sex? Contraception was banned a few months ago because of the drop in population in our city. Vampires can't have their food source dying off. So there is no way I wanted to risk partaking in the act with the possibility of procreation occurring.

Not that I'd have to worry about something like that with a vampire...I think. While they're not undead like the old myths proclaim, their bodies don't act the same as a human's. They don't eat, and the blood they drink provides what they need to survive. Their bodies regenerate quicker, making them hard to kill, though no one with half a brain would try. Vampires are basically superhuman, top of the food chain, with lives so long and features unchanging that it's possible they're immortal, but I haven't read any concrete evidence of any vampires living before the Blood Hunger Plague unless you count the stuff created by the entertainment industry back then.

Diego shifts in his seat, and I notice his discomfort from the silence settling between us as I stare at his thumb drawing circles over my palm. After another moment of him gathering his thoughts, he says, "I'm sorry, Jewel. I didn't mean to make your sisters sound so...coveted. I kind of went off topic from your original question about what your match with me would entail. And to be honest, I hope everything. If you haven't noticed, I find you..." His voice trails off as he thinks of what to say.

"Delicious?" I ask.

He blinks. Diego obviously puts an effort into articulating his thoughts unlike Kingston, who lacks a filter. And I like that about Diego. I can't even believe I'm thinking that thought. I was so set on hating my living arrangements for the rest of my life that the sudden tingles blossoming in my stomach surprise me.

I laugh and curl my fingers over Diego's for a brief moment.

He beams at me. "Teasing me already."

I shrug. "Something I do when I'm nervous."

Grazing his fingers over my arm, he gently turns over my wrist to rub circles on my palm again. And I let him. Something about the way he looks at me with the bright smile on his face, his shining eyes, trying to be close to me without getting into my space without permission makes me wonder if everything I know about vampires is accurate. Because this handsome vampire acts nothing like the savages of the shadows.

"Well, you don't have to be. I know this is a lot to handle, but I want you to know that if we're matched, I'll do everything I can to make you as comfortable as possible in the transition away from your family. I'm close with my brothers and couldn't imagine being away from them, but in your case it's a must for their safety and ours. Also, I can tell you're worried about the other facets of a matching relationship, and you can set whatever pace you'd like. I'm patient and not as needy as my brothers."

"Oh," I whisper. "What do you mean by needy? Like with blood? Um, se—"

"You have a lot of questions. I like that," Diego says, meeting my eyes straight on. "And I promise to answer every last one of them after we finish here. It should go fairly quickly since the blood test elimination." I bet he picked up on the change in my demeanor, and thankfully changed the subject away from all the needs I'm expected to fulfill.

But now I have even more questions. "Elimination? Were Kingston and Austin...?"

His smile turns into a frown. "You look like you'd be disappointed if they were. And here I thought we had a connection."

I wet my lips, nervous how to respond or if I even should.

"It's cool, Jewel. Despite them annoying the hell out of me, I'm close to my brothers and wouldn't blame you for liking either of them."

"You're all really brothers? You look nothing alike." Diego had referred to Kingston as his brother in the lab, but now it seems Austin might be one too. I've never heard of vampire families, only that they have some sort of system in place to maintain order. I don't know much about vampire politics. Donor Life Corp handles all of that as a liaison between humans and vamps.

"Sired by the same vampire. They're my coven brothers, and while we have no human connection, you can say we are still blood-related."

"That makes this kind of awkward."

He chuckles. "More fun. We like a good competition."

And I'm the damn prize.

Grimacing, he says, "Shit. I didn't mean it like that."

A buzzer rings over the door, cutting off anything else he had planned to say to me. But unlike the last few times, no one barges in uninvited. Diego taps a few buttons on the machine and a paper shoots out. He tucks it away, smiles at me once more, and stands up, his full height towering over me as I remain in my spot.

"My time's up, beautiful," he says, glancing at the mirror on the wall for a second before turning to me. "I'll see you in the lobby when the final results come in. Hopefully with my name all over them."

I smile at Diego. I can't help it. "I guess we'll see."

Diego wiggles his fingers at me, stopping in the doorway where I spot Austin bouncing on his feet. The two vampires shake hands, and Diego pats Austin on the back, nearly pushing him in the room to me. The second his gaze meets mine, heat rushes from my chest to flow down my stomach and to my groin. I shift in my seat, startled by the strange reaction of my body upon seeing Austin.

He presses his lips together, stifling a smile for only a second before he gives in and flashes his fangs at me in a grin that both scares and freakishly excites me in a way that leaves me blushing.

"I'm sorry about that," Austin says, taking a seat next to me. He jabs his fingers into a few buttons on the machine, and it whirls to life all over again, beeping with the sound of my thrumming heart.

I cross my legs at my knees, swiveling to face him. "Sorry for what?"

"The titillating side effects of drinking my blood."

I deadpan, surprise stealing the color from my cheeks as I realize the extent of his words. My breathing quickens, sending the machine beeping like crazy. Austin reaches for my hand, but I jerk it away and hold it against my chest.

His brows furrow, the same anguish crossing my face reflecting to me on his. "I'm so sorry, Jewel. I know it was out of line and completely inappropriate behavior."

"Your blood? I drank your blood?" My lip quivers as the words escape. It's all I can think about now that he mentions it. "Side effects? What does that even mean? Am I..." Oheffinghell. It's called the Blood Hunger Plague for a reason, but I thought the supposed pathogen had been eradicated and humans are inoculated upon birth. That's what they told us.

Diego's words about being human before and sharing vampire blood with his brothers through a dad vampire or whatever flit through my mind.

"Am I going to be like you?" I ask.

Austin thrashes his head. "No, you're still you."

"But I drank your blood. *Blood.*" My stomach twists at the thought, and I dry heave.

Austin sucks in a breath of air, unfastens the top two buttons of his dress shirt, and straightens his shoulders. "I can assure you that no harm will come from it. If you feel I've ruined any chance with you, and you want me to withdraw from the matching program, I'll understand. But I do want you to know how sorry I am over the whole situation."

A wave of warmth crashes over me at his words, and I study the sincerity softening his features, making him more boyish with his sad, round eyes and full bottom lip looking so kissable...

I shake my head, pushing the thought away.

He takes the gesture as me not wanting him to withdraw his chance to match with me, and his whole face lights up with a smile that does all sorts of crazy things to my insides. And I still can't stop staring at his bottom lip as it slides between his teeth to better show off his fangs. My heart quickens more, suddenly threatening to ram a tunnel through my ribs to throw itself into Austin's lap, and then my body follows suit, and Austin laughs in my ear just letting me share his chair.

"What the hell is wrong with me?" I ask, catching our reflections in the mirror. "I'm so sorry."

And I'm even sorrier for squirming, because I feel his body react excitedly to mine, and I full on giggle, my face burning and reddening with the blush of my uncontrollable desire, which I now get is what he meant by the titillating side effect from the supposed blood of his I drank.

Austin bows his head to hide his face, and effing shit balls, he's blushing too, something I can't even grasp happening. And it's not even the first time he's done so. Gently shifting my ass off his lap and toward his knees, he slowly brings his gaze to mine.

My giggles disappear immediately, every ounce of laughter slipping away as my fingers slide along his jaw to touch the collar of his shirt. The air thickens around us in a mixture of our heavy breaths, intense emotions, and the heat of my body warming his even through our clothes. I can't help wondering if his blood messed up my brain too. I shouldn't be sitting so closely, absently trailing my finger across his skin, wishing he'd open his shirt more.

He snatches my hand, squeezing my fingers. "There's plenty of time to get to know me physically after we match, but now is the time set aside for your interview and for us to get to know each other some."

"My what?" I swallow, leaning closer. "I haven't prepared."

Ever so slowly, he brings his hand to my face and brushes

away the veil of hair I try to hide behind. "You're the one..." His Adam's apple bobs in his throat, and I swear a tiny breath of a moan escapes his lips. "If you have any questions...now's your chance."

"Questions?" I bow my head, resting my chin on his shoulder, trying to pull myself together.

"Perhaps you want to know something about me?"

I shake my head. "No, I just—can I kiss you?" Who the hell said that? The voice sounded like mine, but just because I can't stop looking at Austin's pouty lips doesn't mean I want my first kiss to be in a room, hooked up to a machine with what I suspiciously think might be a two-way mirror with an audience watching us. And if it isn't, the blinking camera in the corner is.

"You want me to kiss you?"

I tilt my face to the side, my body respectfully disagreeing with my thoughts as I nod my head. "You have kissable lips."

He clears his throat again. "Everything about you is quite kissable, Jewel."

"Yeah?"

"But it's against the rules."

I pout. I can't believe I'm pouting. Or leaning closer. Or—ohmyeffingG. My hands caress the cool skin of his chest, and I accidentally rip a button free. Where the hell did I find the strength to do that? His muscles tighten under my exploring fingers, and he shudders, releasing a growl from his throat.

Shit balls if that wasn't the sexiest noise I've ever heard in my existence.

One second I'm cozy in Austin's lap and the next I'm back in my own seat with Austin standing beside me, bringing a bottle of water to my lips. His chest rises and falls, his lips smooshed together to stop the air from escaping his mouth in what would be obvious gasps.

"I'm really sorry," I say between gulps of water. "I don't usually act like this. Something's wrong with me."

"No, Jewel. You're perfect. Don't apologize for something I'm to blame for. I just panicked in the lab when you blacked out and did the first thing I could think of to help you without much thought of the consequences. The side effects will wear off in a couple of hours. I promise."

"Oh, okay." I release a breath, managing to compose myself the second he steps another foot away. "I was just so confused. I mean, I think you're attractive, but I don't know you all that well, and I've never kis—never mind. It's not important."

He either fills in my blanks or my answer is written on my face because his eyes widen and he asks, "Really?"

"You looked shocked."

"No, it's not that—"

"None of this has had time to cross my mind until..." It's like Austin pulled the cork on my filter before shoving it back in improperly, and my thoughts continue to leak out of me. "The questionnaire was more detailed than I expected is all. You have to give me a break, okay?"

He nods. "Got it. No worries on my part."

The buzzer sounds out, and we both frown at each other. I can't help wondering if my stupid uncontrollable lust might've ruined this for him, because the second he hits the button and the sheet of paper whirls out, a dozen questions fly through my mind.

A knock sounds on the door, and like before, no one barges in. Austin proffers his hand to me, and I let his cool fingers wrap around mine for a brief moment. He pulls away, an adorable smile crossing his lips, though he doesn't show me his incisors this time.

"I hope to see you again, Jewel. I know this got off to a hella awkward start, but I still fully believe we'll be a good match."

"Hella?" I ask.

He chuckles. "I thought you might have gotten your vocabulary from watching the classics."

I can't stop the smile stretching across my lips, and Austin winks, making a gesture that would usually freak me out. My first instinct should be to pale because I shouldn't want this kind of attention from a vampire, but I bite my lip and watch him watch me as he backs toward the door.

He twists the knob, and I straighten my shoulders to brace myself for Kingston's wild banter and stupid irresistible charm, but a strange vampire pushes past Austin and into the room. He slams the door, startling me, and I tense in my chair.

The second our eyes meet, terror rushes over me in a cool wave like all the warmth cascading through me disappeared with Austin.

And then the strange vampire smiles.

Oh, God, please help me. What if this guy is my supposed perfect vampire match?

5

Master

THE INCESSANT BEEPING MATCHES MY racing heart as the unfamiliar vampire leans closer to me from his seat and sniffs my mint-scented hair. I swallow hard, my hands shaking under his scrutiny, and I can't even get myself to meet his gaze to take in the color of his eyes.

"You're prettier than your picture," the vampire says, darting his hand out to push my hair behind my ear. "And thinner, but it suits you. You prefer to be called by your first name, Jewel?"

It takes everything in me not to snap that starvation doesn't friggin' suit me, and it's the main reason I'm even in this chair to begin with. Instead, I suck in a small breath, lift my chin up, and force myself to meet the vampire's blue eyes—not vibrant like Austin's green ones or mysterious like Kingston's nearly black ones or pretty like Diego's gray. This vampire's ordinary blue eyes barely stand out against his pasty skin that I doubt could ever blush. Maybe it's the fact that his backhanded compliment got to me, but I hate this guy already.

"Thanks, I guess, and Ms. Jordan is fine," I say, my harsh voice shocking me.

My words surprise Mr. Ordinary too, because he frowns, turning his gaze to look at his reflection in the mirror. "Okay, Ms. Jordan. You may call me Master Caruthers until we're both comfortable with a first name basis. It seems you've already met the other candidates, so I've requested extra time with you, if you don't mind."

I totally mind. I already want him to leave. Instead, I say, "Sure. That seems reasonable."

He smiles, flashing his fangs at me, but not in the adorable way Austin did. This dude is leering, licking his teeth. He looks like a bite and tear type of vampire. "Good. I looked over your results so far and think we have a lot in common. I wasn't sure about someone with less than average sexual experience unless you lied thinking it would help match you..."

"What?"

"So, you were honest. I suppose the noted hymen from your medical examination should have been evidence enough but with the new laws, I figured there was a shift in—"

I cover my ears, saving myself from whatever the hell he's noting about his observation of human society or his hypothesis of what happens in a world he certainly believes he's far above.

"...but then I imagine it would be quite enjoyable to mold your desires to match mine to really authenticate our companionship."

The shadows of my vision darken, and I stare at my long fingernails while I tune out the vampire's words the second he goes into the sex territory that suddenly makes me feel exceptionally sick. It was one thing for Kingston to tease me over my lack of experience, but this guy is already plotting how our living arrangements will be without even consulting with me.

"Ms. Jordan, did you hear me?" Master Caruthers asks.

I blink a few times. "I'm sorry, what was that again?"

"I asked if you were claustrophobic, because I imagine you'd take to my schedule and would spend the day entertaining me in my tight sleeping quarters. I don't like a lot of space and need to know if breaking you from a fear of closed spaces would be worth it or if I should relent and add additional room."

"You sleep in a coffin or something?" I ask. I always thought that was a myth. Vampires can't stand sunlight, but there are plenty of ways to avoid it.

He scoffs. "I thought you were educated."

"And I thought I'd run your daytime household."

"Don't be ridiculous. I have well-paid security, so there's

no need for you to oversee my affairs. I did not pay the exorbitant amount to try to match with you to include you in my staff. Our time together will be well spent and enjoyable for me."

Bile rises in my throat at his innuendo, and I clutch my hands together in my lap. "Um, that's not going to work for me."

He straightens his back. "Excuse me? It doesn't matter what works for you. You've signed the paperwork. Once we match, you'll return to my home immediately where you'll fulfill your contract. If you do not, your heirs will not reap the benefits."

I frown. "What? You can't be serious, dude."

"*Dude*? You will not disrespect me with your despicable vocabulary."

"Well, you can't treat me like a piece of property to have your disgusting way with," I snap. "I'd rather take a blood debt than match with you."

The vampire roars, sending my hair flying away from my face. I squeeze my eyes shut, bracing myself for the slap that never comes. Something squeaks across the floor, and I glance up, holding my hands to my chest to watch Kingston practically dragging Master Caruthers from the room.

"Your request for extra time has been denied, Roger," Kingston says, escorting the vampire all the way through the door. "Please allow Ms. Sybil to walk you to the lobby where you can wait for the results. And remember, bite the staff and you'll be disqualified from matching for another year."

Kingston slams the door in Master Caruthers's face and spins on his feet to face me. The second our eyes meet, he smiles, but then a sob wracks my chest, and I lose my friggin' shit, making the machine beep like crazy. I rip all the wires stickered to me away and slam my hands against the buttons until it stops.

"What the actual fuck?" I ask, sobbing into my hands, trying not to snot all over the place as the possible fate of matching with Master Caruthers swirls through my head. "I can't end up with that guy. Did you hear him? I'm pretty sure he said he wanted to deflower me immediately. *Deflower.*" I guess I still heard everything the monster said as much as I tried to tune out his words.

"Um, babe. I'm pretty sure I want to deflower you. Right here. Right now. To hell with the rules. The thought of that asshole even looking at you again makes me...unhappy."

I slap his arm, laughing through my uncontrollable tears. "Shut the hell up, Kingston. I'm not having sex with you right now."

"So that means there's hope." He grins, keeping his fangs in check. "And it was only a suggestion. If you allow me to *deflower* you, then he can't. Might make him withdraw." He clears his throat a few times, studying my face for a reaction I clench my jaw not to give him.

Touching my chin, he nudges my head up so I have to look straight into his midnight eyes. His fangs now extend when he smiles at me, but instead of the fear Master Caruthers ignited in me, my racing heart starts to settle. Kingston pulls a silk square of fabric from his pocket and dabs it across my wet cheeks until I stop crying and inhale a deep breath that shudders through me.

"That's better. I don't like what seeing you cry does to me," he says, patting his hand on mine.

I lick my lips to help me swallow through the burning in my throat. "And what exactly does it do to you?"

"Instant boner killer," he quips.

I snort and cover my mouth at the stupid sound that makes Kingston chuckle enough that he might actually be giggling. "You are something else, you know."

His dark eyes flash silver, and he brings my hand up to graze his lips over the back of my knuckles. "Hopefully something you like."

"If it makes you feel better, I'd rather have a blood debt with you than be within a five-mile radius of Master Caruthers."

Kingston leans closer to me. "You really do know how to make a guy feel special. I can't believe you called him dude."

"Me either."

"That's your pet name for me, remember? Now I feel like you need to come up with a new one. I refuse to let that dipshit ruin something so magical between us."

I laugh. "I already have another nickname for you, Kingston."

His eyebrows rise on his forehead. "What is it? Sexy? Hottie? Sex God? I approve of any of those."

"Rule Breaker," I say, keeping my eyes trained on his.

He reaches out and runs his cool fingers along my jaw. "You know me so well, babe. And you know what? I don't want you worrying about matching with Roger Caruthers or the blood debt I wasn't actually going to hold you to. I was only trying to assure a better outcome for me since I wasn't sure how much hell my brothers would give me over my last minute entrance to match with you."

I settle our hands on my knee, allowing him to twine his fingers through mine. I'm not sure how much I believe him about the blood debt, but the fact that his excuse makes my heart pick up pace doesn't make it seem so bad. It wasn't like he forced me to be here. I wanted to be here. "They did sound pretty annoyed."

"Only because they're freaked out about how amazing we are together, babe. Neither had expected one another to both like who you were on paper, but here we are. We're lucky to have made it this far. I'd say a three-to-one chance of you ending up at the Divinity Estate proves all our feelings are right."

"I hope so. If I end up with Master Caruthers—"

Kingston covers my mouth with his hand. "I promise you that you don't have to worry about him, babe."

"How can I not worry?" I ask, even thinking of that outcome making me nauseated. "Can you change the data or something?" Because if he can, then he could change my final match to be him, and I'm not sure how I feel about it. Kingston is crazy attractive, but the moral part of me knows that's cheating, and I'd feel bad for his brothers.

"The idea freaks you out," he says, slightly bouncing in his chair. "I can tell. And the answer is not exactly, because I wouldn't do that to my brothers. They like you as much as I do. I just wish I'd beat Austin to saving your life. I bet he'll get extra points for that, and if not, well he should've taken you up on your request for a kiss. That would've been a first he could never forget, though I doubt he'd even forget you playing lapsies. I'm totally jealous, you know."

"Wait, rewind and say that again."

"I'm jealous as hell, babe."

I shake my head, frowning. "Not that. You said Austin saved my life. You mean by giving me his blood?"

He tips his head back and laughs, but all he does is shake his head. "I see you're purposely ignoring my other remark about him. He'll be delighted you don't care. And so you know, I can be your hero too."

Unlike how Diego thinks before he speaks, or how Austin tries to be careful with what he says, Kingston just spits it all out, making my head swim as I try to keep up with all his revelations. My thoughts jump from Austin saving me to trying to remember his other remark, and I gape at Kingston. "Austin's never kissed someone?"

Running his hand over his face, he pushes his hair from his eyes. "Effing A. I'm a dead man for telling you that."

I tighten my lips, still nervous to tease him. From the little time I've known him, I can tell he reacts to things much more passionately than his brothers—like with throwing the phlebotomist into the wall. I take my chances anyway and say, "Well, the majority of the population probably already thinks that about you."

"If I were dead... You know what? Let them think that." Bringing my hand to his chest, he presses my fingers into his exposed skin under his still half opened shirt from when he showed me his chest earlier. His heartbeat thrums against my fingers, picking up pace as my fingers spread to press my palm completely flat. "If this isn't proof enough, I'll show you how I'm very much alive when we're truly alone."

I blush. "Maybe if we match."

He smirks. "Oh, I do not doubt that we will."

"Diego and Austin seem pretty convinced they will match with me too."

"Just because they think that doesn't mean anything. Who do you want to match with?" he asks, capturing me with his dark eyes. "It's me, right?"

I shrug. "Anyone who isn't Master Caruthers."

He huffs a breath, fake glaring at me. "All right, babe. I can't stand waiting a moment longer. Let's get this over with, so I can prove to my brothers I'm right."

"I didn't think it was that much of a competition. Apparently, appointments were booked solid the whole month. If you don't match with me, you'll match with someone more compatible."

Taking my hand in his, he tugs me from the seat, hits the button on the machine to watch it shoot out the paper with only a few unreadable pieces of code on it, and tugs me along toward the door.

Before he opens it, he leans in, brushing his lips to my earlobe, making me shiver. "Get ready, babe. I'm about to prove myself right."

"You think so?"

"There's no denying it. You're the perfect match for me."

6

The Results

I WAS HOPING THAT KINGSTON was joking about sending Brayla home as a way to assure I wouldn't rush through the Blood Match process to return to her. But he wasn't, and I find myself alone with five vampires and Ms. Sybil, who sits behind the counter, clicking away at her computer. She must really trust these guys since she only glances up once to look at Kingston and me as we walk through the door together.

When the four other vampires all dart their gazes to our interlocked fingers, I quickly tug my hand from Kingston's and cross my arms over my chest. I meet the hard gaze of the strange vampire standing between Diego and Master Caruthers and shrink back under his scrutiny, wondering if he was the vampire who didn't make it past the blood tasting portion of the test.

"Ms. Sybil will assist you now with your results," Kingston says, nudging me toward the counter and away from the group of vampires watching my every movement.

"Does everyone usually watch?" I ask. "The guy I saw matched yesterday was alone."

"His results were narrowed down early, so Caroline knew she would match and chose not to hang around."

"Oh."

"I'd hang around for you, though," he says with a wink.

Abandoning me at the counter with Ms. Sybil, Kingston joins the group I'm too scared to look at again. Whispers of my name sound from behind me, and I swear someone growls. Ms. Sybil doesn't even look up at me as she continues to jab her fingers against the digital keypad in need of a quick wipe down from the smudgy fingerprints created from whatever food used to be in the empty bag on her desk.

A hand slaps the counter next to me, startling me. I jerk my head up to meet the angry gaze of Master Caruthers. He tosses a packet of papers right onto Ms. Sybil's keyboard, and she finally draws her attention up to meet the dull blue eyes of the vampire I'd rather die than match with.

"Here are the hard copies. The disqualification forms are all filled out, and the petition fee should transfer at any second," he says, stepping so close to me that his arm touches mine before he slides his fingers over my hand resting on the counter.

A ding sounds from Ms. Sybil's computer, and she nods her head. "Thank you, Mr. Caruthers. It arrived. I'll need a few seconds to process your paperwork and get Ms. Jordan's all settled."

I peek over my shoulder to catch the sight of Kingston, Austin, and Diego staring at me, though the strange vampire with them tends to something on the tablet he taps away on. The strange look that crosses all my possible matches' faces sends panic rushing through me, and I don't even have to ask them to know something is wrong.

"Congratulations, Ms. Jordan. You've officially matched eighty-one percent with Roger Caruthers of the Shadow Crest Villa. Due to the oncoming sunrise, you will unfortunately be unable to return home to pack any belongings you might want. But don't worry. Master Caruthers will provide everything you need and your next of kin will be notified of the outstanding news through a video announcement."

I gape at the woman and glance to look at my name, along with Roger Caruthers's, light up the screen behind her with a rundown of our compatibility. Our scores are all over the place, and the bonus points at the bottom that push me into the eightieth percentile match zone with him are due to the large fee stated in the small box. We scored so poorly during the interview that he shouldn't be my match.

"But my apartment doesn't have electricity," I say, instead of pointing out the glaring reason we matched, which I still don't believe is possible.

"Your father will receive notification at his place of employment."

"But he's—"

Oh. Fucking. Shit. What the hell happened? Panic tightens my chest. There's no way that I was more compatible to this douche bag than I was to the others. I can't even stand to look at his ageless face with his ashen skin and ordinary blue eyes.

"Please turn to your Blood Match Companion for further information, Ms. Jordan. Mr. Caruthers will happily answer any and all of your questions. And again, congratulations. It was a close one. You almost matched with no one, but Mr. Caruthers generously and graciously accepted flaws of yours he wouldn't have previously." She points at the fee listed on the bottom. "This was due to the edits in his application." Without another word, Ms. Sybil turns her attention back to her keyboard and doesn't even look up as I release a small screech from my mouth.

Sharp nails dig into the skin of my wrist, and Master Caruthers jerks me away from the counter to spin me to face him. My heart throttles behind my ribs, threatening to smash itself to save me, but my panic only makes Master Caruthers leer, flashing his fangs. He reaches his other hand up, petting my hair from my face, holding me in place before I can take a step back.

"My lucky day," he says, leaning closer to me. "I knew we'd match just fine."

Jerking back from him, I turn my face toward Ms. Sybil though the rest of me stays locked in place. "I'd like to petition to be retested and re-matched. I think there was an error in the results."

"I'm sorry, Ms. Jordan. Master Caruthers was the only available match upon completion."

"But what about—"

"The other candidates were disqualified," Ms. Sybil says without looking up from her screen.

"What?" I try to rip myself away from Master Caruthers, but he's too strong.

"Come along, Ms. Jordan. Let me get you home," the repulsive vampire says, pulling me into him to inhale the scent of my hair. His tongue glides along my throat, making me tense. "I can't wait for a proper taste. Do you mind?"

"Hell yeah, I mind," I say, struggling to free myself. "Let me go. You're hurting me."

His smile widens the second before his nails bite into my skin so hard that blood seeps from my wrists to splash across my white dress. My heartbeat pounds in my ears, and I cry out, jerking my knee into Master Caruthers's groin. He roars, shoving me back. The wind knocks from my lungs, and I skid across the tiles, stopping beneath four tall figures. Kingston's chest heaves, his face twisting into rage the second our eyes meet. Austin's wide eyes search over my body in the same panic that leaves me breathless. Diego balls his hands into fists, turning to look from the strange vampire with them and then to his brothers.

"Please, help me," I cry. "He's not my perfect match. One of you three are. I know it."

"Jewel, we're—"

Master Caruthers drags me away by my ankles, cutting off whatever Austin was about to say to me. The raging lunatic of a vampire locks his fingers through my hair and yanks me off the floor to set me on my feet. Twisting me around, Master Caruthers presses his taut chest into my back, forcing me to face the other vampires. His entire body touches mine, and I gag as he grinds against my back, breathing heavy in my ear.

Jerking my head to the side, he exposes my neck, flicking his tongue eagerly across the sensitive skin of my throat. His rough hand slides up my stomach and toward my breasts, and I focus on the looks of horror sweeping across the faces of all four vampires standing before me.

The stranger nods his head at Kingston, Austin, and Diego before disappearing out the front door of the building, and the three vampires glance at each other and then to me. I realize Master Caruthers's actions aren't even about me, and I somehow got caught in a feud between vampires that'll surely end with me ripped to pieces. Master Caruthers purposely rubs our bought Blood Match in their faces. And it looks like his big, stupid ego might actually save me as Kingston steps forward.

One second Master Caruthers lifts his hand to cup my breast through the dress, and in the next, the window cracks under the force of his body smashing into it. Another pair of hands tugs me away, enveloping me so tightly that I can't move as my face presses into Kingston's chest. His heartbeat thrums in my ear, but it's not loud enough to muffle the sudden screech piercing the air, turning my hot blood cold in the process.

Sticky liquid seeps between my toes, and I nearly slip from Kingston's arms. He picks me up, hooking his arm across my butt to keep me from the strange liquid too dark to be human blood as it cascades across the floor and ruins his dress shoes.

I wiggle to turn in Kingston's arms, my stomach threatening to expel what little food and water that remains in it. "Holy shit balls."

"Don't look, Jewel. Please, just don't look," he whispers, running his fingers through my now sweaty hair.

But it's too late. I can't unsee the severed head of Master Caruthers rolling across the floor. And the dark stuff now coating my feet? His blood stains nearly the entire lobby as it seeps from the severed limbs and his still twitching torso.

"They wouldn't want you to see them like this," Kingston adds, shifting me in his arms to cradle me instead of just holding me up off the floor.

The world blurs, and I startle from the too fast movement. Kingston sets me down in a chair inside a sleek office of glass and dark woods before disappearing through an open door. A million thoughts rush through my mind as Kingston's words play over and over in my head. He wasn't trying to prevent me from seeing Master Caruthers. He wanted to protect his brothers from me seeing them. It's then that I know that they're the ones responsible for the lunatic's dismemberment.

I heave a breath, staring at the vampire blood staining the hem of my white dress, a dark contrast from my own red blood decorating the once pristine fabric. I put pressure on the small wounds on my wrists to staunch the bleeding the best I can but seeing the streams trickle down my arms makes me woozy.

"Here, let me help you, Jewel." Austin appears at my side, and I jump, releasing a cry. He hesitates because of my reaction, clutching a first aid kit to his chest. "That asshole was close to nicking an artery. The last thing you need is to lose any more blood."

Dizziness washes over me, but I manage to remain upright in my chair. "You saved me," I whisper. "Twice today."

Austin closes his eyes for a second, releasing a relieved breath. He quickly snaps open the first aid kit and silently tends to my wounds, taking extra care not to touch me too much like he's afraid he'll hurt me even more.

"Kingston told me the reason you gave me your blood earlier." I don't know what else to say. If I even mention Master Caruthers, I might fall apart, remembering his rough arms around me or his slimy tongue licking my neck.

"It was nothing. I'm just glad you're okay. I—"

Flinging my arms out, I surprise Austin with a hug, burying my face into his neck. The second his hand touches my back, my whole body reacts in a mixture of emotions that leaves me on the verge of moaning and crying.

"Let me see if I can find you something else to wear," he says, gently easing away from me.

I hold him tighter. "Don't leave me. I'm scared. What i—"

"It's all clear, Austin. Security has been wiped, Ms. Sybil manipulated to forget, and all traces of..." Diego's voice trails off as I meet his gaze from over Austin's shoulder. "Hey, beautiful. You okay?" he asks me.

I bob my head. "I-I t-think so. Are you? That douche-nozzle didn't hurt you, did he?"

Both Austin and Diego chuckle at the same time. Diego steps into the room, kneeling down in front of me, not even caring that blood still drips from my white dress. He holds one of my hands while Austin still holds my other, and he trails his gaze over me from my feet and back to my eyes.

"We're dandy. I'm just sorry I didn't react sooner. I was in shock over the whole situation," he admits.

"Yeah, Roger petitioned to disqualify us for fraternizing with you before the interview. Asshole couldn't stand that there was no way in hell he'd have matched better with you. I don't even know how he managed the percentage he did. He obviously lied on his questionnaire."

"He paid for last minute edits," I say, watching Diego's gray eyes darken. They must not be privy to Master Caruthers's information.

Diego glowers at the floor. "I'll have Kingston look into that loophole. It was intended to allow someone close to matching to get the chance, not for someone to steal a match out from under another."

"I had no idea you guys filled out questionnaires." I don't know what else to say without losing my shit that Donor Life Corp allows loopholes. I guess I get it, but they're incredibly strict about the rules with humans. It pisses me off.

Austin rubs his thumb across my wrist, just grazing my skin back and forth over and over again, steadying my heartbeat in the process. "How else do you think they test for compatibility?"

"Luck."

"I told you matching had nothing to do with luck," Kingston says, appearing in the doorway. He saunters into the room and comes up behind me, now wearing a different suit and shoes, and rests his hands on my shoulders. Peering down at me, he offers me a smile.

"Just bribery, cheating, and fear," I mutter. "You told me I wouldn't match with Master Caruthers. You lied to me."

You'd think I just kicked him with the hurt that sweeps across his face, darkening his eyes more than I thought possible. He sucks his bottom lip between his teeth but doesn't look away. He leans closer if anything, locking me in place with his brooding gaze before eyeing my hands, taking note that each of his brothers clutches one of mine.

"According to the records, you didn't match with him," he says, cracking his neck while rolling his shoulders. "Roger Caruthers never applied."

I frown. "Huh?"

"You still need to discover your results," he adds. "I mean, if you'd still like to see which one of us you've matched with. Because of the extenuating circumstances, Donor Life Corp will absolve your contract and you're free to return home. But I'd like you to reconsider if that's what you want."

Warmth cascades over me the longer I look into his eyes, and both Austin and Diego squeeze my hands. Kingston strolls from behind me to fill the space between his brothers. He bows forward, slightly nudging my knees apart with his torso so he can get into my face. If it weren't for the unforgiving fabric of my dress, I'd be straddling him.

Fear presses in on me. I steeled myself to be matched. I prepared to match with whoever they put me with, even if it was someone awful like Master Caruthers. But now? I don't even know. I'm scared to find out who could possibly match with me if it's not Kingston, Diego, or Austin. Maybe my sister was right. Maybe there's still another way to survive outside The Boxes.

I clear my throat, finding myself leaning closer to Kingston. "I want to take you up on your offer to forgive my contract because there's no way I want to find out who else was in the running to match with me since you three have been disqualified."

The corner of his lips quirks up in a half smile. "Disqualified? Not according to the computer."

"But Master Caruthers—"

Kingston brings his hand up to my cheek, running his fingers along my jaw. "You'll forget Master Caruthers and everything he put you through tonight."

My eyes widen. "You try forgetting something like that."

Austin clears his throat. "You can't manipulate her memory while my blood's in her system, bro."

Kingston groans, disappearing from in front of me to stand a few feet away. Rubbing his hand over his head, he pushes his hair from his face. "Ah, hell."

I drop my hands from Diego and Austin and push to my feet, closing the distance to Kingston. Anger rushes over me at the thought that he was going to try to use his vampire power on me to erase part of my memory without my permission, a memory I very much need right now so I don't forget what these guys are capable of through all the damn emotions they elicit from the depths of my soul.

I jab my finger into Kingston's chest. "How dare you."

"Babe, please. Let me explain," Kingston says, gently pulling my hand from his pecs of concrete.

"Explain what exactly? That you had me convinced that I was going to match with you or one of your brothers and then you just stood there and did nothing as that vampire basically bought my contract out of spite because you broke the rules."

"I made the rules, Jewel," Kingston says. "So did Austin and Diego. And I can assure you that we didn't break any. Roger tried to force himself through a loophole but forfeited his spot the second he broke open the skin on your wrists. Outside the tasting room, he can't extract more than a finger prick of blood for obvious reasons."

"And I couldn't stand the fact that he made you cry," Diego whispers.

"So you ripped his head off." It's not a question.

Austin clears his throat. "That was me."

I don't know whether to laugh or cry at their revelation and how close I came to having to leave with Master Caruthers and how his massive ego and need to rub in his match was what saved me. If you can even call me sitting in front of three powerful vampires with wicked enough tempers to tear another being to pieces being saved.

"Effing shit balls," I whisper. "This is not how I imagined my night to turn out."

"Sorry, Jewel," all three of them say in unison. They're obviously as torn as I am over everything.

"Thanks. All of you. I mean it," I say, finally finding the strength to meet their intense gazes. "But are you even sure you want to find out who matches with me? Because I'll go through with it if what Kingston says is true. I need this for my family, but I also don't want to see you guys hurt each other or something. I like you all enough and can see a great match in either of you three."

"Only Diego's the sore loser," Austin quips.

"Says the guy who ripped someone's head off," Kingston says with a laugh, chuckling at Austin as his eyes dart to mine.

I reach out and take Austin's hand while fake glaring at Kingston. "Says the dude who weaseled his way onto the match list and tried to trick me with a blood debt."

"Still not sorry, babe," he says, touching my cheek. "Now shall we confirm I'm your perfect match?"

"In your dreams, bro," Diego says.

I roll my eyes and step away from the three of them, though I can see they all want to walk me back to the lobby. I just motion for Kingston to lead the way, and Austin and Diego follow behind me.

Kingston turns around once before we reach the door that'll take us back into the lobby. "Hey, babe, can you do us a favor?"

I twist my lips to the side, not sure I could agree to any sort of favor he might ask of me.

He chuckles. "I'll save the good ones for later, promise, but since you obviously will hate me forever if I try to manipulate your memory when Austin's blood wears off, can you pretend not to know Roger Caruthers."

I blink. "Who?"

He beams me a smile. "Thanks, babe. Go ahead and follow Diego and Austin to the showers and get cleaned up. I'll meet you in the lobby."

"And then I'll be matched and can get the hell out of here?"

All three of them chuckle, and Kingston says, "Fucking finally. Yours was the longest application process ever. You set all sorts of new records for Donor Life Corp."

"Maybe stop scheduling appointments right before sundown," I say, smirking.

Austin touches his hand to my back to guide me faster. "That was my fault. I really wanted to meet you."

Diego leans closer. "Don't let that sweet baby face of his fool you. He's the real troublemaker."

"I think I can handle trouble. And I am sorry it took me so long."

Kingston winks at me. "No worries, babe. You're totally worth the wait."

I don't even know how to react to all of their constant attention, so all I do is smile. For the first time since I rushed into the building, my life doesn't feel like it's about to end. I think I'm as anxious as the rest of them to find out who I match with.

And for once in my life, I'm not even scared. I know my family will be okay. I'll be okay. I'm not going to be a blood slave after all. I might actually get to be a little bit free.

7

The Divine Vampire Heirs

MS. SYBIL LEANS ON HER elbows, staring at her computer screen. Kingston materializes in front of me, startling the woman, and her open mouth melts into a smile. She nods her head at something he says to her, and then she turns her attention to me as I stroll between Austin and Diego as they silently guide me to the counter.

Peering around, I spot no evidence of Master Caruthers' existence. I somehow even managed to get the traces of his blood from my toenails with only a small yet embarrassing amount of help from Austin in the shower. It doesn't help that my body keeps reacting to his presence every time he's in touchable reach. What makes it slightly worse is that he can't stop chuckling about it, which only makes me smile instead of frown because he's cute despite knowing that he is capable of severing someone's head from their body.

"Ms. Jordan," Ms. Sybil says, smiling at me. "You look lovely. A match fit for one of Dark Terrace Ranch's fine princes."

"Princes?" Her sudden nicety digs into me, and I know without having to ask Kingston that he may have persuaded her to be friendlier with me.

"The heirs of Mitchell Divine of the Donor Life Corporation and the heads of the Divinity Estate," she replies, smiling at the three vampires standing behind me.

Peeking over my shoulder, I catch Diego's gaze first, and he shrugs his shoulders. Movement behind him draws my attention away, and I freeze at the sight of the strange vampire from earlier. I blink once, and he stands behind Austin and Kingston with an arm draped over each of their shoulders, studying me with a curious expression without saying a word.

I swallow and smile at him, sensing that he might be *the* Mitchell Divine Ms. Sybil spoke of. For one, his presence alone screams vampire wealth. And two, all three guys smile at the man, who appears to have risen from the Blood Hunger Plague around my dad's age of forty, though Mitchell Divine carries a timeless elegance no human can ever muster.

"Isn't she beautiful, Dad?" Kingston asks, grinning at me

for the millionth time.

I'm taken aback that he'd even call the vampire who sired him that.

"Exquisite." The deep tenor of Mitchell's voice wraps around me, making me smile even more. "I never doubted you boys would match with a fine young woman who can bring fulfillment into one of your lives."

"Thank you, sir," I say and then stiffen. Shit balls. What if I'm not supposed to talk to him? Sudden fear blossoms in my heart, and Austin's cool pinky finger hooks around mine. Kingston reaches up and pokes my nose, wagging his brows at me. Diego beams his huge, heart-melting smile, and I relax a tiny bit.

"You're welcome, Jewel. I'm delighted to bring you into our household." He turns to Ms. Sybil. "Please proceed with the results. I'm sure Ms. Jordan is anxious."

"Me too," the three heirs whisper in unison.

Ms. Sybil nods and taps at her digital keyboard before leaning back in her chair. Everyone turns their attentions to the wall behind her. My name blinks across the giant screen, and I hold my breath in anticipation.

Ms. Sybil's eyes light up. "Congratulations, Ms. Jordan. You're a ninety-nine percent match to...oh."

"Spill it already," Kingston says, sliding up behind me.

He attempts to lean over the counter to look at her screen, but Ms. Sybil taps away at her keyboard, and her monitor turns blue before my picture flashes up on the wall with a few stats about my physical features and various percentages for personality, health, and my blood type.

A second later, another picture pops on the screen next to mine.

Cool arms wrap around me, and Diego spins me so quickly that I nearly lose my balance. "I knew you were my match—nearly perfect. I don't think I've ever seen a compatibility of ninety-nine percent."

I'm tempted to ask him what the one percent is, but he smiles again, and I know it doesn't even matter. Running his fingers up my arms and to my shoulders, he plays with a few strands of my hair, taking me in like I'm the best thing he's ever seen. He looked at me like he was attracted to me before, but something has already shifted between us. It's not love or anything but definite attraction. For the first time in my life, I feel what it's like to be certain of something, and it's how lucky I am to have been matched with Diego.

Diego nuzzles his nose to mine, and I giggle with a wave of anticipation as he puckers his lips while closing the space between us. Shutting my eyes, I lick my lips, nerves and excitement rushing through me at the thought of kissing him—my first kiss ever—and I had no idea how much I wanted to experience such a thing. My whole body aches to press against him, to feel his hands pull me close, to map over my skin in discovery...

Someone hooks their arm around my stomach, yanking me back before my lips meet Diego's. He releases one scary ass growl that makes me stiffen in—oh, shit—Mitchell Divine's strong arms. I jerk my arms up to protect myself, a flash of silver glowing across Diego's gray eyes. A quiet whimper escapes my mouth, and Mitchell spins me away from the others, sandwiching me between his body and the counter.

"What the hell is this about, Dad?" Diego snaps.

The presence behind me disappears, and I blow a small breath through my lips and slowly turn around to face what the eff is going on behind me. I half expect everyone to start throwing punches, but Diego, Austin, and Kingston all gape at the screen behind me while Mitchell tilts his head, giving me an intense once-over that makes me shiver under his scrutiny.

Tears burn my eyes, confusion igniting anxiety through me to tighten my chest.

And then Diego closes the space between us once more and clasps my hand, bringing it to his chest. "I'm sorry, beautiful. I didn't mean to scare you."

"Is everything all right? I thought it was okay to kiss now that we matched." My eyes dart to Mitchell. I'm totally assuming, since I only skimmed the full brochure and signed things without really reading them because I was afraid of backing out. "I'm sorry if that was inappropriate. I got caught up in the moment of learning who my match was."

Kingston clears his throat. "Babe."

I slowly turn my gaze to Kingston, now afraid to even look at him for fear that even though I matched with his brother, I'm still loads attracted to Rule Breaker. I sneak a look at Austin next, and yup. My body does all sorts of funny things when he smirks at me.

"It's Jewel," I say. "I'm sorry, Kingston. You're funny and sweet, super hot too, but you said it yourself that the Blood Match Program would pair me with the one most compatible."

"You sure know how to let a guy down easy, but there's a slight problem with your results," he says.

I frown.

Austin twirls his finger and points behind me. "You should turn around."

When I'm not quick to move, all three vampires close the space to me. Diego and Austin stand at both my sides with Kingston in front of me. Gently grasping my shoulders, he spins me to look at the flashing screen behind Ms. Sybil.

I blink a dozen times and rub my eyes. "Dude, this is a joke, right?"

"No joke, babe," Kingston says.

I swallow, nerves now squeezing my stomach. "Ninety-nine percent match for...*all three* of you? You guys don't even seem that similar."

"Basically, all of the tests filter into three main categories: personality, physical attraction, and nutrients—or mind, body, and blood. We all matched perfectly with you in one of the varying categories and slightly less in the other two—literally, by a minuscule amount. With Diego, you scored a hundred percent match for personality. You'll obviously laugh at each other's lame jokes and—"

"Knock it off, Kingston," Diego says, punching his brother.

Kingston cracks his neck. "You matched a hundred percent in the nutrients category with Austin, so it's not a wonder why the side effect of drinking his blood was stronger than we anticipated."

I raise my eyebrows at Austin, realizing how accurate his original nickname of Hungry Eyes I had given him was.

"Which means," Kingston continues.

I groan. "I think I get it and can fill in the blanks, Rule Breaker."

He chuckles. "Oh, come on, babe. I really want to say it. I mean, I'll beg you if you deny me."

I glare at him, hugging my arms over my chest as he stares at me like he can undress me with his eyes.

Meeting my glare, he pouts.

I roll my eyes. "Fine, dude. If it means that much."

He grins. "As you guessed, I'm one hundred, sexy, amazing, rock-your-world percent match with your body."

Heat claws up my neck, and Kingston has the nerve to flick open another damn button on his shirt, drawing my attention to his lickable chest—lickable? OhmyeffingG. Please, help me.

As the three vampires stare at me with irresistible smiles that steal the certainty I had for my future away from me, I reach out to grab the counter for support. Except I'm not strong enough to hold my weight as my legs give out on me.

Three nearly perfect matches with three extremely intriguing, attractive, basically royal vampires? Holy shit balls. I don't know if this is a blessing or a curse. They might drain me dry in a fit of jealousy or something.

"Jewel? Hey, Jewel. Look at me." It's Austin. "Take a deep breath, okay? Your vitals are off the charts."

"I—" My dry tongue sticks to the roof of my mouth, making it hard to speak coherently, though I can't even think of exactly what to say. "I thought Kingston was supposed to be in tune with my body."

"Annoyingly, Austin's the professional when it comes to human health," Kingston replies. "I trust your sexy body in his hands...but don't get too handsy, bro."

Austin holds a glass of water to my lips, ignoring his brother. "Here, take a slow drink."

Diego links our fingers together. "It's going to be okay, beautiful. We'll get this all worked out."

"Even if we have to Rock-Paper-Scissors for you," Kingston adds.

Austin shoves him. "Not helping, asshat."

"Look, it made her smile," he argues. "You're just scared I'll win."

"Highly doubt it," Diego says.

Austin helps me take another sip. "Seriously."

"Enough!" Mitchell's voice booms through the room. "A Blood Match is not a competition. Jewel is one of your futures and will not be chosen by a back-world game of chance."

"Then how do you suppose we handle this?" Kingston asks. "The likelihood of multiple, perfectly equal matches is unheard of. There isn't some secret bonus questionnaire."

"I'll call an emergency board meeting to discuss the matter," Mitchell says. He closes the space to me, and Kingston, Diego, and Austin all stand up to give the vampire room to kneel in front of me, a gesture I never expected from someone who founded the company our society relies upon for order. "Ms. Jordan, I apologize for the inconvenience this has caused you. I'll assure a bonus package will be given to your heirs."

Slowly, I nod.

"Because it's so close to sunrise, I'll arrange a room here for you with my full staff at your disposal while you wait. You can request anything you'd like. I'll also schedule another visit from Dr. Prajapati to assure you get on the right path to perfect health."

Tears prickle my eyes, and I force myself to nod. Before I can swipe the pesky teardrop away, it splashes to my cheek, and all four vampires look at me like I've lost my head or something.

"Is that unsatisfactory? I promise you the accommodations are—"

"I'm sorry," I whisper. "I didn't mean to offend you, but I thought the pamphlet said that I get one day after the match with my family."

"Your father will be notified, and we'll schedule a visit on—"

"That doesn't work for me. My father is missing," I say. "I'm currently head of my household, so any sort of notification won't reach my next of kin because they're all underage."

"Missing? That wasn't in your file," Kingston says, speaking up.

"I didn't report it."

"Why?" he asks. "We take missing humans seriously. Every donor matters."

I can't stop the fury from swelling through me at his words, but one look from Mitchell Divine stops me from speaking my mind and telling Kingston that donors only matter because they're needed for vampires to survive and not because Donor Life Corp cares about the individual.

I also remember what Diego said about the quarantine. If it were true, it means Dad was going to break the law. Law breakers end up drained and...

"I was scared, okay?" I say, finally responding. "I can't afford our living arrangements by myself, and I know what happens when I can't provide enough. It's why I'm here. And now that I know I'm a match to—to all three of you, it doesn't really matter anymore. I just—please, let me go home and make sure everything is set with my family. The pamphlet said—"

"It's too dangerous, Jewel," Mitchell says. "You're a match to my heirs and with the sunrise—"

"We can send for them," Diego says, speaking up. "That way Jewel doesn't have to leave, and she still gets to see them before their transfer this afternoon."

"This afternoon?"

Diego nods. "Even though you haven't officially matched

with one of us, we will not force your beneficiaries to wait to reap the benefits. No matter what, you belong to the Divinity Estate, so at least that makes things easier."

Belong to the Divinity Estate. While it's technically true, they haven't made me feel like a piece of property.

I release a breath, hoping to myself that it doesn't change the moment I step foot into their household. And I hate myself a little because I didn't even think about Ramona, Fallon, and Dana having to wait. Thank God they don't or else I don't know what we'd do.

"Thank you," I whisper, wiping the tears from my eyes. "You have no idea what this means to me."

Mitchell offers me his hand and helps me to my feet. "Come along, Jewel. I'll escort you to your room while my sons make the proper arrangements."

I shift on my feet and look at the three vampires. "I guess I'll see you later?"

Kingston pulls me into a hug first. "You bet, babe. Call the front desk if you're lonely, and I'll make sure they transfer you to me."

Diego sandwiches me between him and his brother. "Same goes for me."

Austin gently takes my hand when the two of them release me. "I'll stop by with Dr. Prajapati later."

"Lucky bastard," Kingston says under his breath but purposely loud enough for everyone, including me, to hear him.

"Get some rest until then," Austin adds, ignoring his

brother.

Mitchell holds out his arm for me. "Come on, my dear. Your room awaits."

8

Goodbye

RAMONA TACKLES ME, SENDING ME splaying across the soft carpet of my spacious room on the top floor of the tower with a wall of tinted glass that overlooks Dark Terrace Ranch and beyond for miles.

"You have no idea how much I want to strangle you for freaking me out," my sister says, wrapping her arms around me, nearly smothering me into the carpet. "Fallon cried all night."

"I did not!" my little cousin says, standing next to her twin sister only feet within the room.

"That was me," Dana admits. "I thought you were dead,

Jewel. You didn't even tell us bye, you know."

"Yeah, Mrs. Peppers nearly suffocated her with a pillow when Ramona came to pick us up without you." Tears glass over Fallon's eyes, and she sniffles, wiping her face on the dingy sleeve of her shirt that Ramona gave her, passed down from my own collection.

I hold open my arms. "Come here, you two. I'm really sorry about that. It took longer than I anticipated, and I'm a coward and couldn't handle telling you to your faces that I was planning to match."

Dana and Fallon join me and Ramona on the floor, and I do my best to put my arms around all three of them. Ramona's quick to notice the purpling bruise from the blood draw on my arm, and she frowns, grazing her fingers over it.

"Is there no backing out now?" she asks. "God, Jewel. I fucking hate this."

"Watch your mouth," I say, though I don't care if she sounds like me half the time. Mom was the one who hated the fact that we parroted our favorite movies all the time, especially with what she called unnecessary colorful language, which I used to joke about trying to brighten the world with all the color I could.

Thinking about Mom reminds me of Dad, and I can't stop the tears from blurring my eyes. Though I still grieve Mom's passing, her death was sudden and as painless as it could be all things considered. I'm afraid Dad met a horrifying fate.

"I know this sucks, and I hate that I can't bring you all

with me, but you guys will have everything you can ever dream about, and I'm so friggin' happy that I could do this for you," I say, using my sister's shoulder to dry my eyes.

"Damn, you sound like Mom," Ramona says. "And like forty. Which is probably okay because I bet your match is super old."

"I don't know," I admit.

"So, tell us what you do know about him. Is he decent?" Ramona asks.

I open my mouth to tell her about how I actually matched with three vampires, but the way she looks at me, her face paling the longer I take to answer, I'm not so sure she could handle the thought. Things will get sorted out anyway, so it's not like she'll need to worry.

Nodding, I say, "Seems so. And you won't believe this, but he's an heir to Mitchell Divine."

All three of them stare at me blankly. Like me, they have no idea who the vampire is. His name isn't on anything in relation to Donor Life Corp. "Mitchell Divine founded Donor Life Corp."

Ramona gasps and covers her mouth. "You're shitting me."

I shake my head.

"Dad's going to flip his shit when he finds out that you're gonna be a blood slave to the dude that basically screwed all of humanity."

Reaching out my hand, I cover her mouth, practically hissing. "Shhh! You can't talk like that. And Dad, he—" I stop myself from telling her my thoughts of our dad's fate. "He'll appreciate that he'll never have to donate another pint of blood ever again and that none of you will have to either."

"Just you, for-friggin'-ever."

I sigh and shift on my knees to reach for the binder that Mitchell handed me on his way out with everything I need to know about what it means to match with a head of the Divinity Estate. I flip it over to the pages that were missing from the pamphlet on the bulletin board of The Boxes and point to the section about what matching officially means.

She pales even more, and I'm afraid she might pass out. Reaching up again, I tug the box of protein bars from the night table and drop it into her lap. "It's fine, Ramona-Babona. Now you should all eat some of these. They're covered in chocolate."

"Chocolate!" Fallon squeals. "I've never had chocolate."

I grin because I hadn't either until today. "It's incredible."

"Not as incredible as you." Austin materializes in the doorway of my room, and both my cousins and Ramona scream and scramble behind me to the window as far as they can possibly get from him.

Pushing to my feet, I stroll to them and pull the heavy curtain closed, though I know that the window tint protects vampires from the sun. Austin doesn't come any closer, turning his gaze from me and to my family, a look of concern crossing his face.

"I'm sorry, Austin. They've never been in the same vicinity as a vampire before," I say, rubbing soothing circles on both my younger cousins' backs. "Hey, guys. It's okay. Austin is the vampire I matched with."

"You mean one—"

I hold my finger up, shaking my head at him. "He's been very kind to me, and you don't have to worry about him. He doesn't bite."

Austin chuckles at my words, making me blush. They didn't come out how I intended, and I can nearly hear Kingston making a joke about Austin only biting if I want him to, especially because we matched perfectly for the nutrients category.

"I'm sorry to interrupt your family time, Jewel, but your friend from last night was causing a commotion in the lobby, and—"

"Brayla's here? God, please don't tell me you guys threw her out or something," I say, letting go of my sister and cousins to close the space to Austin.

He clasps my hand, stopping me from leaving the room. "I brought her up but just wanted to make sure it was okay with you."

"It better be okay with her!" Brayla yells from somewhere in the hall. "Because I'm the reason she got to match in the first place last night when your rude ass secretary tried to deny Jewel's application and then that cocky ass vamp—"

"That cocky ass vampire took exceptional care of your friend last night," Kingston says, nudging Brayla into the room.

Ramona and my cousins scream again, and I scowl at Kingston and motion for him to stay back. Brayla pulls from his feeble hold on her and dashes across the room, tackling me the same way Ramona had, but neither of us hit the floor. Kingston sets Brayla on her feet and Austin rights me on mine before trailing his eyes over me to make sure Brayla didn't hurt me. I don't know if I should be thankful or offended that they think I'll hurt myself or worse at any second because I'm supposedly fragile. At least they care.

"Please don't do that again," Kingston says. "Jewel's practically starved and needs to be handled gently."

Brayla gives me a funny look. "I heard Jewel say that guy was her match. Why do you care?"

"Hey, beautiful. I brought food for you and your family if you all are hungry," Diego says, peeking his head into the room. At least everyone's too surprised to react this time.

"Thanks, Diego. There's never been a time one of us wasn't hungry," I say.

His brows crinkle, and I notice that Kingston was wrong about Diego laughing at all my lame jokes, because he obviously doesn't get that I have to make light of life to keep my shit together, so I don't wallow in a pool of self-pity.

"Never again, Jewel," he says, giving me a quick hug. "Promise."

"Are all vampires outside the shadows this doting?" Brayla asks. "Because now I'm starting to regret that I put off the Blood Match Program an entire year."

The three guys glance at each other and then look at me like I'm the one who can somehow answer her question.

"That's right. Brayla Diggs, nineteen, family of four. Lives with both parents and an infant brother. Wants to match due to parents aging out of the donation process," Kingston says, repeating what was part of her initial application.

Flicking my hand out, I swat him on the shoulder. He doesn't even move or flinch. "Kingston."

"Sorry, babe. It's a habit," he says. "And we really need to work on your strength. I don't think you could even kill a fly with how weak that arm of yours is."

"What the hell is going on?" Ramona asks, drawing everyone's attention to her. "I've studied the Blood Match Program, and this is nothing like the papers said. A matched vampire keeps their donor away from other vampires. It's a stipulation. What's your deal, dude?" she says to Austin. "You better not think you can get away with passing my sister around. I'll file the paperwork that says you breached your agreement."

I crinkle my nose at her comment. "Ramona, it's not like that."

"Ya sure, Jewel? You're making googly eyes at all three of them. What have they done to you? Did they brainwash you?"

Ramona steps closer, pointing her finger at all three vampires. She grabs me by the front of my dress, and I stumble toward her. Kingston releases a low growl from his throat a second before both Diego and Austin follow suit.

"I'm going to report this to the center," she adds.

I tense. "Ramona, shut up."

She places her hands on her hips. "Make me. This isn't

right, Jewel."

"Ramona!"

"Jewel, watch out!" Fallon screams.

Spinning on my feet, I crash right into Kingston as he closes the space to me. Holy effing shit balls. My sister struck the dangerous nerve of all three vampires, and now I'm terrified of how they're reacting. Their charm and attractiveness threw a blanket over my head, making it nearly impossible to remember that I'm a human and they survive on my blood. I'm the prey in their world no matter if we're all compatible matches. If one of them loses control, I can't stop them, and I'd be forced to live with the consequences of forgetting their very nature—instincts now focused on my little sister.

Sucking in a deep breath, I yell, "Get out! All three of you!"

Austin wraps his arms around Kingston and yanks him back, breaking his focus on Ramona. The snarl crossing his face melts away, leaving behind wide eyes and a gaping mouth—an expression that mirrors the fear racing through me.

"Babe, I'm—"

"Get out," I repeat. "All of you. I will not stand for this. Just leave me alone. You will not ruin my last day with my family, understand?"

Without a word, Kingston, Diego, and Austin disappear from the room, moving so fast it's like they vanish into thin air. I take a few shaky steps forward to my sister and hug her against me before turning to Dana and Fallon to hug them too.

Brayla slides an arm over my shoulder. "What the eff was

that about?"

"It's nothing."

"You can't lie to me," she whispers. "There was some seriously intense vibes going on with you and all three of them."

I swipe a bottle of water from the small table and take a small sip, clearing my throat. I didn't want to have to tell anyone this, especially because it'll all be settled by nightfall. The last thing I need is for my family to worry even more, but they're obviously not going to give up until I give in and tell them the truth.

"I don't even know how to say this," I start, wringing my hands together. "Because it's been a weird night."

"I was right," Ramona tells Brayla. "They're brainwashing her. I heard vamps can use mind control."

I sigh, shaking my head. "It's not that, Ramona."

"You wouldn't even know, Jewel. They can make you forget."

"No, I definitely know I'm not being messed with." Kingston couldn't do it because of Austin's blood in my system. I don't say that, though. No need to have to explain why he tried to my stressed out and anxious sister. And I really do want to forget about Master Caruthers. "And you're right about the intense vibes, Brayla. Everything's a little strange and they're all trying to figure out what to do because this situation has never happened before—"

"What situation? Just spit it out, Jewel," Ramona snaps.

"I matched with Austin...but also with Kingston and Diego. Exactly ninety-nine percent each."

"What?" Brayla practically yells. "You matched with *three* vampires? What the hell are they planning to do?"

I shrug. "I'll find out tonight."

Ramona groans. "This is so messed up."

Opening my arms for her, I pull her in for another hug. "It's not so bad. I actually kind of like all of them."

"Jewel, gross."

Sighing, I tug away. She should know it's a good thing that I do. Life would be hell otherwise. "I'm just saying that no matter what happens or who I end up with, I'll be okay, Ramona-Babona."

She sniffles. "You better be, Jewel-Babewel. Because if you're not—"

I cover her mouth, stifling her words, and force my mouth to smile. "I will be. And you all will be okay, too. I promise."

I just hope I can keep my word.

9

Blood Match

"FIVE MINUTES, MS. JORDAN," MS. Sybil says from her spot behind the counter.

Groaning, I turn away from her and throw my arms around my sister first and then take each of my cousins next, before hugging Brayla last. She rocks me back and forth in her arms, pulling me away from my family and toward the door where an armed man stands by the first non-broken car I've seen up close. The sleek silver metal sparkles in the sun, but it's as quiet as the rust buckets permanently stationed next to the curb on Starlight Row as a reminder of how far the human race has fallen.

"You sure you're going to be okay, Jewel?" Brayla asks. "I mean, while they don't look like Chomper Jonas, they look like they want to devour you in all sorts of ways that make me worry, because...you know."

Warmth blossoms over my cheeks. "I'll be fine. I don't think it's going to be like that."

"Yet. Because damn, Jewel. The shadows would be less scary if it were filled with..."

I cover her mouth with my hand. "Ramona's going to hear you. Or they will. Kingston has a big ass head already. I don't want him thinking—never mind. Don't worry about me. Worry about yourself. I want you to be careful. If you want, I can see if I can get them to postpone your appointment. You're eligible for a few more years."

She shakes her head. "We promised always to do this together, and Mom's scared for Dougie. He's not growing like he should be because of how much the quality of rations has diminished. I want to do this for him."

I can't blame her. Dougie was a surprise to Mr. and Mrs. Diggs, considering Mrs. Diggs was considered too old for childbearing. Dougie's birth was all anyone in The Boxes could talk about since he's the only infant on our floor. Thinking about his birth reminds me of what Diego said about the quarantine, and it makes me wonder if maybe there was more to the miracle—or curse, depending who you ask—than we know.

"I'm going to miss you so much," I say. "Don't forget our

plan, okay?"

"Definitely won't. Mom promised she would make sure to check in on your family every day, so they'll be able to pass along my letters." Because once you match, all ties except to your family are severed. But since I'm certain Brayla will match, our families can pass things along to us. It won't be the same as meeting in the stairwell every morning, but it'll have to do. "And maybe you can use that sexy neck of yours to possibly get one of your Prince Hungries to arrange a meeting between us."

I laugh, nodding my head. "Anything for you, Bray-Bray."

A buzzer sounds through the air, drawing my attention to the doorway that leads to the elevators. Mitchell Divine appears, and he crosses the lobby to stand in front of Ms. Sybil, whispering something to her while keeping his eyes directed on me.

"Is that...?" Brayla asks.

I nod my head. "Mitchell Divine."

"He's hot."

Mitchell's mouth twitches up in a smile, and he winks at Brayla, sending the color draining from her face. Ramona groans from behind us, and I swivel to face my sister, clutching her backpack to her chest.

"Jewel, the board is ready for you," Mitchell says, appearing before me. Only Fallon whimpers this time. "You can trust that your heirs will arrive safely to their next destination before nightfall and once you're settled at the Divinity Estate, you may notify them. It's up to your match to make visiting arrangements."

"So, you've chosen?" I ask.

He doesn't respond to my question, flicking his gaze to Brayla. "I've also arranged a ride for Ms. Diggs. Please make your goodbyes quickly. Everyone's getting impatient."

Because he blatantly ignores my question about his decision, I let it drop. I guess I'll find out soon enough. I haven't even seen Kingston, Diego, or Austin since I yelled at them to leave, and now I'm feeling all sorts of anxious about it now that I can't hide behind my family visit any longer.

Nodding my head, I return to Ramona's side and hug her for the millionth time. I cup her face in my hands and kiss her forehead. "I expect you to do great things, Ramona-Babona. Please try to keep Dana and Fallon from killing each other over who gets what room."

"Man, am I going to start sounding like you now that I'm in charge?"

"I'm sorry it has to be this way. You shouldn't have to be the adult before you're even one."

"You shouldn't have to be one yet either."

Wrapping my arms around her tightly, I hug her hard enough that I hope the feeling stays with her as long as possible. "It is what it is. And don't worry so much. This is a good thing.

"Is it?" she questions.

I nod. "You're free. You never have to donate blood. You'll never be hungry. I heard you get hot water, too. It's awesome."

Her bottom lip quivers and she blinks her tears away. "Thank you, Jewel-Babewel. I love you forever."

"I love you always and infinity." I smear her wet cheeks with my fingers. "And you know what? We're going to find Dad. He'll be home in no time, and then you can have all the fun you want. Maybe even find a nice guy—"

She cuts me off with another hug. "Just take care of yourself, okay? Don't let them push you around or make you feel less than them. I know your rights. I'm not afraid to speak up." She has never been. She gets it from Mom.

"Jewel will be well provided for," Mitchell says, stepping closer to offer me his arm. He must realize we'll have to be dragged apart to finish a goodbye I hate so much. "You have my word, young woman. She's in Divine hands, and we have the deepest respect for those in the program."

I only get a few seconds to say goodbye to Dana and Fallon, and Brayla holds them back as they try to run after me. Despair rushes through me that I'm another person leaving their lives, especially after Aunt Dottie and Mom, but I know they'll understand.

Mitchell Divine guides me away, and I look at my family one last time as the armed man escorts them to the silver vehicle. I'm slightly jealous they all get to ride in a car, something I never even imagined doing.

Soundlessly, Mitchell taps a screen near the elevator and the doors slide open with a ding. He guides me on, and I grip the rail at the sudden motion of being lifted dozens of stories in the air. I tense, bracing myself. The Boxes only have the stairs to get to the top floors, but I might prefer them over feeling like my heart slips into my stomach.

The elevator comes to a halt, and Mitchell turns to me. "This shouldn't take long. We only need your final approval and for you to sign some paperwork."

"Okay." My voice practically comes out a whisper.

I summon the courage to ask him again who I've been matched with, but the elevator door slides open to reveal a long, sturdy table with the most vampires I've ever seen in my life. Four men and two women sit at the table with an empty leather chair at the head with a stack of papers and a shiny gold pen next to them in the space in front.

I flick my gaze around the room, my heart picking up pace when I catch sight of the Divine heirs huddled in the corner of the room. Kingston leans against the wall with his legs crossed at his ankles. Austin sits in a wide leather chair while Diego perches on the arm of it. None of them smile at me, making my anxiety worse. Everyone stares at me as Mitchell leads me into the room. I lick my lips, my hands shaking, and I glance in the guys' direction once more and smile through my nerves.

"Can I have a second to talk to your sons, sir?" I ask Mitchell, trying to stop myself from looking at the silent vampires watching my every move.

"I suppose that would be okay," he says, guiding me toward the head of the table.

He releases my arm, and I shuffle toward the corner of the room. Kingston straightens his back while both Diego and Austin get to their feet to close the distance to me. I take a moment to look into each of their eyes, feeling my heart race even more.

"I need to apologize to the three of you," I start. "I was out of line earlier. Whatever happens now, I want you to know that I think you're all pretty great, and I appreciate everything you've done for me and my family."

Kingston envelops me in a hug first, burying his face in the crook of my neck. "No worries, babe. The way you talked to me—hell, it was hot."

I groan. "Kingston."

He chuckles and spins me toward Austin. The blond vampire grasps both my hands between his and brings them up to rest his chin on them while pulling me close to him. His vibrant eyes sparkle in the light, and I can't help myself from staring at his lips.

"You promised me you-know-what would only last a few hours," I whisper into his ear, purposely not saying the words out loud due to the audience zoning in on me.

Austin flushes and smiles, showing off his fangs. "It did," he whispers, brushing his lips to my earlobe, making me shiver. "It's all you now."

I pull away, baring my teeth while crinkling my nose. Well, that's embarrassing.

Diego draws my attention to him as he shifts on his feet, his looming height shadowing over me. He opens his arms, and I gingerly step forward into them, heat stirring inside me at the memory of our almost kiss.

"Kingston was right, beautiful. You shouldn't apologize

when it was our poor behavior that caused you to react like that. Forgive me?"

How could I not? I don't think I've ever felt such sincerity.

As I pull myself away and look at the three of them, a blip of sorrow washes over me because I know two of them will be disappointed by the outcome. My matching wasn't supposed to be a competition, but it sure feels that way because two of them lose. Two of them will have to go through the process all over again to find another match.

Jealousy sneaks over me at the thought. How messed up am I for even thinking that way?

"Ms. Jordan, if you're ready, we'd all like to carry on with our nights," a woman with vibrant red hair says from her position at the table. She leans on her elbows without smiling.

I bob my head and shuffle to the head of the table where Mitchell pulls out the chair for me. All three brothers follow behind me and take spots next to their dad to peer at the paperwork laid out on the table for me to read and sign.

I skim over the first page with all of my information on it without spotting what I'm dying to find out. "It doesn't say who I've been matched with." Swiveling in my seat, I turn and look at Mitchell and then to Kingston, Diego, and Austin.

"Due to these unforeseen circumstances, the board decided to put the final matching decision onto you at the recommendation of the heads of the Divinity Estate."

"What?" I ask. "I get to pick?" Holy shit balls. I was not prepared to make such a decision. I mean, how can I even decide? The whole point of the Blood Match Program was to do the decision making, setting my fate into motion, and me accepting a life not of my choosing. But now? If I make a choice I might regret, the fault falls on me.

"Yes, Ms. Jordan," a serious man with silver hair responds.

I frown at the paperwork, sweat beading along my hairline. "I think I would have preferred Rock-Paper-Scissors," I mutter under my breath.

Kingston chuckles from behind me, and I cringe. If he heard it, then everyone else in the room did, too.

"I mean, I don't know. It's—"

"If you'd please finish reading the contract before you, you will take note that an immediate decision isn't necessary. You've been given thirty days to respond, allowing ten days with each heir to help in your decision."

"In rotation," Mitchell says. "To be fair."

Oh shit.

Ah Hell.

What the actual—

"Okay," my mouth says without consulting with my brain. How my poor mind, blood, and body will handle such an arrangement freaks me out. But another, quickly dominating part of me, can't stop the stupid grin from crossing my face because for once a major life decision falls into my hands. Hell to the yeah.

With the way Kingston chuckles again, I stiffen, wondering if I accidentally mused my thoughts out loud. But only the three brothers smile at me, and I know immediately it's because I agreed to the weird arrangement that reminds me of what Diego said to me during our interview about him and his brothers being capable of playing nice and sharing, though I have no idea what he was referencing before.

"Sign here, here, and here," the woman closest to me says. "This states you agree to a temporary match with Kingston, Diego, and Austin Divine. It also states that you may cancel two contracts without explanation before your thirty days are up."

The man across from her taps another sheet. "This clause is in place to temporarily limit personal blood donations and also means that you agree to allow your matches to accept blood from the gen. pop. We understand the intimacy of personal blood donations, so you must agree and sign here to proceed."

The intimacy of personal blood donations? Is he for real? I mean, maybe for a vampire, but I don't like to think of where my blood goes once it ends up in a vial...

I swallow. "They've agreed to allow me to use—"

"Babe, that's personal information," Kingston says, sliding his hands around my shoulders. "You don't have to explain anything. This is purely for the record. Everything else will be discussed between us later."

Ah, hell. What am I getting myself into? Why do I love how his damn words make me feel? A discussion of the sorts sounds awkward as all get-out, but now I'm interested to see what they expect.

I nod my head and sign all the documents as quickly as

possible without asking any more questions since one of the six board members explains each thing in terms I can understand. When I set the pen down, everyone stands from the table, and Diego helps me to my feet.

Mitchell turns to me and takes my hand, kissing my knuckles. "Welcome into my coven, Jewel Divine. I have a feeling you'll be quite happy."

He disappears with the others, leaving me alone to face Kingston, Diego, and Austin in the grand boardroom with a view of the glittering lights of Dark Terrace Ranch below. I stand awkwardly, shifting on my bare feet under their scrutiny. While my mind still can't wrap around what I've gotten myself into, my body agrees with Mitchell Divine and is embarrassingly happy as all three vampires take a step closer to me.

I clear my throat, my heart beating so hard that it'll tunnel through me and to the floor at any second. "So, um. Who's first? I mean—shit balls. This is—"

"The bomb," Austin says, smiling at me. "Because now I get the chance to prove myself to you."

"It's *da bomb*, bro," Diego says.

I laugh. "I never heard of that one."

Kingston slides his arm around my shoulder. "I think we can all agree that teaching Jewel more back-world slang can wait. I don't know about you, but I'm over this place and would prefer to take our girl home."

Our girl. Oh, man. "I'd like that."

"Good, because the car's waiting for us out front," Austin

says.

"The car?" I don't know why I'm surprised. "Someone's driving us?"

"Yeah, me." Diego slides his fingers through mine, tugging me with him with Austin and Kingston right on our heels.

"You?"

Kingston grins, moving in front of me in the elevator. "Don't worry, babe. I'll keep you safe."

Austin touches my shoulder. "And if he doesn't, I'll make you better."

"Fuck. Me," I whisper and cringe the second the words escape.

They all chuckle.

I blush, holding my hands up. "None of you better say anything. You know what I meant."

Kingston pokes my nose. "Of course we do. And babe, I promise this will be all sorts of fun."

"Or awkward," I say.

"I guess we'll see, huh?"

I guess so.

10

The Divinity Estate

COOL FINGERS RUN ACROSS MY cheek, stirring me from sleep. "Hey, babe. We're almost home. You don't have to wake up if you're tired, but I thought you might want to see things for yourself."

Opening my eyes, I glance up at Kingston grinning at me. His hands hold me in place as I lie curled on the seat with my head resting on his suit jacket piled up on his lap. I press my hands into the cool leather seat, wincing as I struggle to sit upright, still weirded out by the world blurring around us as Diego drives the quiet car down the empty road with the only noise sounding from the tires gliding over the smooth pavement.

I stretch my arms over my head, ignoring the dull ache from the bruises across the bends of my elbows. "How long have I been asleep?"

"About an hour," Austin says, swiveling around to look at me from the front seat.

"An hour?" That doesn't make sense. We had been driving for at least ten minutes when I laid down, and it only takes an hour to run across Dark Terrace Ranch.

"About fifteen more to go."

"Where is this place exactly?" I ask. Because I've never heard of the Divinity Estate. I had assumed they lived in one of the towers along the perimeter fence or in one of the big houses hillside. Shifting, I peer out the window that suddenly disappears down into the door. Cold wind whips my hair, and I take in the lightless landscape stretching into a black void of nothing into the beyond. "Where's the city? Why is it so dark out there?"

"That's the ocean," Diego says.

"The ocean?" I had no idea we were close to the ocean. "We don't have to swim or anything, right? I didn't know we were near the coast."

"Really, babe?" Kingston tilts his head to look at me. "You can see the ocean from at least a dozen buildings in Dark Terrace Ranch."

All the world maps were destroyed after the Blood Hunger Plague when the cities were redefined in The Divide, and the only time I've ever seen a map that wasn't of our own city was on a movie about a road trip. I couldn't figure out how to read it with the screen paused and the characters lacked navigation skills, so I gave up trying. The digital maps around the city tell us exactly where we are, how far it is to the place we need to be with exact walking instructions, and also what's off limits. I don't even need to look at them anymore. No one does.

"Did you not look out the window in your room today?" he prods, reaching out to touch my leg.

"I did."

"It's kind of hard to miss."

I frown, shrinking away from him to hang my head out the open window. The way he looks at me makes me feel dumb for not noticing the ocean or knowing the information that we were by water. A million responses burn on the tip of my tongue, but the sudden quiet inside the car stops me from snapping at Kingston to tell him that of course I didn't know we were near an ocean because I lived on the fifth floor of my building, and it wasn't high enough to see over the wall. And I didn't notice any damn ocean from my room today. All I saw were buildings and hills forever.

A cool hand slides over my knee, but I refuse to look away from the darkness. I try to imagine what the black stretch of nothing looks like in the day time and wonder if it's clear like the faucet water so I can see the marine life in real life that I've only ever seen in movies and old magazines.

"I think her room was on the east side," Austin says, breaking the silence. "So there's no way she could have seen it, Kingston. I'm not even sure donors have access anywhere above the seventh floors unless they work the towers."

"Oh," Kingston says. "It slipped my mind."

"Jewel." The cool fingers touching my leg squeeze my knee gently. I turn away from the strangely fragrant wind and realize Austin touches me as Kingston stares out his own window. "I can take you down to the beach on my night if you'd like."

His night. Two days away. Tonight belongs to me as I get settled, but tomorrow starts the first of thirty. Funny enough, Rock-Paper-Scissors ended up determining who got to start the rotation. Diego gets to spend time with me tomorrow, Austin the next, and Kingston last. I expected a lot more complaining on his part, but he bragged to his brothers that it gives him more time to plan how he'll win me over—my life and matching now a competition like one of the old match-making reality shows I bet inspired the Blood Match Program, though Kingston mused something about online dating, which I guess is how humans used to meet when we were allowed the best technology of the time.

"I don't know how much fun I'll be at the beach," I say. "I don't know how to swim."

"There's no swimming in the ocean here. This area's restricted as a marine life preservation center. Donor Life Corp puts in a considerable amount of effort to protect the wildlife, trying to reverse years of damage caused by—it's mostly just for looking." Austin smiles at me, gauging my interest in his suggestion.

I peer out the window once more and nod. "Sure, I'd like that."

"Me too."

Diego slows the vehicle coming up to a towering wrought iron gate right in the middle of the road. Two armed men stand in front of it and stroll up to the car to peer inside. The bigger of the two vampires bends down and sticks his head right into my window, startling me, and Kingston slides his arms around my waist to rest his head on my shoulder.

"Sorry, Ms. Divine. I didn't mean to scare you. Security requires I take a visual count of all passengers," the vampire says, straightening back up.

I don't say anything.

"Have a good one, Pedro," Diego says. "You too, Walt."

Diego navigates the car through the open gate and waits a moment for it to close behind us. The headlights cut across a black paved road along a steep hillside surrounded by tall trees. I've never seen so many in my life. I can't stop myself from leaning forward between the front seats, practically perching on the center console. Diego beams his brilliant smile at me, hitting a button that brightens the headlights even more.

A sweet, tangy aroma drifts in through the open windows, and I can't help taking deep breaths to fill my lungs with such an amazing scent. The lush greenery of the hillside reminds me of Austin's sparkling eyes, and I bet it's even more magnificent under bright rays of sunshine, though I might never get to see the full extent of it if I must adjust to a vampire schedule.

Bursts of bright orange and yellow colors decorate the roadside trees, and I shift to look at Austin, who's already watching me with a smile spread across his face. "Are those oranges?"

"And lemons. There are also some cherry trees somewhere. Grapefruit, plums, apricots, avocados, and some other fruit trees. We have a vineyard as well."

"You are so lucky," I say and then realize that fruit wouldn't be something they'd care about.

"It gets harvested for Dark Terrace Ranch," Kingston says.

"Not in The Boxes. I think I've had an orange once when I was a kid."

"You refer to the Central Plaza Tower as The Boxes?" Diego asks.

I suck my lip between my teeth, thinking about our tiny one-room apartment where I shared the floor space with Ramona, Dana, and Fallon even though two of us could have squeezed together on the couch. It wasn't until after Dad disappeared that we moved into his bed.

"You'd understand why if you've ever seen—" Something huge and black steps right into the middle of the road, causing Diego to slam the brakes. Kingston locks his hands to my legs while Austin stops me from flying forward with his arm.

I scream out, scrambling to the backseat as another humungous animal emerges from the trees. Kingston hugs me to him, releasing a small chuckle into my hair. I pant, trying to suppress my fear and calm my racing heart, realizing that the two animals aren't even coming near the car.

"You better get used to them, beautiful. The cattle own this mountain," Diego says.

"Zebras and goats too," Kingston adds.

Slowly pulling away from Kingston, I bring my attention to the two cows moseying their way onto the other side of the road into a grassy area that descends down the mountain. Blush burns my cheeks, because now the guys probably think I'm a naïve girl who freaks out over stupid shit like surprise cows.

While we don't have them in the city—or many other animals for that matter—I know what they are. I've tasted beef a few times over the years when Mom made hamburgers for Dad's birthday because it was his favorite thing to eat as a kid. While the most experience I have with cows is rushing past the way too expensive bloody cuts of beef at the market, I've seen them in plenty of movies.

"Before any of you start thinking I'm ignorant when it comes to anything outside of Dark Terrace Ranch, I know what a cow is. I was just surprised," I say, feeling like I need to justify my embarrassing reaction.

"You do startle easy," Diego says, twisting in his seat.

Kingston hugs me tighter. "But I don't mind."

Whatever weirdness that was between the two of us over the ocean thing seems to have passed, and I remind myself that this might be an adjustment for everyone. The guys couldn't have been more clear that Blood Matching with me was more than being a live-in donor, but it's still hard to wrap my mind around it. I'm almost worried to let my guard down, because what if they're only acting this way so that I'll choose them? What if things change? What if I piss one of them off and get ripped apart? *If you die, you die. Ramona gets to live regardless.*

Diego continues to navigate up the winding road and past a wooden building where I spot more cattle lounging around for the night. I've never seen so much greenery in my life that I can't stop myself from constantly sticking my head out the windows, crawling throughout the car to do so.

After what feels like the longest journey ever, Diego turns off the main road and enters through a well-lit gate that swings open automatically after he presses a button. I bounce in my seat, wishing he'd slow down just a little so I can take in all the intricate details carved into a stone wall that turns into a grand staircase entrance to a breathtaking terrace of a house that looks like a palace.

"Whoa," I whisper, practically hanging my entire torso out the window to get a better look. I've never seen anything like the Divinity Estate. In Dark Terrace Ranch, everything is made of steel, concrete, and tinted glass. The materials of the buildings surrounding the terrace come to life as a piece of art in smooth stone.

"Wait until you enter the grounds," Austin says, reaching for my hand again. He swings my arm for a moment before releasing me to exit the car.

Diego opens the door for me, helping me out. I stroll next

to him, ultra aware of his fingers on my back with Kingston leading the way. Austin keeps my pace at my other side, holding onto the small bag that Ramona had brought me of things she thought I'd consider important.

Practically flying with me up the stairs, Diego doesn't give me much of a chance to look around. Austin points out four guest houses at the top of the grand staircase, three currently occupied with people I'll supposedly meet some other time. Huge fountains with white statues stream water in arches into small pools.

Kingston laughs when I giggle and point at one of a little boy peeing and spitting water at the same time. "Dude, that's ridiculous."

"The original owner had a taste for art that we've kept," Austin says. He points at a looming statue with what looks like people with dog heads. "It's all original. Quite the eclectic collection. That one dates back supposedly three thousand years."

Bright lamps light up the property, allowing me to see everything as well as I would if it were daytime except for where Diego mentions that the ocean stretches in the west. A few people rush about the property—all human—but none of them stop to greet us, keeping their heads bowed and their attention on the ground.

"You'll find the outdoor pool over that way," Austin motions, continuing to give me a quick tour on our way around the vast property toward the main house. "And the indoor one is under the tennis courts."

I only nod because it's not like I'll be jumping into what looks like incredibly deep water of the expansive pool made from shimmering rock, tiles, and concrete with still water that sparkles with the pool lights and the moon reflecting on it from above.

"If you go through that door there, it leads to a movie theater, but you can also access it from inside," Diego muses. "You can ask one of the staff to show you how to work the movie library, but all of our rooms have TVs."

Their rooms. I release a breath at the thought.

"Yours does too," Austin adds, surprising me.

I catch sight of the three of them looking at me. My cheeks burn again under their scrutiny, and I feel extra self-conscious, because I don't want any of them to know how nervous I am about all of this. It seems weirdly too good to be true, because of how nice they're treating me. As much as I want to just go with it, I can't help thinking about how upset Ramona was or how she accused me of being brainwashed. Because she was right. They could do it, and I wouldn't even know. And this is only the first night. They'll treat me exactly how I want to be treated until I choose one of them to officially match with, and then who knows?

Thoughts of Master Caruthers and his well thought out idea of my purpose flits through my mind, making me shiver. They might all have their own plans just waiting for me.

But then Diego smiles without flashing his fangs, pulling me from the dark fear scratching through the attraction I never knew possible to have toward not only one vampire but three.

Kingston grasps my arm, taking over for Diego, who releases me without complaint. I catch the three brothers sharing a silent conversation with their eyes, and I wonder if they can somehow read minds.

I gulp at the thought.

But if they can, none of them react to me or everything that swirls through my head.

Kingston tugs me to a stop outside an intricately carved grand entrance with a huge door made of iron, gold, and dark glass. Lifting his hand, he brushes strands of my dark hair from my face, bowing his head slightly toward mine, so I give him my undivided attention instead of drinking in all the details of the stone façade of the palace.

"We weren't joking in the car. What you say goes, and as per your contract we must always receive verbal consent."

"I did agree to hugs," I muse, holding a straight face. The second I was alone in the car with the three of them, Kingston handed me a private contract that would remain between the four of us, including a list of things I was comfortable with them doing without proper consent.

"And hand holding," Austin says.

"Cheek kisses," Diego adds. "But I have to warn you about my poor aim."

I laugh and roll my eyes.

"Though you may do as you wish with us without asking, babe. You want to make out all night on our night and not with my brothers on theirs, that's fine by all of us," Kingston says, grinning.

I giggle, heat warming my insides. Diego rubs his neck and then combs his fingers through his short hair while shaking his head. Austin meets my gaze with a soft expression, not giving anything away.

"Or if I want to kiss them on their nights and not you on yours," I say.

Kingston fake glares at me. "Unlikely, but yeah, okay."

I release another laugh and slap my hand against his chest. "I don't think I've ever met someone as cocky as you."

"You sure you can live with such an egomaniac?" Diego quips.

I shrug without really responding. The other part of our personal agreement in the car was that none of the guys were allowed to ask me about either of them in regards to anything intimate, which is fine by me. It not only will help with jealousy, but it also assures that I don't feel obligated to do the same with the others if I don't want.

Austin attempts to punch Diego in the arm, but he's quick to move and open the door, though a man in a suit holds it for the four of us to enter. I gawk at the eclectic foyer filled with antique furniture from dark tables to plush rugs covering shiny tiled floors. A sparkling chandelier glitters, sending rainbow fractals of light across my white dress.

"Welcome home, princess," Austin says, teasingly. "I'm going to grab you a few things to eat if that's okay. You need small meals frequently for a while."

I nod. There's no way I'll deny an offer of food. "Are you going to continue to feed it to me, too?" I joke, because it seems that everything I've eaten in the last twenty-four hours came from his hand.

He chuckles. "You bet I am now."

"And I'm going to grab you a few necessities," Diego says. "Kingston will show you to your room."

Diego kisses me on the cheek, giving Kingston another one of their intense mind reading looks, and the second he disappears after Austin, I'm tempted to ask Kingston what that was all about, but he slides his fingers through mine and nearly makes me run to keep up with his long legs.

"So, I need to apologize," Kingston says, tugging me along with him down a massive hall with huge ancient-looking paintings hung along the walls.

"Apologize? For what?" I ask.

"For being an ass in the car. I wasn't thinking when I commented about you not knowing that Dark Terrace Ranch was located on the coast. You just—it's easy to forget that you didn't live the same life as me. I don't have a lot of experience with donors—I mean, humans. Sure, Donor Life Corp employs a great number of humans, but I mostly deal with the vampire clientele."

"That sounds so weird to me. You look like you're my age and not like someone who should be in charge."

"I'm not in charge, but I do help out. And for your information, I'm two years older than you," he replies, keeping a straight face. "At least physically."

"So how old are you really?"

He fakes shock and touches his hand to his heart. "You can't ask a vampire that question, babe. It's rude."

I roll my eyes. "By your enthrallment toward back-world language I'm going to assume that maybe I should call you gramps instead of dude."

He lifts an eyebrow. "Ouch, babe."

I laugh. I can't help it.

"You're lucky I deserve this from you," he murmurs. "For the ocean thing. But I hope you don't hold it against me. Austin might be more perceptive from his experience in human health, but I'm a quick learner."

I smirk and reach up to touch his cheek. His ability to recognize my feelings makes him extra attractive right now. I can almost forget our initial meeting. "It's okay, Kingston. I won't. I know you didn't mean to offend me, and I didn't mean to react like I did. I'm still trying to figure out how to deal with all this. I've never had my own room or a real view. Or three incredibly smart and attractive guys who keep trying to feed me." Who I'll feed in return...

"It's all in our plan to fatten you up," he says, flashing his fangs, like he read my mind.

I deadpan.

He laughs again. "Come on, babe. I'm *slightly* kidding. But seriously. Everything I want to do with you might break you."

OhmyeffingGod. "Dude."

"What? Teaching you some valuable self-defense moves or how to drive or horseback riding can be dangerous."

I blink.

"What?"

I narrow my eyes at him, sliding my hands up his shoulders to hook around his neck. "That's not what I expected you to say, Rule Breaker."

Trailing his gaze from my eyes and down my throat, Kingston leans in and whispers, "We can do whatever is on your mind, too."

I get caught in his dark gaze. "You're bad."

"And you like it."

He jokingly snaps his teeth at me before pulling himself away to take my hand again. With his sudden quick breathing, I realize how hard it was for him to step away from me. And right now, I wish he hadn't. I'm dreading the moment we reach my room where he'll leave me alone.

"So this is your suite. If you continue down the hall, you'll find Diego on the first left. Austin's is the last one in the hall past Diego's, and mine is the first door on the right in the opposite direction. Don't hesitate to visit at any time. The whole rotation thing isn't set in stone, and it technically applies to nights only."

He opens my door for me, revealing a surprisingly modern room compared to the rest of the estate I've seen. And it's huge. Three times the size of my tiny apartment and a billion times nicer. A four-poster bed with a canopy rests on a raised platform against the far wall. Heavy curtains cover huge windows, and a tinted-glass door leads to what looks like a balcony. A sitting area lies on the opposite side of the bed with a plush couch, cozy recliner, coffee table, and the biggest TV I've ever seen. An arched doorway leads to a massive granite, metal, and glass bathroom while another one leads to a huge walk-in wardrobe with hundreds of pieces of clothing neatly draped on hangers.

"We'll have a tailor come by to size you in the morning," he says, motioning in the direction I look.

I nod. "Sounds good."

"There's a phone by your bed. Our extensions are listed on them, and as soon as I receive the number for your family in Haven Springs, it'll be automatically added. I expect in the next hour or so." He shifts on his feet, looking around. "Austin and Diego will both come by in a bit but feel free to send them away."

"I thought you said you played nice with them?"

"I was only thinking about you," he responds. "I can imagine this getting...exhausting."

I purse my lips, rubbing them together. "I'm not taking your bait."

"Damn."

Closing the space to him, I wrap my arms around his neck and hug him for a moment, feeling his heartbeat against my chest. His hands rub the length of my back, combing through my hair, and he pulls away slightly to look at me.

"I don't have to go, you know," he says, trailing his gaze away from my eyes and down to my mouth.

Standing on my tiptoes, I brush my lips to his cheek. I nearly agree that he can stay, but something holds me back. I don't know if it's the intensity of his gaze or the obvious attraction between us, but either way, I'm afraid to give him any sort of impression until I get a feel of how things are going to be around here. After spending so much time with him and his brothers the last two days, I need a moment to process and breathe. "I think you were right about me being exhausted, but thanks for everything. I never thought I'd say this, but I'm kind of glad we matched even after the crap you pulled."

"Just kind of?"

I lean in close again, touching my lips to his ear and whisper, "Don't make me regret it, okay? See you around, Kingston."

He sucks in a small breath as I pull away, his gaze glued to my lips for a long moment. I know if I move even a millimeter, I might give in and kiss him even though he doesn't ask. I can already see it in his eyes that he's determined to get me to make the first move, but I'm too nervous. Not now. Not tonight. I'm acting on adrenaline and the strange excitement constantly crashing over me, knowing that even if this turns to shit, I'll still be out of The Boxes. I'll never have to deal with curfew or worrying about shadow vampires. And I know my family will always be safe.

Kingston notices my hesitation and expands the space between us with a smirk crossing his lips, reading me without needing me to breathe a single word. “Good night, Jewel. Hopefully I’ll see you sooner rather than later.”

11

Personality Match

RAMONA LOOKS PAST ME, STARING at the room behind me, a funny look crossing her face. The video feed projects over the white wall over my bed, and I sit at the end with my pillows at the foot of the bed, crossing my legs at my ankles.

"That's your room?" she asks, moving around like she could look past me more if she tried hard enough.

I nod, grinning. "Yeah, so you can stop worrying. There's no cage or chains or whatever the hell you were obviously imagining."

"And none of them have bitten you yet?" she asks.

I roll my eyes. "Not unless I give them permission. I get to have my blood drawn like usual, at least for the next thirty days."

"Fuck, Jewel. Thirty days being tossed between three vampires? That's so messed up. Don't you think it might be safer to just pick one now? Your odds for long term survival will be better."

"Ramona, stop," I say, throwing a pillow at my sister on the screen. "Don't talk like that. I'll be fine."

She groans.

I pout, pulling my knees to my chest to rest my chin on them. "I mean it. I don't want Dana and Fallon to overhear you."

"They're passed out. I don't think I've ever heard either of them snore so loud," she says.

"So, it's good there? Everything that was promised?"

She nods, her worry lighting up into excitement as she looks around her new home. I can't see much of it, but I spot the glow of a TV behind her. "The fridge is bigger than me. And it's filled. Fruit, Jewel. Greens. Cheese too. I want to eat it all, like now."

I smile. "Do it. Your monthly allowance is more than what Dad made in a year. You get a bonus because of..."

"This messed up bullshit?" she asks.

I shrug. "Come on. Just enjoy it for me, okay?"

Bobbing her head, she holds up a half a peeled banana and waves it at me. "Oh, I am, but I can still worry."

I reach over and grab the plate of food Austin brought earlier and show her the muffin wrapper and a grape stem. "I have a personal chef and a vineyard, so don't."

"Don't forget why," she mutters.

Like I could ever. Kingston's joke about fattening me up didn't go over my head. I know that if I can reach my proper weight I can offer more blood. "Ramona-Babona, I won't."

A chime rings from her side of the video feed, and she glances away from me. "Hey, Jewel. I have to go. I need to get the girls up for orientation and the official Haven Springs tour. Will you call me tonight?"

I frown. "It has to be before sundown, okay? And I'll see about when I can visit you."

"Hopefully soon. I already miss you so much."

I blow her a kiss. "Miss and love you, too."

She waves once and the screen disappears as she disconnects. I flop over on the bed and gaze toward my windows, realizing that the sky lightens with the coming dawn. The only thing planned for my day, according to Kingston, is a tailor supposedly stopping by to adjust some of the clothing, but I don't know when.

I should sleep, because I've been up the whole night and barely slept a few hours on and off since the matching announcement, but I'm not used to sleeping alone. The gigantic bed doesn't help and the fluffy pillows can't replace being smothered by my cousins in my sleep. I also can't suppress the strange feeling brought on by the whole house, like I'm being monitored. Maybe I am.

Strolling from my bed, I make my way to the balcony door and turn the knob, half expecting it to be locked. It opens with ease, and a cool breeze plays with my hair, sending tresses dancing from my neck.

I gape at the expansive property, blooming with morning flowers and dew-covered greenery. The collection of fragrances tickles my nose, and I automatically inhale a few deep breaths. Trailing my fingers across the cold metal railing, I stroll the length of the balcony to a few potted plants near two chairs and a small table. I bend over to sniff one of the pretty white flowers, touching its soft petals with my fingers. I wonder if anyone would say anything if I picked a couple to bring inside.

I don't get the chance to contemplate it much, because a loud beep sounds from below, and I catch sight of a man tending to the huge garden. He calls out to another human, and they both glance in my direction, but neither responds as I lift my hand to wave. It's the strangest thing. Even the moody man in the last apartment on my floor back in The Boxes would greet me if I said hello first. But maybe they're not allowed. I want to find out though.

Before I get the chance to ask, a huge shadow crosses below, and I jerk my head toward the sky and spot a massive bird gliding on an air current in the direction of the...holy shit balls. The ocean looks exactly like it does in the old movies from this distance—a long stretch of royal blue that blends into the sky. I wish I could get a closer look, but it's farther than I expect from this huge top of the hill palace I still can't believe is real.

A gust of wind makes me shiver, pulling my hair from my neck, and I turn around to head inside my room when I notice a figure in a tinted-window a little ways over. From its sheer size, I think it might be Diego, watching the world light up from behind the protection of the dark glass. I lift my hand and wave, and he waves back, just watching me for a moment.

I turn away from him and enter my room, peering around the vast space, suddenly feeling lonelier than ever. I don't know if I will get used to having so much space without my sister. The knowledge pulls at my heartstrings.

Glancing at the phone with the extensions to the guys' rooms glowing on the digital screen, I consider calling Diego, but the idea of doing so seems lame considering he's just down the hall. So I gather my nerves, stroll to my bedroom door, and peer into the hallway. I half expect for an armed guard to stop me, but silence greets me.

"Just go," I tell myself out loud. "You know he's awake."

I step into the hallway and saunter in the direction of Diego's room, staying on the soft floor runner until I reach the first door on the left like Kingston had told me. An intricate design decorates the sturdy wood door, and I raise my hand to knock but then hesitate. What the hell am I even doing? I should turn around and go back to my room and force myself to try to sleep, because I need to get used to it and Diego promised to pick me up at sundown.

As I turn around without knocking to rush back to my

room, the door swings inward, and Diego offers me a heart-melting smile like he's so happy to find me standing at his door. His gray eyes sweep over my body, and I tighten my jaw, really regretting not putting more thought into coming here because I'm wearing a slightly too big and a little too short to be worn without pants T-shirt. But there was no way I was wearing any of the selection of bedtime attire folded neatly for me in the top drawer of a built-in—clothes obviously not actually made for sleeping.

"Everything okay, beautiful?" Diego asks, propping himself on the doorframe.

I bounce on the balls of my feet, hugging myself. "Yeah, it's fine. I just couldn't sleep and saw you were awake. I hope you don't mind if I'm here."

"Definitely not. It's still early for me. Kind of like if you went to bed with the sunset, you know?"

"That makes sense. I never put much thought into it. Dark Terrace Ranch has a pretty strict curfew, and luckily I've never had to deal...um, I mean, I don't have a lot of experience with vampires outside of the shadow dw—" I snap my mouth shut. Eff me. I can't even manage to get out a sentence without probably saying a dozen things that might offend him. "I'm sorry."

He reaches up to touch my warm cheek. "Don't apologize. I'm glad you don't have much experience. I know what Starlight Row is like for humans but especially donors, even during the day."

Especially donors? I knew Donor Life Corp lied about our

donor bracelets stopping vampires from attacking. They do what they want, and the city vampires aren't called shadow dwellers for nothing. They lurk in the shadows and out of the sun, especially in the morning in an attempt to get close to the early risers. And there are a lot of them.

"Oh." I don't know what else to say. Feeling slightly self-conscious that I'm standing in a T-shirt in the hall, I shift on my feet. I play with the hem of my shirt, pulling it down more, and look around, allowing silence to fall between us. "Okay, well, I should probably go back to my room."

"Why don't you come in?" he asks, stepping back. "I should've asked you that first instead of making you stand there."

I hesitate, looking past him into a suite even bigger than my room. "Um, I..."

"We can watch TV or something." Now he's the one shifting on his feet. He might actually be nervous, which shouldn't make me feel loads better like it does.

Slowly, I nod and step inside. I don't want to be rude or weird. I need to start getting comfortable with this, and I'm supposed to be with him tonight, anyway. Watching TV with him is something I can handle. It's less nerve-wracking than anything else I can think of. I still can't get over the Blood Match questionnaire, even if Kingston said no one was privy to the detailed results apart from the computer, though what Master Caruthers mentioned about my physical...ugh.

Diego takes my hand, yanking me from the gross memory,

and guides me across the grand room with all dark furniture, warm red rugs, a perfectly made bed with dark gray sheets and soft-looking pillows, which faces a giant wall-mounted TV. But we don't stop there, thankfully. A separate room with a black leather sectional couch that faces a blank wall hides nestled in the back of the suite and away from the heavy-curtained windows.

"Hungry or anything?" he asks, motioning for me to sit down.

I shake my head. "No thanks." Now that's something I never thought I'd ever do—reject an offer of food. But I'm really not hungry. The only complaint my stomach has is from the sudden nerves bunching inside me that pick up my heartbeat.

Diego disappears for a moment and returns with a thick blanket that he offers me as he sits down at my side. I was so nervous before in the hallway that I didn't realize he wears soft cotton pants and a T-shirt, and I prefer it on him compared to his dress clothes.

"What do you feel like watching?" he asks, shifting to mess with a tablet he pulls from a side pocket of the couch. A projection lights up the whole wall, which I realize is covered by stark-white fabric. I've never seen a movie on such a big screen.

"Whatever. Nothing with gore," I say, suppressing a yawn. The couch is as comfortable as my new bed, and my body picks now to remind me how long I've been up.

"Romance?"

I crinkle my nose.

He chuckles. "Why doesn't that surprise me?"

"How about a comedy?"

"Sounds good to me."

Diego glides his finger over the movie library so quickly that I don't get a chance to look at the small movie posters. A familiar, long-gone production company logo flashes across the screen, and I twist on the couch to look at him.

"I've seen this a dozen times. It's my favorite," I say.

He grins. "Mine too."

"So dumb it's funny, right?"

Nodding, he drapes his arm over the back of the couch and shifts, bumping his knees into mine. "I didn't even know you could still get a copy of this in Dark Terrace Ranch."

"You can't." I swivel to ease back as the movie starts. Curling my legs up, I summon my bravery to lean into him to get comfortable, which makes him smile at me. "My dad kept my grandpa's entire movie collection and his DVD player. We have two hundred and fifty-seven movies from before the—" I stop myself. Diego would know this. Human entertainment dropped immediately with the population size.

There is only one movie theater in Dark Terrace Ranch, but for one, I'd rather buy groceries than pay to see a movie I probably would hate, and two, the shadow-dwelling vampires love the movies in the day. They have designated screens—which is basically all of them. I don't care what they say. The skylight that separates the facility with a beam of sunlight isn't exactly effective security to someone hungry and determined.

"You'll have to tell me what you had, so I can pick a few new things you haven't seen," he muses, running his fingers over my shoulder, playing with my hair.

I stifle another yawn and nod, sinking deeper against him. Exhaustion settles over me, and I struggle to keep my eyes open for the movie. Diego continues to play with my hair, trailing his fingers lightly over the bare skin of my arm.

"Hey, beautiful," he whispers, nudging me.

I blink a few times and can't believe the credits roll across the screen. "It's over?"

He chuckles. "I should walk you back to your room so that you can sleep. I need some as well."

I pout, and I mean full on sticking out my bottom lip friggin' pouting, and I can't believe it. But I also can't believe how comfortable this spot on the couch next to Diego is.

"Or we can stay right here," he whispers.

I nod and sink lower as he shifts down to lie behind me. My back rests against his chest, and his cool arms slide around my sides to pull me closer against him. "If it's okay. I've never slept alone before."

"Whatever you want, Jewel. I don't mind."

"Then I think I'll stay."

A screeching alarm blares through the room, ripping me from the strangest dream ever. One second I'm dreaming about lying naked on a table, bleeding into crystal goblets for a room of faceless vampires, and the next thing I realize, I'm clutching Diego's neck as he flies to his feet.

He releases a growl, attempting to cover his ears without dropping me. I raise my hands and cup them for him, staring at his angry gray eyes, his fangs extended out, his muscles bulging but his hold remains gentle around me.

"What's going on?" I yell, cringing. If the sound hurts my ears, I'm sure it has to be awful for him.

"I don't know. Stay here, okay?" Diego sets me on my feet, and I do as he tells me, only creeping toward the doorway to watch him from the sitting room of his suite.

As he reaches the door, the alarm shuts off, leaving my ears ringing. His bedroom door flies open, and he tenses, sliding a scary-long sword from a stand of a dozen or so weapons I hadn't noticed. What the actual fuck.

I scramble back, wondering if we're under attack. I didn't know this kind of thing happened to vampires. Sure, there were security guards at the base of the hill, and even The Boxes had an armed guard, but I never imagined I'd have to deal with threats now—not under the care of three vampire heirs of Donor Life Corp.

"She's gone. Someone took her! The sirens will keep everyone down for five minutes, and you wasted one. What the hell took you so long? Come on. Her last call out was at sunrise to her sister. We'll be lucky if she's even still alive." It's Kingston.

I shuffle toward the archway and catch sight of him rushing into the room with Austin behind him. The two vampires stand rigid with wild eyes, fangs flashing, unsettlingly scary like when

Master Caruthers was about to be ripped apart.

"This could be about Roger. Word must've gotten out," Austin says next. Shit balls. They asked me not to mention his demise, but I had no idea that this could've been the reason why. Now, I don't know how I'll ever sleep alone.

Diego slides his sword back in its sheath. "Calm down. I for—"

"Calm down? I'm going to ki—"

I suck in a sharp breath, clutching the wall. Both Kingston and Austin's heads jerk in my direction. They glance from Diego to me, and I take an automatic step back into the sitting room as a wave of indecipherable emotions crosses both their faces.

Kingston appears in front of me first, his dark eyes softening when they meet mine. "Babe, you're okay." He holds his hands out, just running them along the silhouette of my body without touching me.

I nod.

Cool arms wrap around me from behind, and Diego rests his chin on my shoulder. There must be some unspoken rule between the three brothers about touching me when I'm in one of their rooms, because Austin inspects me too but keeps his hands tucked in the pockets of his pajama pants.

I can't stop the smile crossing my face, seeing them dressed for bed. I knew vampires slept, but it's just weird seeing them like this. And then I remember what I'm wearing and where I am, and blush flourishes over my chest and warms my neck, sending my heart racing. Austin's Adam's apple bobs in his throat, his gaze running over me, the same hungry look I noticed in his green eyes surfacing like the first time I saw him.

"Jewel couldn't sleep," Diego says, breaking their intense gazes on me. He lets me go only to grab the blanket from the couch to wrap around my shoulders, covering my state of being half undressed. "So we were watching a movie."

"And then I actually did fall asleep," I admit, not wanting anyone to assume anything even if everyone knows that it could be a possibility, though intimacy outside who I'm with remains private.

"Which sounded like good sleep," Diego whispers in my ear, making me tighten my jaw, reminding me of the weird ass dream.

"It was a nightmare."

"Didn't sound like it," he teases.

I laugh and shift, hiding my face against him. "Stop it."

"Yes, please do. Diego, because of your carelessness, we need to let security know that Jewel is safe before they start interrogating the guests and staff," Kingston says, clearing his throat. "And Jewel." He sounds so serious using my name.

I force myself to look at him, despite wanting to sink to the floor and hide under the blanket away from all of them. He looks ready to chide me over worrying everyone, which annoys the hell out of me, because the days are supposed to be mine. How was I supposed to know that people would flip out if I left my room? No one said anything. "What, Kingston? No one told me I was supposed to stay in my room. The days are supposed to be my time regardless of what I decide to do with them."

Kingston wets his lips, rubbing them together. For the first time, he's not telling me the first thing that pops into his head. He was serious last night when he told me he'd catch on quickly to be more empathetic.

"Hey, beautiful," Diego says from behind me. "Next time you leave your room, you have to remember to notify the staff where you're going."

"I was supposed to notify someone?" I ask, spinning to face him. "No one told me that."

"It was in the contract," Austin says, speaking up.

"Not the one between us." Because I actually read that one. Now I wish I had paid more attention to the other one presented to me by the vampire board, but it wasn't like there was a chance I wasn't going to sign it. And I was nervous.

"It's okay, babe. Diego screwed up, too. I'm pissed at him, not you. You just scared the shit out of me. You're my dream match and if anything happened to you I'd—"

"Tear someone's head off?" I ask, glancing at Austin. He blushes, and I reach out and nudge his shoulder, bringing his gaze from the rug and to me. "Which if it's someone like Master Caruthers, I think I'm okay with that."

"Good to know," Austin murmurs, touching my hand still on his shoulder.

"Because as you probably know, there are a lot of people

like that guy out there," Kingston says. "And no doubt every single one of them wants a piece of you."

I shudder. "Great, now I don't think I'm ever going to be able to sleep alone."

Narrowing my eyes, I look at the three of them, expecting at least Kingston to make a joke out of the situation or insinuate something that'll make me all sorts of flustered. But all he does is press his lips together to hide his smirk, his dark eyes saying everything his mouth doesn't.

"Jewel, we didn't mean to scare you over this," Austin says. "And the possibility is unlikely. You're safe here, okay? The security measures are in place just in case, and knowing where you are helps the staff properly care for you if you're not with us."

Three different chimes go off at once, and Kingston pulls a small electronic device from his pocket at the same time as Austin. Diego hugs me closer against him, allowing his to ring from the night table near his enormous bed—a bed I can't stop looking at now. Because I'm still tired and my nerves are frayed, and all I want to do is hide.

"So you guys good to handle it?" Diego asks. "I think Jewel wants to get a little more sleep."

His words summon a yawn from me, and I cover my mouth in embarrassment. Neither argue or even give me weird looks. They thankfully accept that I'm safe and okay with Diego and nod their heads.

I hug Kingston first and then do the same for Austin. "Sorry again for freaking you out. I'll see you guys later."

Diego holds my hand as we watch them leave. Turning to me, he slides his arms around my neck to pull me against him so his body completely touches mine. He nudges me back to the couch, but I push him toward his bed.

"The couch is nice and all, but your pillows look amazing," I say. "Can I sleep there?"

"Of course. I'll take the couch," he says.

Diego guides me across the room and scoops me up to set me on the way-tall bed. Brushing my hair from my face, he leans in and gives me a whisper of a kiss on my cheek, inhaling a small breath of my scent in the process.

I clutch his hand and stop him from going back to the couch. "Cuddle with me?"

He grins. "Anything you want."

"You probably think I'm a wimp for being afraid to sleep by myself," I say.

Pulling me close, he says, "No, beautiful. I don't think that. And as much as I enjoy this, I hope your fear won't always be the reason you come to me or why you stay."

I smile at him and tuck my head against his chest, listening to his soft breathing. "It's not the whole reason, Diego. I do like you."

"Good. Because I really like you."

12

Human Sensibility

RAMONA FROWNS AT ME AS I hold up a shimmering gray dress that I think will match Diego's eyes. I'm pretty sure at this point, I'll never see my sister smile again, which sucks, because I could use it.

Diego walked me back to my room two hours ago where I met with the tailor. The old, silver-haired woman wouldn't even look me in the eyes. Her team of five people raced to alter a few dresses for me to choose from tonight with a promise to adjust enough clothes for the rest of the week. One even commented about not wanting to do as much as they planned because I'd just get fattened up.

I tried not to let it get to me, but the staff of the Divinity Estate pales in good manners compared to the families in The Boxes. They whisper too quietly for me to hear and so far have kept their answers short.

"It's too nice," Ramona finally says. "You shouldn't pick something that might make you appealing. Try whatever the hell that thing is over there." She motions to my bathrobe draped across my bed.

I roll my eyes and hold it up. "I'm sure everyone would love how easily accessible my body is in this."

She groans, and I laugh. Making light of something like this makes it easier not to freak out. Because no matter how friendly or cute the guys are, they will depend on me for my blood.

A soft knock on the door draws my attention away from my sister, and I shoot my gaze to my balcony door now open to allow sunlight in.

"Give me a minute. I have to close my outside door," I call out. Turning toward Ramona, I puff out my lip. "I'll call you tomorrow, okay? I want to see Dana and Fallon too."

She purses her lips. "I'll see what I can do."

She disconnects the line, making me frown. The last time I called, my cousins were sleeping. This time, they were apparently hanging out with some new friends they met on their tour of Haven Springs. I know it's only been a day since I've seen them, but I miss them. It's the longest we've ever been apart since they moved in with us.

The door to my bedroom flies open, and I jump from my bed and rush toward my balcony. Whoever designed this room before the Blood Hunger Plague didn't account for the future residents to be vampires or else they wouldn't have aligned the two doors. But I wanted natural light. Tinted glass makes it feel like night all day long.

"Diego, stop!" I yell, heaving a breath, fumbling to get the door closed. He wasn't supposed to be here until after the sun set.

"Ms. Divine, doors are to remain shut unless being used to pass through no matter the time of the day," a feminine voice snaps.

I blink a few times, getting used to the sudden dimness of my room and meet the bowed head of a girl around my age, clutching a small wooden box in her hands. She enters my room completely and closes the door, sweeping her gaze across the clothes spread out over the bed and one of the couches in the corner.

"I'm sorry. I didn't know," I say, strolling back to my bed.

"Like you didn't know about alerting security to your whereabouts." Her sharp tone makes me feel dumb. "Someone could have been hurt because of your irresponsibility. Half the staff thought the misters were going to end their contracts on the spot, and you know what happens to the humans if that's the case."

I don't, but I can tell it can't be good. "It won't happen

again."

"It better not. The shock alarms caused some concern for our elite guests, and it's best not to draw attention, which the misters will unintentionally do. Word spreads incredibly fast, if you know what I mean. I'd hate for something to happen to you due to your carelessness, Ms. Divine."

I jerk my attention toward her, feeling the threat laced around her comment of concern as it sinks into me. She has a lot of nerve to say something like that, especially because I could tell one of the guys, but the last thing I want is to have them flip their shit over a girl who's trying to survive as much as I am.

I clear my throat. "Thank you for your concern. Now if you'll excuse me, I have to get dressed."

She brings her gaze from the floor and smirks at me. Blond hair sticks out from under her black cap, and for the first time, I realize how the only skin on her body that shows is her face and hands. She wears black from neck to shoe and looks well-built and well-fed. Another perk of working for the heirs of Donor Life Corp, I suppose.

"The dark blue one over there." She points to a dress I immediately discarded because my bathroom towel covered me more than the dress. "It's Mr. Diego's favorite color, and it'll match the gift he asked me to deliver. Also, don't forget to wear your hair up to show it off."

I hug my arms across my body, staring at the wooden box she sets on the table near my door. "Thanks for the suggestion."

"You're welcome, Ms. Divine. I'll wait outside to escort you to the lab."

"The lab?"

She raises an eyebrow. "For your blood."

Oh, that. "Yeah, okay. I'll be quick."

In normal circumstances, I'd get to wait several weeks to donate, especially because of the extra blood I'd given for the match testing, but apparently drinking Austin's blood helped rejuvenate me and now I'll be giving a small amount daily.

Before I could even muse my thoughts about why Donor Life Corp doesn't do it for everyone, Austin said that the side effects were too risky and left it like that. It's probably a good thing, since I couldn't even stop myself from crawling into his lap. I can see a lot of vampires taking advantage of that. He didn't say as much, but he might've bent the rules a little for me. Kingston isn't the only rule breaker.

"Take as much time as you need, Ms. Divine. It's not me who truly waits on you." With her words, the girl turns around and exits my room, closing the door behind her.

Staring at the blue dress she suggested, I contemplate wearing it for all of a second before changing into the gray one Ramona warned me against. The tailor managed to alter the shimmering, flowy fabric in all the right places, accentuating my breasts by cinching the sides down to my waist.

After seeing the diamond and sapphire necklace in the box Diego sent to me, I twist my hair up into a braided bun and pin it in place with a few sparkly clips I found on my crowded vanity table. I skip almost all the makeup because I don't have time to mess around with it except for successfully applying a sweet smelling, sheer rose-colored lipstick.

I look around my room for a moment and realize there aren't any shoes to be found. I didn't wear any here either, seeing as someone discarded my only good pair at the Blood Match Center with the rest of my clothes.

Stepping into the hallway, I find the girl waiting for me with her head bowed toward the floor. She reminds me of how Brayla and I used to run through the city, because the last thing you want is to have a vampire catch you staring at them.

"Unless you're being escorted by one of the Divines, I suggest you drop your gaze to the floor at all times," the girl says.

"Is that a rule?"

"You might not be part of the staff, but you're still obliged to follow human rules and basic sensibility. I mean, if you want to ensure you get to where you're going safely. The Divines aren't the only vampires around here, and while the others usually respect the staff, you don't want to do anything to provoke their attention. Don't you know that some vampires can control your mind? If that happens, I guarantee you can't report it to one of your misters."

"Oh." It takes everything in me not to turn around and run back to my room to wait for Diego to pick me up to take me to the lab himself.

"Did you remember to notify security?" she asks, without moving.

"Ah, shit," I mutter. It's going to be harder to remember than I thought.

The girl sighs and waits for me to hit the call button by my door to let the gruff sounding man on the other end know that I'm heading to the lab with the girl, who tells me her name is Laurel, and then I race behind her to keep up.

After heading down a winding stairwell in a tiny tower and through an old entertainment room with two pool tables that seem more like art pieces than used for fun, we reach a long, dark hallway with old tapestries hung along the walls with a single heavy door at the end.

Laurel knocks on the door once and turns around to strut away without even saying goodbye. I shift on my feet, nervous about whoever I'm about to find on the other side of this door in this dark hallway.

It suddenly swings open, and I tense, preparing to run away if it's one of the elite vampires Laurel mentioned, who might also be the same ones the guys freaked out about earlier. I tilt my chin down to stare at the floor runner in case, taking in a few nervous breaths.

"Wow," a familiar voice says before a cool hand touches my bare arm. "You look radiant, Jewel."

I trail my gaze from the floor to confirm that my mind isn't messing with me and that Austin is indeed the one touching me. Throwing my arms around him, I surprise him with a hug, making him laugh.

"You have no idea how happy I am to see you," I say. "No

offense, but your house kinda freaks me out a bit."

"And I bet Laurel didn't help any," he says, motioning for me to follow him inside the room. "I can talk to her if you want."

My eyes widen. "Please don't."

"Did she threaten you?"

I thrash my head back and forth, sending stray strands into my face. "It was nothing, Austin. I just didn't realize there were so many rules and things I needed to know just to cross the house."

He sighs. "I'm sorry if she frightened you. She's a good employee, but she can be a little crass, especially with new people. You might call her possessive since she grew up here under the care of her mother. A know-it-all, if anything."

Which means every human here feels like family to her. Except for me. "No worries. I'm just glad it was you behind this friggin' intimidating dungeon door."

Austin smirks and guides me into what Laurel referred to as the lab, but it's not like any of the labs I've been in. Where the donation center was stark white and cold, with old chairs and yellowing counters, this room contains a comfortable looking bed, tan walls, and opaque glass cabinetry to hide all the equipment.

"I hope you don't mind if I tend to you," Austin says, rolling out a machine from a closet. "My brothers and I agreed that I'm to oversee your health, which includes the blood draws, so there won't be any mistakes like last time."

As per my initial Blood Match contract, I've released my rights to make medical decisions and consented to entrust my health to the vampire I matched with. My vampire will agree or disagree with medical advice on my behalf, which means that no matter how awkward this might be, I have to follow through.

I swallow, remembering the physical the doctor at the Blood Match Center gave me and start to sweat just thinking about having to go there before I even *go there,* if I ever *go there,* with Austin.

"Um, do I need to get undressed?" I ask quietly.

"I thought we could at least have our first night together before—"

I smack Austin's arm, releasing a breath. "Austin! You sound like your brother."

He laughs, reaching up to cover my hand with his. "I'm pretty sure Kingston would have just told you yes to your question. With me, I'd like the date first." Rubbing a hand up through his hair, he grins at me, his cheeks flushing, reminding me how flustered he got when he admitted that he'd given me his blood and that there were some interesting side effects.

I scrunch my nose, refraining from telling him that he's probably right, though I know Kingston would be at least half joking about it. "So, no physical?" I ask to change the subject.

"No, you're all good there, Jewel. I'm just going to enter in your current stats to follow your progress and extract a small vial of blood."

I release a breath. "Okay, that I can handle."

Austin explains everything to me as he does it, keeping the conversation light. When he's through drawing the small vial of blood, he hands me a piece of hard candy and watches me pop it into my mouth. The sweet cherry flavor bursts across my tongue, and then he hands me more.

"You're as sweet as these, you know," I say, popping another into my mouth. Austin's been nothing but professional and friendly, acting completely opposite than what I'm used to when it comes to blood donations.

"Glad to see Austin's taking good care of you, beautiful," Diego says from behind me. "And you look stunning. I knew that necklace would look perfect on you."

I twist on the bed and smile. "Thanks. I don't think I've ever looked so nice."

"Then you didn't see yourself last afternoon," Austin murmurs.

I bat his shoulder and then allow him to help me to my feet. He tosses Diego the vial of my blood. Knowing he's going to drink it, I turn away and glance at the wall. Austin touches his hand to my lower back, and I force myself to smile past the weirdness. This is what I agreed to. I've been donating blood for months. But just knowing Diego drinks my blood reminds me that this isn't all fun and games. He could very well be my permanent Blood Match, counting on me for sustenance. It's how he survives.

"Ready?" Diego asks, linking his fingers through mine to

pull my attention away from the wall. "I thought I could feed you, then maybe we could head to the gym and work on building up your muscle tone. End the night with a movie you haven't seen."

I nod my head. "Sure, that all sounds great."

"Have a good night, Jewel," Austin says from behind me. "Take it easy on Diego. He might not realize it, but I know you're stronger than you look and could kick his ass."

I laugh. "You bet I will."

Diego chuckles. "Now I'm definitely going to let you."

13

Blood Spill

DIEGO STANDS WITH ME OUTSIDE my door, hooking his fingers around my waist. I'd be lying if I didn't say I had an amazing time with him, even if my whole body aches now. After having dinner on the terrace overlooking the outdoor pool, where I had things I've never eaten before like the huge meatballs in the most amazing sauce, Diego put me through the most intense workout ever, where after he joked he could help me wash my hair in the huge shower. We ended the night with movies in the actual theater with popcorn for me and blood in a goblet like the ones I dreamed about the night before for him.

He was nice enough to ask if it was okay, and I agreed. Might as well get used to it, though something about knowing it wasn't my blood made me feel weird.

"You want to come back to my room?" Diego asks, leaning closer. He captures me with his brilliant smile, the gesture lighting up his whole face, making him even more handsome. I study the sharp curve of his jaw, his soft brown hair curling around his ears and unstyled.

I almost nod, but a part of me holds back. If I go to his room, I might never want to leave, and I know that's unfair to both Kingston and Austin. I haven't had time to give them much of a chance, and I'd like to.

Instead of responding with a rejection, I stand up on my tiptoes and he bends forward to meet his lips to mine. I kiss him sweetly just long enough to feel him tighten his grasp on me. He beams his brilliant smile again, his gray eyes sparkling in the soft light. That was better than I imagined my first kiss to be—sweet and soft and teasing enough that I can't wait to try it again.

I grin, rubbing together my lips. "I had a really great time, Diego, but I spent the day with you yesterday and—"

He brushes his fingers to my cheek. "Hey, you don't have to explain. While I'd love to spend the rest of the day with you today, I get it. I know you like my brothers too."

"I just want to give all of you a chance."

"And you're amazing for that," he responds, peering around the hallway. "Walk me to my room?" Diego must suspect that my mind is made up to already head that way, where Austin's room is supposed to be the last in the hall. I'm grateful he doesn't point it out.

I nod. "Sure."

Diego smiles at me while closing his door, and I only hesitate for a minute, peering around the dim hallway. For a split second, I consider running back to my room to change out of my dress, but then I hear soft voices coming from that direction and then footsteps.

Bowing my head, I stare at the patterned floor runner leading down the hall, longer than I had expected it to be. All the doors remain closed, and I try my best to ignore all the possible things that could be hidden behind them.

I spot a set of double doors at the end of the hallway and pick up my pace, practically running. The creepy feeling I had in the basement returns, and I spin to quickly glance behind me at the empty hallway. Maybe I should've gone back to my room and just called Austin to pick me up, because his suite seems to be in its own wing, and now I worry that I possibly turned and went in the wrong direction somehow by accident, all because I was too afraid to watch where I was going.

A door slams from in front of me, and I spin to look, but the hallway remains empty. Another door closes behind me, and I startle, jerking back around. Whoever it is moves too fast for me to see, purposefully messing with me. Instead of opening the closed door to confront them, I start to run. I'm mega friggin' scared and want to find Austin.

"Ms. Divine!" a voice calls out. But it's too late.

I crash into a solid body and topple over, landing with a thud on the floor. Laurel sneers from above me, holding a tray with a cup and a pitcher in her hands. She looks once at the doors behind her, then in front of her, and yells out and drops the tray right on top of me. Warm liquid cascades over my face and chest, shocking me.

I freeze, panic squeezing my chest at the sight of the blood dripping from my hands from swiping them across my face to clear my vision.

"I'm so sorry," she says, holding her hands up without touching me. "You ran right into me. Why weren't you watching where you were going?"

"What's going on out—" Austin inhales a sharp breath from somewhere behind me.

Laurel backs away even more, her hands held up, her head bowed. "Mr. Divine, it was an accident. Allow me to clean this up."

Except it wasn't an accident, and Austin releases an unsettling growl from his throat. Laurel purposely dropped the pitcher of blood on top of me. It's like she wanted to get a reaction out of Austin, and his eyes flash silver as I blink on the floor.

I meet her gaze that dares me to call her out on her lie and prove that my loyalty now lies with vampires instead of humanity—something I worried about Ramona thinking the last two times I spoke with her. I don't take Laurel's dare.

Another much lower growl escapes Austin's mouth as he

looks between her and me, his eyes practically burning invisible tracks across my body bathed in blood.

Squeezing my eyes shut, I cover my face with my hands, and whisper, "Please don't bite me."

Austin sucks in another sharp breath. "Ms. Mendoza, please excuse us."

"Would you like me to retrieve another—"

"Leave!" he yells at her, making me flinch. Out of my three vampires, Austin's the last one I had expected to react like this, but behind his sweet charm hides a predator vicious enough to sever a man's head.

I whimper, staying completely still on the floor like Dad told me to do if I ever found myself on the receiving end of a vampire's fury. If I can't flee, I shouldn't fight, because it might make things worse.

A shadow darkens my eyelids. "Jewel, I'm sorry," Austin whispers without touching me. "Please don't be afraid of me. I didn't mean to scare you. I was confused and thought that Laurel—"

Sitting up, I meet his concerned green eyes. "It was an accident."

"I know. But seeing you covered in blood..."

"Made you hungry?" I cringe at my question.

He laughs. "Funny enough, that was not my first thought. I was worried you had been injured."

"No, I'm fine. Just wearing your...dinner?"

Without thinking, I reach up and tap my bloody finger to

his pouty bottom lip. His nostrils flare, his eyes darkening. Something within me keeps me from moving or jerking away. My finger absently continues to glide over his bottom lip where his tongue slides over the blood, and he gently sucks it off my finger.

My eyes dart from his, a whole bunch of conflicting emotions rising in me as I lose myself in his intense stare. It's then that I realize he's only wearing a towel around his muscular torso and my dress rests hiked up on my hips.

"Damn, babe. Can you please deliver dinner to me next?" The sound of Kingston's voice snaps me out of the pull slowly tugging me closer to Austin.

Austin releases a low growl from his throat, making Kingston laugh. Turning from his brother, Austin helps me to my feet, carefully shifting my sticky hair from out of my face. Kingston steps forward, glancing at the mess on the floor and the blood all over me, but he doesn't reach out to touch me or anything.

"What happened anyway?" he asks. "I hope one of the staff didn't make you serve Austin."

I shake my head. "It was an accident."

"It was Laurel," Austin says. "Who happened not to get a single drop on her."

Kingston frowns and glances at me. Sweat prickles on the back of my neck. He looks ready to fly at me to cup my face, look into my eyes, and demand I tell him what really happened, because it only takes one look at both of them to know that they know I'm not telling them everything.

"Just let it go," I snap. "I'm fine."

"That's beside the point," Kingston says.

"Please," I whisper. "Drop it."

"Unruly members of the staff need to be put in their places, especially when it comes to you, babe. I know all this is new to you, but if she purposely did something to jeopardize your safety, then we must—"

"Kingston, please. It was an accident. I was scared and running and didn't see her."

"Running from what?" Austin asks, gently taking my hand.

"I don't know. My imagination, I guess."

The two vampires share one of their mind-reading intense looks, and it takes me shifting on my feet to get them to look away from each other. Kingston slowly nods his head, taking me in once more.

"But I'm fine now. I swear," I add. "I just want to get cleaned up."

"I can walk you back to your—"

I shake my head, cutting off Austin's words. "Can I stay?"

He nods his head, a whisper of a smile crossing his mouth. "Of course."

"And I'll make sure everything's as it should be," Kingston says. "Don't have too much fun with Austin, babe."

"Oh, but I planned on it," I retort, raising my eyebrows at him.

He chuckles and groans. "I guess I'll be plotting all day to see how to top it."

Oh, boy.

Kingston flicks his fingers once at me and disappears, leaving me alone with Austin in the hall. With one more look around, Austin guides me into his room, completely different than Diego's. Where Diego's room was dark and modern, Austin's contains red woods and glass. His sitting area consists of two recliners and walls of books instead of the projection screen. I've never seen so many books—way more than the rickety shelf at my old high school. And they're just as old.

"Cool collection," I say, pointing into the room.

"Just some of my favorites since they don't print hardback editions anymore," he says. "Do you like to read? Your literacy was one of the reasons I applied to match with you. It's pretty uncommon, you know."

"Education was important to my parents," I say, a blip of sadness washing over me. Who knew that their need to see me and my sister got somewhat of an education would be one of the reasons I ended up here.

"Well, I'm happy to teach you anything you'd like."

"Maybe after a shower," I muse, turning to glance at the archway to a gleaming bathroom.

Austin motions for me to follow him, and he presses a few buttons on a digital screen to start the glass enclosed shower. Steam fogs through the air, warmth sinking into my cool skin. I don't move for a moment, turning my gaze to Austin's ripped body and the towel still hanging around his hips.

He remains utterly still while I continue to drink him in. "Everything you need is already in there. I'll see about having someone bring some food."

"Actually, can you help me first?" I ask, turning around and lifting my hair to show him the zipper of my dress.

He swallows, his Adam's apple bouncing, his arm muscles flexing as he curls his fingers. And then he quickly steps forward and eases down the zipper. Once his fingers drop from my back, I turn around, but Austin's already gone.

I release a breath and stare at my horrifying reflection in the mirror. I hope this isn't a sign of how my life at the Divinity Estate will be—me, covered in blood, and more confused than ever.

Thankfully for now, it's not my own.

"Hey, Jewel," Austin whispers.

I roll over directly into his arms. Sweat prickles my forehead as I pull myself from another weird dream—as similar as the one the night before of me naked and bleeding on a table—but this one was slightly different, because I imagined Laurel standing at the head of the table, clutching a knife I'm sure was responsible for the wounds.

Fluttering my eyes open, I face Austin on his bed, my arms caging both our heads while his hands hug my waist. He stares at me for a moment before letting go to brush the damp strands of hair from my eyes. I shift closer, pressing my warm face into his bare chest and listen to the thrum of his heart beating against my ear.

"I had the weirdest dream," I whisper.

"Sure looked like it," he says, rubbing his fingers along my back. "Sounded like it, too."

I tilt my head up toward his and purse my lips. "Well, that's embarrassing."

He chuckles and shifts me up, kissing the top of my forehead. Tracing my finger along his stomach, I follow the line of muscles down to his navel as tingles course through me at the memory of the first time we were alone together after he had given me his blood.

"We should get up," he murmurs.

"Or we could just stay here all night." Whoa. I think Kingston's lack of filter wore off on me, because I didn't intend to say that out loud.

He groans and pulls me to my feet, smiling the whole time as he does so. "That's incredibly tempting, and I might kick myself later for saying this, but I wasn't joking about wanting a proper date with you."

My cheeks flush at the idea of what could happen after a date with him, because I feel like I'm experiencing an everlasting side effect from his blood. I can't stop looking at his full lips and how soft they probably feel.

"I almost forgot about the beach," I say, bouncing on the balls of my feet.

His smile melts into a frown. "About that. We're going to have to reschedule it for another time. None of us think it's a good idea to take you from the estate alone, and I don't exactly want tonight to be a group affair."

I smirk. "So then we can just stay here."

He shakes his head and laughs. "Come on. I promise we'll have fun."

Austin practically drags me with him through the large estate and out the enormous front door to the terrace. I had expected to have to stop by the lab, but he guides me down a concrete hill and past a huge tennis court and to the door of a building seemingly built into the hillside with huge arched glass windows that allow in the purple twilight with the moon hanging in the sky. Neither of us even changed, and I wonder what exactly he has in store.

Blue and gold tiles glitter around a remarkable facility with marble and glass light fixtures and white statues decorating the outskirts of an impressive indoor pool lit only with the soft light from above. Intricate gold patterns decorate the arched walls with huge beams that stretch across the ceiling. The pool extends into another ornate room with more shallow water.

"Since I couldn't take you to the beach, I thought we could swim here," he says.

I frown. "I can't swim."

"Yet."

I grin and let him tug me into the shadowed archway of a changing room with showers extending along the wall. On a tiled bench built into the opposing wall rests a bathing suit and a couple of towels.

"Go ahead and change, and I'll be right back," Austin says.

He exits the quiet room, and I stare around for a moment to make sure there aren't any other doors for people to pop out of. When I summon my courage, I undress from the long T-shirt I borrowed from Austin and slip into the black and white polka dotted one-piece bathing suit. My dark hair cascades around my shoulders, and I quickly braid it and knot it in place.

"Are you dressed?" Austin asks from outside the door.

I hum my response, and he re-enters the room and drinks me in from his place by the door. His burgundy swim trunks show off the V of his hips, and I can't help myself from checking him out for the millionth time. From a suit to a towel, and from pajamas to swimwear, he looks hot in anything.

"Perfect fit," he says, closing the distance between us. "I hope you don't mind if we swim first and then we can eat together poolside. Unless you're hungry now..."

I slide my arms around him and push him toward the exit. "You promise you won't let me go, right? The deepest water I've been in was stomping through puddles after the rain."

"You're safe with me. I promise."

I nod and lean forward, surprising him with a kiss. What I expect to be timid, reflecting my nerves and lack of experience, explodes into something that leaves me breathless like he's been waiting his whole life to kiss me, explore my lips, catch up for what he's been deprived of.

He reacts with the hunger I sometimes notice in his eyes as

he slides his hands down my back and to my butt, not exploring my curves but using them to get me closer. He picks me up so quickly that I can't stop myself from curling around him, giving in to his desire to be with me on a different level than a need for my blood.

He craves me as much as I crave him, devouring my kiss like I've been starving him of my affection. And I realize I might have been just as starved for his. All the pent up desire I've been carrying explodes in a hot wave through me, and I deepen our kiss, caressing my tongue to his without wondering if he likes it because he moans deep in his throat, shifting me on his hips to feel the full extent of excitement I elicit from him.

I'd have never guessed that Austin lacked any sort of experience like Kingston said, because his lips meld perfectly with mine, his fingers firm yet gentle as they memorize my body. My own fingers glide across his taut arms and his shoulder blades, combing through his tousled but still sexy blond hair.

The world shifts, and my back presses against the cool wall. "Is it okay if I continue?" he asks through a gasping breath.

"Yes," I manage to say, kissing him again, squeezing his body between my thighs as I attempt to guarantee not even an inch of space falls between us.

He touches his forehead to mine, his handsome face blurring from his closeness. "Just tell me if I need to stop."

I suck in his bottom lip, summoning another moan from him that makes me smile through a kiss. As his mouth explores mine with our entangled breaths, my whole body reacts to his touch. His hand trails up my side to cup my breast through the bathing suit, and I release a gasp and a moan and a pleading whimper the second his fingers move away. He breaks from my lips, kissing me tenderly down my jaw and toward my neck, his fingers awakening something raw inside me I had never known I could feel.

I pant, surprised by the wave of fear and lust battling it out until my mind processes what my body begs for, nearly sending me over an edge I'm not sure I could ever return from. Austin's fingers travel down my stomach, inching lower to touch me in a way no one has ever done so. I squirm at the agonizing pace of his hand sliding past my naval, and I grab his fingers to show him it's okay and that I want him to explore me more.

And then his teeth graze the skin of my throat, and I tense, my body on the verge of exploding as I almost scream for him to bite me.

"Austin, stop," I manage to say instead, my breath heaving with my expanding chest.

He pulls away and meets my wide eyes. "I'm sorry, Jewel. I got carried away. I didn't mean to make you nervous. I wasn't going to bite you. I promise."

Resting my head on his shoulder, I inhale another deep breath, trying to suppress the freaky desire and disappointment from his words. What the eff is wrong with me? I don't care how attracted I am to Austin, I know I can't possibly really want him to sink his teeth into my skin...right?

"Don't apologize," I say with my face away from him, my

cheeks and chest, basically my whole body still humming with tingles. "I liked it...maybe a little too much."

He buries his face in the crook of my shoulder. "I moved too fast. I just—I like you. More than I imagined I would. You're beautiful, funny, and smart. Sexy as hell."

I lean back to touch his cheek. "I think you're pretty amazing too."

He kisses me once more. "Really?"

"Why do you sound surprised?"

"No reason. I just hope that never changes."

14

Phantoms

I GLARE AT MY SISTER'S projection. "I don't care if they're having fun. Go get them."

Ramona's jaw twitches, and she peers past me like she'll catch sight of one or all of the guys hanging out in my room. "Fine. But we don't have a lot of time to talk today."

I frown. "You can't make time? Come on, Ramona-Babona. I miss you."

"I miss you too, Jewel." She glances past me again, making a weird face. "The girls are coming now."

The screen blurs and Dana and Fallon both crowd the

screen, beaming huge smiles at me. Their hair, the same shade of brown as mine, shines with a luster I've never seen. And they already look healthier with rosy color tinting their cheeks. I'm pretty sure Fallon's even wearing makeup.

"Jewel! We've been waiting forever to talk to you," Dana says. "You know we waited all day yesterday."

I grimace for a second before composing myself. "You did?"

They both nod.

"I heard you were having fun," I muse, spotting Ramona staring at me from behind them, her lips hidden in a line. I know my sister better than I do anyone in the world, and the strange feeling I had during our last conversation resurfaces as she subtly shakes her head at me. "I'm so glad you like it there."

"And what about you? Are you okay?" Fallon says. "They're not chaining you up or anything. Ramona said they might."

It takes everything in me not to react to the fear Ramona clearly instilled into their heads over my situation. "It's honestly been great. Better than I ever imagined."

They both deadpan. "You don't have to lie to us to protect us. Ramona said—"

Fallon and Dana scream in unison, their eyes widening as they stare at me through the phone. Fear rushes over me, a creepy sensation, the same one I got in the hall when I ran into Laurel, raises the hairs on my arms.

I shift and look behind me at my empty room. "What's

the—"

Ramona yanks the phone from my little cousins. "Hey, Jewel. We gotta go. This is a lot for them, okay? Take care of yourself."

"Ramona, wait," I say.

She disconnects the line, her projection disappearing from the wall. A door slams behind me, startling me to my feet. I spin around and search my bedroom again. Fear sinks into my stomach as the silence gets to me. I rush to the phone on my nightstand and pound Kingston's number, but he doesn't pick up.

I grab my robe and pull it over the new cotton pajamas that waited for me on my bed after Austin dropped me off. I asked Kingston to give me an hour so that I could call my sister, and now I wish I had taken him up on his offer to call her from his room.

Strolling across my bedroom, nerves bunching my muscles, making me feel worse than after my work out with Diego, I dart to my door and smack the call button and wait for the voice to respond.

"I'm going to Kingston's room," I mutter and exit without waiting for a response.

I peek out into the hall, finding it empty, and turn the opposite way of Diego's room to make my way to the first door on the right, which turns out to be as far away as Austin's room. Anxiety squeezes my chest the farther from my room I get, and I feel like the first time I did when I found myself on Starlight

Row and two blocks from the safety of my apartment after sunset. I can feel the weight of someone's stare, but every time I turn around to look, no one's there.

But then I hear footsteps and someone softly breathing. I spin around to look behind me again and cold fingers brush against my neck, lifting my hair. I freeze in my spot, clenching my jaw, keeping my eyes trained on the floor.

"Please don't hurt me," I whisper.

The hand disappears along with quiet footsteps, and I release an uncontrollable sob using my hand the best I can to smother the sound. I can't draw attention to myself. Not here. Not now. If someone other than one of the guys hears me, I'm screwed.

A silhouette blocks the dim light from my blurry vision, and I scramble back, falling onto the floor. I hold my hands up protectively, screaming out again. "Don't touch me!"

"Kingston, what the fuck," Diego snaps.

"It wasn't me." Another figure kneels next to me. "Jewel, hey. Hey, babe. Look at me."

I blink away my frightened tears and focus on Kingston, searching my face with his dark eyes. Flinging my arms out, I launch myself at him and knock him on his back, burying my face into his soft T-shirt.

Fear continues to strangle my voice, and the only thing that comes from my mouth is another sob and a wheeze of breath. Kingston gathers my trembling body into his arms, rubbing his hands up and down my back, trying to push the fear out of me. One second I'm in the hallway, and in the next, he sets me on his unmade bed and slides in beside me, hugging me in his arms without saying a word until I finally manage to pull myself together.

Kingston carefully touches my chin, guiding my face to look at him. "You're safe, babe."

"I wasn't though," I whisper. "Someone was in my room."

He frowns, his shapely brows nearly covering his dark eyes. "Only the three of us and Laurel have complete access to this wing, and Laurel was with me. No one else has permission today."

"Is there anything else I can do for you, Mr. Divine?" Laurel's sweet voice draws my attention away from Kingston and to her as she sets down a plate of food along with a pitcher of what is surely blood on the table near the door. "Perhaps something else for Ms. Divine. She looks like she might faint."

"You're excused," Kingston says, waving her off, turning his attention back to me.

Laurel smirks once, dropping her gaze back to the floor, and then disappears after shutting it behind her. Her smug look sinks under my skin. She looked delighted by my state of fear, probably assuming I deserved it for my first morning here. But another part of me senses there's more to her. I haven't survived Starlight Row for as long as I have because of luck. I know who to trust and who I can count on not to toss me into the shadows at the first sign of trouble, and Laurel would gladly shove me into a mass of hungry shadow dwellers without a second thought.

"I don't want her to have access to my suite anymore," I say. "Only you, Diego, and Austin."

"Okay, babe. But why?" he asks. "Is this about the blood spill yesterday?"

I shrug. "Maybe."

"It'll take a few days to authorize another staff member. Can you hold on until then? I'll make sure she stays away from you, but we—meaning me, Diego, and Austin—still need someone on this floor to assist with our needs." Like serving blood. He doesn't say it, but I know it.

Shuddering a breath, I nod my head. "Yeah, I can handle a few days. I just—I'm sorry. Something scared me."

He purses his lips. "Maybe it was the ghosts."

"Ghosts?" I squeak.

He chuckles, shaking his head. "I'm kidding, babe."

I groan and shove him, but he's quick to close the space between us and pulls me back into his arms. I let him hug me until the fear finally dissipates, and Kingston leans back to peer into my eyes.

"That's better. As much as I like how clingy you get when you're freaked out, I'd much prefer you cling to me because you hate the space between us."

I laugh and rest my head on his shoulder. "Who says I don't."

He hums under his breath. "Hold onto that thought and do me a favor."

"A favor?"

"I'd appreciate it if you'd take off the robe. My brothers are coming down the hall now. Not fair that I've found you in a damn sexy T-shirt with Diego and then hand feeding Austin his dinner in the hottest dress ever. It's my turn to make them jealous."

I snort, covering my mouth with my hand, annoyed that a stupid sound escaped me. "I suppose I could do that."

He grins as I untie the robe and helps me push the soft fabric away from my neck. His smile falters, and he droops his chin, raising an eyebrow at me. "What are you wearing?"

"Pajamas."

"Those are—" He sighs, yanks his shirt over his head, and hands it to me. "Never mind, put this on."

Laughing, I shrug into his shirt over my plain cotton one that matches my cotton pants, taking a moment to devour his delicious muscular body with my eyes. He bites his lip between his teeth, grinning at me while flashing his fangs, clearing enjoying my reaction to seeing him shirtless.

I raise my fingers to his skin, gliding them across his built chest, grazing his nipples, and then switch directions to touch his flexing abs. A knock sounds on the door, and I freeze, but Kingston brings his index finger to his lips to shush me before I say anything.

"Come on, Kingston," Diego says. "You're the one who asked me to get Austin."

Kingston sighs. "Fine, but make it quick. I'm pretty sure

my babe's going to be better than okay."

The door swings open, and Diego and Austin come in, both smirking as Kingston pulls me even closer, practically sitting me on his lap. I go along with it and hang my arm across his shoulders, giving both Diego and Austin a smile just for each of them.

"You know, Kingston. I'm surprised you asked Jewel to put on clothes rather than take them off," Diego says. Without having to ask, I know both he and Austin heard our conversation on their way over.

Kingston groans. "I'm failing miserably at this."

I shift in his arms, smirking. If Diego and Austin heard our conversation, then I know Kingston knew they would hear it, and he's trying to poke at my pity. I consider calling him out but decide to let him think he's clever. Propping my chin on his shoulder, I run my fingers over his bare chest and down his stomach again. "You're not failing. I might prefer it this way."

He inhales a sharp breath and grabs my hand, bringing it to his lips to kiss my knuckles. "You two, out. I assure you Jewel's fine now and will be safe and content with me."

"But what about the person in my room?" I ask.

Diego and Austin both tense. "Someone was in your room? Kingston—"

I half expect him to brush off my fears, to tell me it's all in my head, but he kisses my temple and says, "If someone was on this floor, they're gone. I'm restricting Laurel's access as soon as we transfer in a replacement just in case. She'll be promoted to the guest houses with a bonus as to not draw attention."

"You think she let someone up?" Austin asks.

Kingston shrugs. "She was with me during the incident, so I can't be sure."

"I should talk to her," Austin says.

Diego shakes his head. "Better to not show our suspicions and to just keep a better eye on her."

"Agreed," Kingston says.

"What about the person in my room," I ask again. "Whoever it was, they touched me in the hallway. I know I'm not imagining it."

All three guys look at each other, sharing a quiet conversation. Just when annoyance begs me to open my mouth to insist on one of them telling me what the hell they're thinking about, Austin meets my gaze. "We'll do a sweep of your room and the rest of the floor, but you shouldn't worry too much."

I blink.

"Word could've gotten out, and it might have been someone just curious to see you," Diego says.

I frown.

"Yeah, babe. If that person wanted you, you'd be dead already."

Covering my eyes, I inhale a long breath through my nose. Their words do nothing to help with the fear building inside me and freak me out even more. Because they're right. The phantom vampire in my room could have ripped my throat out before I would've been able to call for help.

"Nice work, dude," Austin says. "You scared her again."

I pull myself together and meet each of their eyes. Diego half smiles at me, hiding any and all of his concern over the situation. Austin balls his hands into fists, failing to hide his frustration. Kingston's pouty mouth mirrors mine, and he hugs me against him again.

"Go ahead and make sure everything's clear," Kingston says to his brothers without looking away from me. "Ask security to double up and do more frequent checks. Also, no unauthorized vampires in the main house during the day until further notice."

"Got it and agree," Diego and Austin say in unison.

"Jewel's not to be alone," Kingston adds.

I open my mouth to argue and stop. I can tell it isn't up for discussion. The thought of being under watch all the time gets to me, but it's not like I want to go back to my room alone now. I knew I handed in my freedom to give my family theirs, and I don't mind being with the guys, but it's the thought behind it.

"Ever?" I ask.

Kingston slides his fingers through mine. "We'll respect your privacy, but yeah. Never alone."

I nod, meeting all their gazes. "Okay, never alone it is."

Kingston points to the door. "Now get out, you two. You've had plenty enough time with our girl. I have some catching up to do."

Kingston strolls out of his bathroom naked, rubbing a towel through his wet hair. He heads toward his wardrobe without looking in my direction. Syrup drips from my piece of waffle onto the plate as I gape at him from my spot perched in a chair at the small table in his office. His skin glistens, still damp with shower steam, and it takes everything in me to turn my gaze away.

"Breakfast good?" he asks from his spot across the room.

"Mmmhmm," I muse, shoving another bite into my mouth.

His light footsteps draw closer, and I know he's purposely slow and noisy, because he's capable of moving so quickly that it's like he materializes in front of me. But not this morning.

"It's not going to work, Kingston," I say, peeking through my eyelashes as his silhouette blocks out the light in his bedroom.

"What do you mean?" he asks.

I peek again and turn away. Ah, hell. "I'm not going to throw myself at you because you present me with this weird ass opportunity."

He chuckles. "I have no clue what you're talking about. I'm offended you think I'm so easy. For your information, I hate dressing in the bathroom. If you choose to look, that's on you."

"Kingston."

"There's nothing to be ashamed of, babe. We're a hundred percent match for body, so of course you're going to like what you see."

If my cheeks could warm anymore, they'd surely set my face on fire. His soft laugh proves how much he enjoys my reaction, so I inhale a deep breath, straighten my shoulders, and open my eyes to meet his.

Holy shit balls. Thank God.

Kingston grins at me, leaning in the doorway, wearing a light gray pair of boxer briefs. With his dark eyes and seductive smile, his hard abs and prominent V pointing down to the obvious bulge I desperately try not to stare at, he reminds me of one of the fragrance models from an old magazine. But hotter.

I throw my napkin at him, and he snatches it mid-air and drops it back to the table. "I do like what I see," I admit, giving him another once over. "But—"

"No buts. Let's leave it at that."

I roll my eyes. "But I want more than that hot body of yours. And these games you're playing—no more."

"Games?"

"Last sunrise with the whole favor thing. You were trying to make me pity you over some awkward as hell moments with your brothers. You don't need to be jealous because I was scared to be alone and rushed to Diego, forgetting what I was wearing or how I went from pure panic, thinking Austin was going to attack me to shoving my fingers with someone else's blood on them into his mouth."

"Austin would never attack you," he says. Out of everything, that's the one thing he chooses to comment on, and I can't help the smile crossing my face.

"I know that, Kingston," I say, getting to my feet. "Just like after last night, when I was freaking out, I knew I could come to you. And you didn't disregard my feelings or brush me off. You held me the whole day even though I friggin' snotted on you from crying."

He scrunches his nose. "That was pretty gross, babe."

I laugh, sliding my arms around his neck. "So, do you get that you don't have to try to seduce me with that pretty damn hot body of yours or play games with me to get my attention. Because I like you. A lot. And if you want some of my affection, all you have to do is ask."

He raises an eyebrow. "You're going to make me—"

I shut him up with a kiss, caressing my lips to his just enough to tease him and make him moan deep in his throat. His hands travel down my sides to rest on my hips, but he keeps space between us, letting me take the lead. I slowly pull away, afraid to give into my desire to press harder to him, to give him permission to explore me in the way we both want. But I know if I let him, I might not stop.

Because as my life spirals out of my control and into the hands of my three vampire matches, I want to hold onto the girl who grew up in Dark Terrace Ranch. The girl who never imagined a life like this or how much she'd actually enjoy it. I need to remind myself that as much as I want to hold on, some things I have to let go. But that doesn't mean I have to let go of all of me. Just the parts I no longer want to live with.

"That was the best kiss of my life," Kingston whispers against my lips, just holding me close without closing the space again.

I smirk.

"You don't believe me?" he asks.

"No, I believe you," I say.

"Good, because you're the only one I ever want to kiss. And hug. And touch. Lots of touching."

I softly nip his lip between mine, making him moan again. "You forgot devour."

"And all you want to do is test my self-control."

"It is rather fun."

15

Happy Surprise

"SO, YOUR BROTHERS ARE GOING on our date?" I ask Kingston while smiling at Diego and Austin over his shoulder.

He rests his chin in the crook of my neck. "They're helping me escort you to our destination."

"I'm kind of surprised you don't want to stay here. Austin said—"

"Something came up at the Blood Match Center." He frowns, his pouty lips extra kissable.

"Oh, you mean this isn't a date. You're taking me to work." I hate the fact that disappointment washes through me, and I'm sure my expression mirrors Kingston's. Spending the day with him so far was nothing short of interesting. He was right about me enjoying sleeping next to him, because though he doesn't need another ego boost, he's an amazing cuddler.

And after what he exclaims was the best heart-to-heart conversation that assures we'll be close forever—in the form of a joke I know he's at least somewhat serious about—I was looking forward to our night. Under all the sarcasm and pickup lines hides a guy I know I could contently match with. *If he doesn't change the second you do...if you do.*

Kingston hugs me tighter, groaning into my skin, making me shiver as his voice vibrates over me as he apologizes about having to return to my "dreadful hometown." I never in a million years thought I'd ever return to Dark Terrace Ranch, but I was wrong—Kingston, Diego, and Austin are the heirs to Donor Life Corp after all.

He straightens his back and peers down at me. "This isn't how I imagined my first official date with you would go, but I swear I'm going to make it up to you. Please, please, please don't hold this against me."

"Only if you keep holding me against you," I say with a laugh. He's not the only one who can fire back flirtatious banter, which his sad face looks like it could use.

He exaggerates a groan and turns to his brothers. "I quit. This is my formal resignation."

"Careful, Kingston," Diego warns. "That's grounds for disqualification from being matched."

"What?" I say.

Kingston turns to me and cups my face. "Don't worry, babe. There's no way I'd purposefully get disqualified from a match again, especially with you. And hold onto that thought about my body against yours, because I promise I will make it up to you."

This is the second time I've heard about Kingston's mysterious disqualification from an apparent match he applied for. I'm annoyed at the sudden jealousy coursing through me, but I decide to drop it and say, "Shit happens, dude. You don't have to make it up to me. Whatever time I get with you still makes me happy."

Glancing behind him, he shares a look with his brothers. "You and that back-world mouth of yours gets to me every—can I just kiss you?"

Confusion crinkles my brows. "Huh?"

"I asked if I could kiss you." He licks his lips, his dark brows puckering with nerves I don't think I've ever seen him carry. It could be because of me or the night, but something has him on edge. I can feel it, though it's not my place to ask why. "Please, Jewel. I want nothing more from this night than to kiss you."

How could I say no to that? This is one of those moments where I kind of wish he didn't need to ask permission, because being surprised with a kiss might make this less weird with his brothers only feet away.

I stare at Kingston's mouth, wetting my own lips in anticipation, and then dart my gaze to his brothers behind him. It helps that Diego and Austin remain expressionless, amused if anything, and then they turn away. "Yeah, okay," I manage to say, knowing I'm taking way too long to respond.

Closing the space, Kingston brushes his lips to mine, pulling me to him by my butt to press against me. Something about the change of plans or how nervous he acts does nothing for the constant anxiety fighting to control the state of my chest and my thrashing heart. But I force those feelings away and lose myself in the warmth blossoming from me to steal the chill from Kingston's skin. I soak in his need to be with me to take it as my own. Kissing him deeper, I glide my hands over the solid muscles of his back from over his suit. He parts his mouth open and caresses his tongue to mine until I react more fervently, nearly gasping, my body begging for his hands to roam away from my lower back.

He pulls away first and smiles at me, reaching up to touch my face. "You know, we can just run away together. Screw the world."

"Kingston..."

He sighs. "You're right. This might not be an ideal date, but that kiss of yours did help start things off how I imagined, and I will be thinking about it until I can devour you in the best way possible later."

I bat my hands to his shoulders, shaking my head with a smile. "Later seems like a long time away. I don't know if I can wait." My teasing makes him moan in his throat, and I laugh and wag my finger at him.

"Don't worry, beautiful," Diego says. "I won't make you."

Kingston intakes a sharp breath without commenting or looking toward his brother. I kind of like seeing how much he seems to hate the world in this moment. Hate his position at Donor Life Corp. I bet it's not often he's ever complained. I never thought I'd get pleasure from knowing that I'm the reason he does.

"Babe," he whispers. "You're enjoying this, aren't you?"

I bite my lip and smile. "That obvious?"

"I deserve this," he mutters.

But I don't believe that's true. I wrap my arms around him and bring my face close to his. "How about to make up for the fact that you're not going to get much alone time with me, I waive the whole asking permission for a kiss rule for tonight."

He reacts by flashing his fangs and immediately presses his lips to mine, stealing my breath away. "You're amazing, you know."

"Remind me to schedule something at the office during my night as well," Diego says from the front passenger's side door of the car.

"While these two plot to get pity kisses, I'll gladly stay home with you and take what you offer." Austin winks at me, opening the back door with an excited smile.

I roll my eyes and stop in front of him, touching his cheek. "Don't drive too crazy, okay?" I tell him instead of commenting on his dig at his brothers.

Kingston slides in behind me. "Oh he will, babe. If you thought Diego was bad, just wait. Austin and I made a deal to guarantee you cling to me for the next hour."

"Only an hour?" It took longer than that to get here with Diego's crazy driving.

He misinterprets my question like I don't think an hour in a speeding car is long enough and chuckles. "No time to waste, babe. We'll take our time on the way home. Promise."

I bob my head and slide farther across the seat to sit behind Diego, not liking the looks of the space between the seats I nearly flew between the last time I was in the car. Diego beams at me when I touch his shoulder, and Kingston ends up taking the middle seat, draping his arm over my shoulders to pull me into him. Austin adjusts the mirror, hits a few buttons, and the car lights up without a sound.

"Seatbelt, Jewel," Austin says.

Kingston mutters something I can't hear under his breath at his brother. "You don't trust me to hold onto her?"

Both Austin and Diego swivel in their seats in a silent warning, making Kingston reach for the belt to snap the harness around me. Everyone smiles at me in some sort of weird anticipation like they can't wait to see what I'll say next. Both Kingston and Diego stay turned toward me while Austin flicks his gaze to me in the mirror. The car takes off, sending me back in the seat. I release a short scream in surprise, and Kingston chuckles again, snuggling me to him.

Austin speeds, the eerie silence of the racing car getting to me. Kingston wasn't lying about Austin driving fast to the city. I lose track of time, shifting uncomfortably in the seat. Kingston says something to his brothers, and Diego touches my knee. Nausea rolls through me, the dark vehicle suffocating me so much that I hang my head as far forward as possible. I'm afraid if the ride doesn't end soon, I'll throw up.

"I need out," I whisper. I can't figure out why it's so unpleasant this time. This drive was nothing like the one to the Divinity Estate.

"Soon, Jewel," Austin says.

"I don't feel good."

Rubbing his hand on my back as I lean forward again in the seat, Kingston tries his best to soothe me. "We're coming into the city, babe. It'll be over soon," Kingston says, touching my chin to get me to look at him. "And so you know, I regret my decision asking Austin to drive."

Austin puts the car into park, but the world still feels like it's moving around me. "I didn't know she'd get motion sickness. She was fine on the way up."

"Because I'm clearly a better driver out of autopilot. If you would've listened to me about sticking to the highway, she'd be fine," Diego says. "You should've just opened the windows."

"I'd prefer not to have to deal with surprises in front of our girl. Safer to deal with puke than..." Kingston shuts his mouth, quickly unfastening me from the restraints to get me out of the car. "Doesn't matter. We're here, and you'll feel better soon. Thanks for not puking your brains out on me, babe."

I nod my head without saying anything, their conversation swirling through my mind. I never expected the three of them to be on edge, especially together, but they rush me toward the door to the Blood Match Center, keeping me tucked between their muscular bodies. And I thought they were just hurrying to get me home last time. At least I'm not out of my mind scared like I've been most of my life. I can't even believe I appreciate the fact that I wouldn't put it past them to rip someone apart on my behalf. That should not be a hot quality. But with my guys, I suppose it is.

Kingston slides his fingers through mine and tugs me across the lobby. I manage to compose myself, my stomach already tons better since getting out of the car. I'm slightly annoyed that once again, I'm barefoot, but I still don't want to ask about it. I think it has something to do with who I am, and luckily, the floors are sparkling clean just like the steps outside.

Nodding his head, Kingston acknowledges the people sitting in plush chairs across from the area separated off for the humans that come after hours for their daytime appointments. I've adapted pretty well to the reversal in my schedule, but it still feels funny eating what I'd call dinner food at a time I'm used to eating breakfast.

A few vampires rise to their feet, setting down small glasses of blood. Diego intercepts the only woman in the room, giving her an air kiss as she obviously stands on her tiptoes in her already towering heels to get a good look at me from over his shoulder. Her fingers run down his arm, and annoyance rises in me, pushing away the last bit of car sickness.

Kingston squeezes my hand, drawing my attention to him. "Are you jealous, babe?"

"I—um..." Am I? Friggin' A. I'd never hear the end of it from Ramona if she knew that I was upset over someone touching one of the guys whom I might provide sustenance to for the rest of my life, however long that may be.

As much as my good sense wants to deny it, I know my matching is more than that, and I feel threatened by this incredibly beautiful woman especially with the daggers she glares at me. I'm a Blood Match, not a vampire. What if when things are through and I make my decision, this amazing way of life ends and whoever I pick decides my real place belongs only to their fangs? I'd end up on a table, bleeding out for a room of vampires just like the stupid dream that has plagued me since my Blood Match.

"Maybe. I'm sorry. It's just..." I let my thought hang in the air. There's no way I'd ever admit what's going through my head. I signed up for this. I knew the risks, which were worth it to save my family. But I expected to go into this scared and had embraced a fate opposite of what I've experienced. I don't know how I'll survive if things change. Because I like Austin, Diego, and Kingston—probably more than I should.

"You don't have to worry, babe," Kingston says, bringing my hand up to his mouth to kiss. It's almost as if Kingston can read my mind, but I think it's more. He's a perfect match for my body, and no matter how much he teases me about sex, I know it also means he can read me without me having to say anything. "Diego only has eyes for you, no matter how much I wish he didn't."

I stifle a weird ass coo sound that threatens to escape my mouth at how Kingston always manages to assure me about his brothers, though he wants me to pick him. I admire his love and loyalty.

Kingston nods in Diego's direction, and we both watch him shift out of the female vampire's reach. Diego glances over his shoulder at me and grimaces, making a silly expression to make me smile. She steps closer while he steps back another foot, peeking at me again, begging me with his pretty gray eyes to listen to Kingston about him.

"See?" Kingston says.

I look over at Diego again, and holy shit balls. If that lady vampire could rip my head off with her mind, I'd meet my final donation, like yesterday, because she obviously heard Kingston's conversation with me. I know Diego did.

Kingston twitches his fingers at her, and I swear a hiss escapes her mouth, sounding out to me even from all the way over here. I nearly shove myself under his arm to escape her death glare, hugging him so tight that he quickens his pace and corners me in the open elevator.

"You're gonna get me slaughtered poking the beast like that," I whisper.

Kingston tips his head back, releasing a loud laugh. He covers my mouth with his cool hand before leaning in to stop me from talking with a kiss instead. Scooping me up higher, he props me on the railing and presses against the tight fabric of my dress, expertly hiking it up so I can straddle him.

"While you'd technically be the one responsible for such a tragedy referring to Katherine Duchanne as a beast, I promise I won't allow her the honor of even breathing the same air as you again."

A growl erupts from behind us, and I tense, seeing the elevator door still open and Katherine scowling at me from across the lobby, now alone. Diego and Austin appear inside with us, startling me for all of a second, and I release a breath as Austin hits a button to close the door. Kingston kisses me once more and then slowly peels himself away, straightening my dress for me. He sets me on my feet, turning back to the door. I watch the floor numbers count up from behind the wall of hot vampires, and rest my chin on the crook of Kingston's neck, stretching up to see.

"I can't allow you into my office tonight, babe," Kingston says, craning his neck to look at me. "So, I've arranged a room for you on the top floor. Austin and Diego will be with you, but I also have a surprise to encourage you not to turn them into your sole form of entertainment."

Austin chuckles. "But we don't mind if you do."

Kingston heaves a sigh when the elevator doors open. Spinning around, he meets me for another kiss, hugging me to him while groaning against my lips. "I miss you already. I do hope you enjoy your surprise."

"See you later," I say, watching him exit the elevator.

He stands there, sticking out his bottom lip to make me laugh, until the doors slide closed. Both Austin and Diego shift toward me, allowing me to fill the space between them. I rest a hand on each of their shoulders until we reach the top floor. Diego takes my hand, exiting first, but he walks slightly ahead with Austin right behind me. We stroll like this the length of the long hallway until we reach a door with Kingston's name etched onto a gold placard. He didn't arrange just any room. He arranged his room, and I realize that of course he'd have somewhere to stay in this looming tower. He was here on my matching day before the sun had even set.

Diego touches my cheek. "Wait here with Austin for a second."

He presses his palm on the digital pad, turning the light green, and enters the room probably to make sure it's clear. A loud scream pierces my ear, and I scramble back, falling into Austin's strong hold.

"Don't hurt me. Please! What is all of this even about? I'm not supposed to be here until—hey, aren't you one of Jewel Jordan's Blood Matches?"

I break away from Austin, disobeying Diego's instructions to wait outside, and rush into Kingston's tower suite. Brayla's confusion morphs into excitement, and she scrambles away from the wall and rushes toward me only to be intercepted by Diego and lifted off her feet.

I bat his arm. "Diego, put her down."

"She was going to tackle you," he says, setting her on her feet without arguing.

I glare at him. "No, because I was going to tackle her first."

Throwing my arms around Brayla, I squeeze her against me until we land on Kingston's bed where I rock her back and forth, laughing and crying at the same time. We were both prepared to live the rest of our lives maintaining our friendship through letters passed on by our families in Haven Springs, and I can't believe she's here.

"This is the best surprise ever," I say, hugging my best friend again. I shift to look at Diego and Austin. "If I yell loud enough, think he'd hear me?"

"He and the whole building," Diego says.

"I guess I'll thank him later," I muse and then blush at how my words sound with the way I practically hum them.

"If this isn't bribery, then I don't know what is," Austin says. "Maybe we need to establish a few more rules."

Oh jeez. I pull myself away from Brayla, who zips her lips when I hold my finger up to her to motion for her to stay in her spot. I cross the room the Diego and Austin. They both stop talking, silencing their hushed conversation obviously about me.

"I'm struggling to keep up with the rules already," I say. "So, please. No more. Even if Kingston's trying to bribe me, which I honestly don't think he is, you guys know this is supposed to be his night. He'd have much rather spent it with me back home and not here, no matter how excited seeing my best friend in the entire world makes me."

"You have that wrong, beautiful. He'd absolutely disagree and would gladly give up his time if he saw you right now," Diego says. "I can only hope to figure out something that could make you this happy."

Austin reaches out and touches my arm. "And the rules aren't for your sake, so you have nothing to worry about, Jewel. Just some things we've all agreed on to make things easier."

"Like the no touching me in each other's bedrooms?" I ask, smirking.

Diego chuckles. "Unless initiated by you until you make your final decision."

I rub my hands down my cheeks at the reminder. "Why do I even have to? I like you all."

Heat rushes into my face, and I spin away from them before I can see either of their expressions. One look at Brayla's twisted lips proves how crazy the thought is. I could never provide enough sustenance for three vampires. And though the guys make me feel like my blood isn't what it's all about, I know when it comes down to it, it definitely is.

Plopping on the bed next to Brayla, she slides her arms around me, hugging me without a word. I ignore the weight of Diego and Austin's stares, begging me to look up at them. But I don't want to. I don't want to think about any of this right now. I want to be with Brayla and ask her how everything has been now that my family and I are gone.

"You can look up," Brayla whispers into my ear. "They stepped outside."

Easing myself away from her, I peer at the cracked open door where Austin and Diego now wait on the other side, trying to give me the privacy I desperately need.

"I'm sorry, Bray-Bray. You shouldn't have had to witness that," I say, clutching her hand between mine. "How's everything going? Did you eat?"

She nods. "Way too much. I was kind of worried Ms. Sybil was purposely trying to fatten me up, but you know me."

"Can't turn down a meal," I say with her in unison.

We both laugh.

"You look amazing, Jewel. The healthiest I've seen you in what seems like forever. I'd ask how your three boy toys were treating you, but I can tell it's obviously good. I don't know why Ramona's so flippin' freaked out by this. It's not like she's the one who gave up her life. She should be damn thankful to have you, and I'll tell her as much."

"You talked to her?" I ask.

"Yeah, apparently she has enough stipends to bribe Jimmy to let me use his phone."

"Jimmy?"

"Security Steve. The night guard. Definitely doesn't seem like a Jimmy, right?"

My mouth forms an O.

"Anyway, Ramona has called me every day this week. She's worried about you. Thinks that you're..." Her gaze darts to the cracked door.

"That I'm what?"

"I don't want to say it. I know they can hear me," she admits.

I roll my eyes. "It's not like they're going to do anything. She's my sister. Despite what she thinks, they are amazing."

"You sure they're not passing you around to others like some main course?" Brayla presses her lips into a thin line, forcing me to hold her gaze. "Ramona said you were with an unfamiliar vampire twice now the other night, and he had the nerve to scare Dana and Fallon when they were on the phone with you. Like seriously, who the hell does that? She's considering not letting them talk to you anym—"

One second I'm perched on the bed with my best friend, and the next, Austin holds me against him while Diego sits in my spot in front of Brayla. She releases a screech, scrambling away from him.

"Another vampire?" Diego asks. "The only vampires allowed within reach of Jewel are me and my brothers."

Fear erupts in my heart.

Brayla darts her gaze to mine, her saucer eyes glassing over. "Don't hurt her. I'm sure Ramona made a mistake. Jewel wouldn't—"

Austin flips me in his arms, concern pinching his brows. Without him having to say it, I know he doesn't assume anything bad. He knows I would never invite a strange vampire into my room let alone allow one to see my sister. I haven't even let the guys do that yet. "We were hoping you were wrong but at least twice? Damn it."

My bottom lip trembles at his words, tears blurring my eyes as I try not to cry at the thought that I was right. A vampire was in my room this morning, and it wasn't even the first time. He could've easily hurt me, ripped open my neck, or killed me even, and there would have been nothing I could've done about it.

I thought living in Dark Terrace Ranch was scary, but I felt safer holed away on my fifth floor apartment with our one security guard than I do in this moment. Because there, I was just a donor—a faceless nobody—but with the heirs of Donor Life Corp, I am someone. I'm the Blood Match of all three of them.

A tear splashes my cheek, but just as quickly as it wets my skin, a finger swipes it away. "Beautiful, please don't cry," Diego says, appearing on my other side. "We'll make sure no one gets close to you again."

"I hate this," I whisper. "I'm going to end up being too much work. You're going to regret that I matched with you."

Silence falls over the room, and more tears fall on my cheeks. It's Brayla that comes to me next, summoning her courage to shove herself between two vampires to hug me. She pats my back until I manage to even my breathing.

"And what happens when I make my decision? None of you could possibly protect me by yourselves. And why should you? I'm your personal blood donor."

"Don't say that," Austin says.

I clench my fingers into fists. "But it's true! How could it be any different? I'm a donor and you're vampires. I wouldn't even be here if my friggin' dad didn't get himself killed or taken or whatever the hell happened to him because of vampires."

"Beautiful, we—"

Shaking my head at Diego, I say, "Please. I need a minute. Just leave us alone for a minute." Because I'm afraid of what else I might say as my situation sinks in.

The guys disappear, leaving me with Brayla, and I feel like utter and complete shit. They didn't deserve to get the brunt of my anger. They've been nothing but sweet and gentle and kind. Considerate. But in this world that only provides to those who have something to offer, I can't help losing myself to the reality of it all.

"Jewel," a masculine voice says from the open door to the room.

I stiffen, recognizing Mitchell Divine's voice without having to look up. I pry my gaze from my hands, clutching Brayla's so tightly that her fingers change colors, and force myself to give the founder of Donor Life Corp my respectful attention.

"It's nice to see you again," Mitchell says.

Kingston appears at his side, his jaw tight, and I have a sinking feeling that they both heard me a moment ago.

"Thank you, sir. It's lovely to see you, too," I manage to say, keeping my voice even.

He turns his attention to Brayla. "Ms. Diggs, I apologize for interrupting, but I must ask that you excuse us. My son will see to it that you return home safely. It seems we have some unforeseen matters to take care of tonight."

I suck in a sharp breath. It's worse than I thought. My big mouth just got my best friend kicked out of here, and it might be the last time I ever get to see her again. I throw my arms around Brayla, hugging her, trying my best not to cry into her hair. As much as I want to beg for another few minutes, the dominant, screaming part of me that wants to survive keeps my pleas locked up tight inside me.

"Please explain everything to Ramona for me," I whisper. "And take care of yourself. I love you, okay? You're my best friend. Always. No matter what."

Kingston crosses the room away from his dad and to me, gently tugging me to my feet and away from Brayla. Our eyes meet, and he gives me a look that stabs me right through the heart. And I know whatever we had together has been shattered, and I don't think I'll ever get to put it back together. I'm not even sure I'll survive the next five minutes as my admission about my feelings toward some vampires hangs in the air.

"I'm sorry, Jewel. I must compel Ms. Diggs of your meeting tonight," he says. The use of my name stings more than it should.

"Kingston, please. My sister. She—"

"This is for both your safeties after what she's told you," Kingston says.

I guess word does travel fast.

I reach out and clasp Brayla's hand. "I love you. They can't take that from us no matter what."

She nods and swipes her tears from her face. "Don't forget

what your parents taught you."

That I'm more than what my vein has to offer. I nod without saying it out loud.

Kingston tugs Brayla away from me, glancing at me every other step as he exits the room. His dark eyes shine with indecipherable thoughts, and I try my best to project my regret over my uncalled for words in my moment of panic.

"Shall we walk?" Mitchell Divine asks from his sudden place in front of me.

He holds out his arm, and I take it without argument. I expect to see Diego and Austin waiting in the hall, but it's empty, and I'm alone with the man who might very well end my life this second.

I don't make it more than three feet out of the hallway when Mitchell spins me around on my feet, covers my mouth with his hand, and leans in to look into my eyes.

His eyes flash silver in the light. "Don't scream."

I couldn't if I wanted to.

"I need you to listen carefully, Jewel."

Ignoring him is the last thing I could do.

"Now I need you to tell me something."

"Anything," I murmur into his hands, my mouth speaking without my brain's consent.

"I need you to tell me the truth."

16

Mind Control

TEARS SPILL FROM MY EYES, but something grips my body, leaving me incapable of moving. Mitchell Divine swipes his fingers over my cheeks for me with a calm look softening his hard features.

"Are you afraid of me?" Mitchell asks.

Once again, my mouth opens automatically without my permission. "Yes." It's now that I realize he's getting into my head, turning me pliable to answer anything he wants with his mind manipulation, something Kingston swore to never use on me.

And I despise it. Mitchell never gave me the chance to answer by my own freewill.

"Why?"

As much as I try to clench my jaw, my mouth still opens to respond. "You might kill me."

"What about my sons?"

I glare. "Yes."

"Why?"

"They might never forgive me," I answer, the response surprising the both of us.

"Elaborate."

I attempt to squeeze my eyes shut to break his hypnotic gaze, but nothing happens. The best I can do is curl my fingers into my palms, biting my nails into the skin of my hands. "I said some terrible things that I regret all because the vampire I owe a blood debt to will not leave me alone even though I'm matched to others."

Mitchell scowls. "A blood debt for what?"

"I don't know."

"What is his name?"

"I don't know," I say, my mind swirling at the revelation escaping my mouth.

"What does he look like?"

"I don't know."

Mitchell roars into my face, blowing stray strands of hair from my eyes. My body impulsively reacts, my nails biting deeper into my skin, shooting pain through my hands and up my wrists. Warmth blossoms in my enclosed palms as blood pools and seeps through my fingers.

I automatically jerk my hands to my face protectively. Mitchell freezes, his nostrils flaring, his fangs flashing. Fear steals my breath, squeezing my heart so hard I'm sure it'll explode and kill me any second.

He releases me and disappears down the hall.

I get to my feet, fear making me gasp for breath.

"Jewel," a voice whispers. I jerk to peer behind me.

The world spins, and I land on my knees, alone in a strange, grand suite of pristine whites and pattern grays. Black furniture with ornate crystals and sparkling metals decorates the main living area of the room, the space sleek and modern compared to the Divinity Estate.

My bloody hands stain the white carpet as I push myself to my feet. Taking a deep breath, I suppress the turmoil shuddering through me and manage to get back up.

A door swings open to my right, and I swivel to face it, praying to see either Kingston, Austin, or Diego arrive to collect me. But it's none of them. The vampires fly across the room faster than I can open my mouth to scream out.

An eerily familiar man covers my mouth with one hand while squeezing my waist with the other. He drags me through the doorway he came through, and I flail, kicking my legs, trying to pry myself from his grip. Katherine materializes in front of me, locking the door. Both vampires intake deep breaths in unison, sending panic through me.

Flipping me around in his arms, the strangely familiar vampire smiles at me, his eyes flashing silver. "My precious Jewel. How good it is to have a moment with you again. Tell me how happy you are to see me and mean it."

My eyes widen as he burrows into my mind the same way Mitchell did. But this is a million times worse. He's not prying information from me; he's manipulating my very emotions. A smile crosses my face, and my hand reaches up and touches the vampire's cheek, running my bloody fingers across his sharp jawline.

"You have no idea how happy I am to see you," I say, my mind now at war with my body.

The vampire snatches my hand from his face and flicks his tongue across my palm, tasting the blood seeping from the half-moon punctures aching on my skin. His brilliant blue eyes capture me, and my body reacts without my permission, inching closer.

"We won't be apart forever, my precious Jewel. I promise. Paying off your father's debt will be rather enjoyable. I can't wait to hear you beg me to drain you dry when the time comes."

His sharp words cut through me. Terror seizes my mind despite my placid body, relaxed in his arms as he continues to flick his tongue across my palm. Katherine glares at me from behind him, positioned by the door with her arms crossed. She releases an annoyed sigh, drawing his attention to her and away from me.

The second our eye contact breaks, I regain control of my body. I swing my hand out, slapping the vampire man across his face in an attempt to get him away from me. He only smiles, flashing his sharp incisors at me.

"A fighter like your father," he says, gripping my hands between his. He yanks them up, lifting me off my feet. "And probably just as ignorant. Lucky me."

"If you hurt me, the Divines will rip you apart," I say, forcing my voice to stay even.

He chuckles, shifting to hold me with one hand. "What an interesting notion. I can see their possessiveness, considering how they broke the rules for you. I thought you would surely get disqualified if I had made you tardy."

Realization stabs at me. I knew something was weird about the day of my application. There was no way I could've been late. "No one broke the rules for me."

"Tell me the truth, Jewel," he says, trapping me again with his gaze.

I try to clench my jaw, but my words still escape. "They don't break the rules. They make them. They'll rip you apart like the asshole who tried to match me out from under them." I cringe, agony coursing through me the harder I try to resist.

"You might've been right in your speculation, my lover. But no worries. Things will right themselves in due time," he says to Katherine. I've never been so thankful that he didn't ask me more. His eyes flick back to mine. "I can't wait to see them fight and turn on each other after you reject two of their proposals. Lucky for them, I really do share and will let you see this through. Having an in with the Divines might be worth the effort." His words poke right at my fears, cutting the seams to rip them open.

"Lover, they're coming," Katherine says. "You promised me."

The man sighs and gets close to my face. "Forget this conversation. Forget me in your wake but hold me dearly in your dreams, precious Jewel. Remember I'm coming for you. If anyone asks, you've come here to clean your wounds."

"Lover," Katherine whines. "Give her to me. I want a taste. I never did get mine."

The man drops me to my feet without letting go of me. My knees buckle and pain bursts in my arm as he stretches it out, offering it to Katherine. She extends her fangs, her nostrils flaring. I release a whimper, tears burning my eyes, fear leaving me gasping.

A crash sounds from outside the door, drawing the vampires' gazes from me. The man drags me back to my feet, leans in, and brushes his lips to mine. When he pulls back, he whispers. "Close your eyes. When you open them, you won't remember a thing."

The world shifts, my body flipping to smash into the slick tub. Hot water sprays across me, pouring in my face. I choke and spit, flailing. My mind whirls with a million thoughts, and I scream out. Hands lock around my body, pulling me up from the spray of hot water. I cry and swing my arms in an attempt to free myself.

"No, no, no, no. Please, don't," I say. "Just let me go."

Fingers encircle my wrists, trying to pry them from my face. "Jewel."

"Please, there must be some other way to pay my father's debt. Please, just don't bite me."

"Beautiful, it's okay. Please, look at me. Open your eyes."

The familiar voice wraps around me, snuffing out the overwhelming fear ignited inside me. Hands brush over my eyelids, swiping at the hot water burning down my face. I heave a breath and prepare to tell Diego to go after Katherine and the strange vampire, but another cool pair of arms envelops me, soft lips brushing mine, and I open my eyes to meet Kingston's dark gaze.

"Take a breath. You're okay. We got you," Kingston says.

"What happened, Jewel?" Austin asks from beside Kingston, reaching out for my hand. "You're bleeding. How did you even get in here? Mitchell said—"

"Your dad scared me," I admit, my head fuzzy as I remember how he cornered me and yanked answers from my mouth without my permission. "He used his mind control to interrogate me. My body reacted, and I hurt myself. I ran here to clean my wounds. I didn't—"

Something feels wrong.

Easing back from Kingston, I peer around the large bathroom, catching my reflection on the floor-to-ceiling mirror inlayed with the tiles. My skin glows pink from the burst of hot water from the still running tub, but why is it on when the sink would work just fine?

"Jewel, who was with you?" Diego asks.

I frown. "No one."

"Babe, I know I promised never to manipulate your thoughts, but will you let me in?" Kingston asks, pulling my attention from Diego to him. "Someone else has been messing with your mind."

"Your dad," I say, my breath quickening. "And you promised me, Kingston. I—no, please. I'm scared. No one was with me. It was your dad. He did this. He's why I'm here."

All three guys frown, sharing a silent conversation with each other. Kingston presses his lips into a line and leans forward to hug me. Austin and Diego each take one of my hands, careful not to touch the aching cuts.

"Please forgive us," they all say in unison, "it'll never happen without your permission again. After what you said to Brayla..."

Tears burst from my eyes at the memory. A mixture of emotions clouds all three of their faces, the words as fresh and painful as the cuts burning my skin. I hug Kingston first, pressing my forehead to his for a second before I kiss him.

"I'm so sorry. I was just overwhelmed and—" I turn toward Diego next and open my arms for him to hug me. "I'm an awful person." Shifting again, I throw my arms around Austin. "I don't deserve to match with any of you. I can't excuse what I said."

"Babe," Kingston says. "You're not awful or undeserving. You're afraid. Your fears are valid, and you shouldn't be ashamed of your feelings."

"Yeah, beautiful," Diego says. "While we can't completely know what it's like to be you or what it's like to be in your position, we understand why you're afraid. Look at the asshole who tried to match you away from us."

I shudder at the thought of Master Caruthers. "It's just that this is all so hard."

"Picking one of us?" Kingston asks.

I shrug. "All of it. I don't want to hurt any of you, but I also can't forget my place."

Austin asks. "Your place?"

"As your donor."

Kingston pushes my wet hair from my face. "Babe, you read the papers. You signed the contract. You know this isn't just about supplying blood to one of us."

But I can't suppress the ugly thought that tells me otherwise. "For now."

"Forever, Jewel," Austin says.

"That's a long time," I whisper.

Diego gives Kingston a look, and he bobs his head. Motioning me closer with his brother's approval, Diego slides his arms around me. "That's the point, beautiful. We're fully willing to commit to you."

"And rock that sexy ass body of yours," Kingston adds, smirking at me. "Hopefully later."

I release a laugh, the trembling fear finally washing away. Both Diego and Austin groan, shaking their heads at Kingston as they get to their feet. They leave the bathroom first and head back into the bedroom, and I can't help wondering if they're purposely giving Kingston a moment alone with me.

"Come here, babe," Kingston says, motioning me into his arms. "I need to kiss you for a moment. And then we need to figure out why you're in here, soaking wet, even though I love what it does to that clingy dress of yours."

Crinkling my nose, I reach out and poke Kingston's bottom lip, realizing a second too late that blood still coats my fingers.

Kingston's eyes darken, his nostrils flaring, but not in a way that freaks me out. His tongue slowly glides across his lip, sending a wave of lust over me. Desire tightens his jaw as a mixture of emotions and deep-seated hunger engulfs him, but it's not only a hunger for my blood. His eyes travel from my lips to my nearly see-through dress, damp and sticking to my chest like a thin veil over my skin.

My lips crash into his as I react first. My body demands to be as close as possible with my sexy vampire gazing at me like I'm the best thing he's ever seen. The thought of space between us becomes nearly unbearable, and I press into him until he falls back onto the floor with me on top. His hands glide down my body, mapping every inch of me through the tight fabric I wish would relent as it grips onto my legs. In a quick motion, Kingston flips me off him and onto my back, ripping the hem of my dress in the process.

My body arches into him, and his fingers dig into the flesh of my hips to align our bodies with him between my legs and only our clothing separating our skin. His cool fingers tease my skin, running along the hem of my dress bunched at my hips. I gasp as his touch brushes over my thigh and then shifts to run up the length of my body to tangle in my wet hair. He kisses me deeper, his tongue exploring mine until I gasp, now breathless.

He breaks away from my lips, moaning against my throat, the sensation tingling across my skin. I grab the front of his shirt and fumble with the buttons until he quickly unfastens them to allow me to slide my hands across the smooth, muscular skin now peeking out. He moans into my ear, his fingers suddenly slowing down despite mine speeding up to trail down his torso toward his belt.

He doesn't let my hands get far, his fingers lacing with mine to ease my hands up over my head, giving him access to my body, but he doesn't take it. His weight slowly sinks against me just enough to make me gasp in anticipation.

"Jewel, I—I have to stop," Kingston whispers, resting his chin on my shoulder to breathe into my hair. "If I don't stop, I'm going to ask you to—"

"Don't ask," I say, surprised by my own words.

He moans and kisses my throat. "Jewel, you don't mean it."

"I do."

He groans, rolling off me only to pull me with him. Shifting me in his arms, he cradles me, cuddling me to him to kiss me softly once more. He nuzzles his nose to mine and smiles, releasing a shuddering breath as we both try to get our desire under control.

"You have no idea what you do to me, babe," he whispers.

"*Me*?" I ask. "What about what you do to me?"

"One hundred percent body," he says, smiling. "You just wait until I have you to myself with no one about to come in."

I press my hands to his chest, laughing. The door to the bathroom swings open right after his words leave his mouth, breaking my gaze from Kingston's. Mitchell Divine stands tall in the doorway, his gaze flicking over me in Kingston's arms. Austin and Diego stand behind him, smirking at Kingston, who releases another quiet groan in my ear.

"Not sorry to interrupt, bro," Diego says, "but time to go. Building's clear. Best to get out of here before word spreads about the lockdown and the evac."

"Did you manage to tell Kingston anything, Jewel?" Austin asks. "Whoever attacked you knew their way around here and slipped past security in a dead zone."

"I already told you it was—" I turn my gaze to Mitchell. "It was your dad who scared me. I was afraid of bleeding everywhere, so I came in here to clean my wounds." I wish they'd quit asking me. I know what happened. Mitchell forced me to tell him why I was afraid, and... Damn it. My head throbs just thinking about it.

"But you were in the tub," Diego says.

I swallow, fear rising in my chest just when I finally managed to breathe again. "Maybe I fell in."

Austin inspects me from his spot. "With scorching water. You're lucky you didn't get burned more."

"Kingston, if you're too afraid to do it, allow me," Mitchell says. "She signed the contract. You already have her permission. You don't need it again."

Mitchell steps closer to me, and I screech, covering my eyes with my hands. "No! Stay away!"

Three deep growls sound through the room, reverberating through my bones. Kingston rubs his fingers across my wrists until I slowly pull my hands away. Mitchell purses his lips, looking from between me and his sons.

"I can't do this to her. I promised her," Kingston says.

Diego kneels next to us, touching my cheek to get me to turn away from Kingston. I just wish they'd do as they said and get me out of here. Something about this room freaks me out. But I can't remember why. It was Mitchell and his mind manipulation. It was—

I release a sob. "What's going on with me?"

"We want to find out. If you'll let me try. We're a perfect personality match. You can trust me with your mind." Diego pets my hair and reaches to coax me away from Kingston. I half expect him to hold me tighter, but Kingston shifts me over, just content to hold and kiss the back of my hand. Austin gently rubs his hands over the tops of my bare feet, and I can tell he's assessing the condition of my body the best he can without giving me a full physical.

"I don't know. Are you sure it was another vampire? All I remember is him," I say, pointing at Mitchell without meeting his gaze.

"I know you're scared, beautiful. I know this is fucking hard as hell on you, and I hate it. But I'm asking you to let me into your head. I promise I will be careful, and you don't have to answer anything you don't want to. We just want to see if maybe you forgot something. Because even though you keep saying my dad was the one, I think someone else got to you, too. This doesn't add up."

I suck in my bottom lip in contemplation. "Can it just be me and you?"

He glances from me to look at Kingston and Austin, and they nod. "Yeah, just me and you."

"Okay," I whisper. "I give you permission."

Diego cups my cheeks in his hands. "I'll be quick, and we'll hopefully get this asshole."

"Then we can go home?"

He smiles. "Yeah. Anything you want, beautiful."

17

Blood Debt

THE CITY SPRAWLS INTO DARKNESS through the wall of windows of Diego's suite. The whole top floor of the Blood Match Center's tower is dedicated to the Divines with a cluster of small rooms facing the east wall intended for guests, like the room I stayed in previously.

I sit between Diego's legs, facing him on the bed with my hips straddling his waist without being in his lap. His gaze trails from my eyes to the soft fabric of one of his spare dress shirts I wear like a too-big dress.

"You ready?" he asks, sliding his hands around my waist to

smooth over the tense and aching muscles of my back.

"I don't know. I'm so nervous," I say.

"I can help with that. I mean, if that's okay."

I nod.

Diego kneads his fingers down my spine, expanding his hands over my lower back, just working the muscles for a minute, sending tingles through my whole body. He peers into my eyes, silver flashing in the depths of the gray color. "Take a breath and relax. You are safe with me. You can tell me to stop at any time. I'll start with some easy, non-related questions and commands and work my way to what happened tonight, okay?"

I clear my throat. "Okay."

Leaning in, Diego captures my gaze. "Keep your eyes on mine until I tell you not to."

Heat flushes my face, my body reacting to his voice by slackening in his embrace.

"Take a breath."

On command, I inhale and exhale.

His serious mouth quirks up in the corner in a tease of a smile, one I wish he'd give me in completion. "You're doing great. How do you feel?"

"Disappointed." Whoa. The words escape my mouth before my brain has a chance to give my usual automatic response that I feel fine.

He frowns. "Disappointed, why?"

"You won't smile, and I need it." Shit balls. That's embarrassing. I sound whiney as hell.

Chuckling, he teases me by offering me a wide smile, showing off his fangs and everything. "Better?"

"No."

"Tell me what I can do to make you feel better," he says, still smiling at me.

"Kiss me." My eyes widen the second the words come out of my mouth. It's like my mouth has a mind of its own and the rest of me can't do anything to stop it.

His smile fades, his gray eyes darkening. My body eases closer, and I lick my lips, wishing with everything in me that he relents to my rebellious mouth and does what it says, because my mind caught up already, and I agree. A kiss from Diego will definitely improve the situation.

"I'm sorry, beautiful. I'm not going to kiss you while your mind is open like this. If you still want me to after, I'll gladly give you everything you want."

I sulk, annoyance washing through me at the fact that he won't kiss me and because I'm pouty about it. My heartbeat picks up, anxiety tightening my nerves as I suddenly have the need to ask him to release me.

He tilts his head without breaking eye contact. "You okay, Jewel? You're tensing up."

"Something's wrong. I don't like this."

"Will you hold on for five more minutes? I'll be quick with the questions."

I nod. "Five minutes."

Clutching my face between his hands, he bows close

enough that I can see the silhouette of light around my form in his dilated pupils. "Did someone demand you forget something tonight?"

"Yes."

"Can you describe him or her?" His intense stare burns through me, prying at a piece in my mind that ignites a blip of pain behind my eyes.

"I—I don't know. I don't remember." My mouth automatically provides the response for me.

Diego leans closer, so the only things in focus are his eyes. "Describe the vampire who made you forget."

Blue eyes. Tall. Sharp features. Suit. Thin lips.

A dozen features swirl through my mind as a fuzzy image erupts from my memory. I swallow, opening and closing my mouth to tell Diego what I remember, but the second I try, the image fades. "I don't remember."

"Jewel, describe the vampire."

Tears blur my eyes, panic clenching my muscles as my mouth tries to cooperate but something inside me claws at my brain, making it impossible to think. "I can't."

He narrows his eyes. "Tell me why."

"I can't," I repeat.

Pressing his fingers into my temples, he glares at me, his eyes glowing silver. Pressure swells in my head, but I can't look away from Diego. "Jewel, tell me why."

I release a scream, agony clawing through my mind. My head pounds so hard the edges of my vision shadow. I fight with myself to keep my mouth shut. I can't answer his question. I'll die if I do.

"I said tell me."

"He won't let me remember outside my dreams!"

A guttural sob rips from me, pain exploding in my head, the whole world spinning and hazing. Diego breaks his stare and tugs me closer to shift me in his lap. He hugs me against him, petting my hair with one hand and smearing tears with the other. I heave a breath, my placid body tensing, my muscles aching all over again.

"I'm sorry," he whispers. "I'm so sorry. I know that hurt, beautiful. But I'm done. It's over."

My head lolls, my chin dipping to touch my clavicle. "I didn't say anything useful. You have to try again." I can't believe I even say the words, my vision still blurry from allowing Diego into my head. But what he did wasn't what made me feel so bad. It was something else. Something dark and vile just simmering below the surface. With enough prodding, he could pull it out. I know it.

He rests his head on my cheek, twining our fingers together. "I can't, Jewel. The vampire basically put explosive walls on parts of your memory. If I set them off, I could hurt you. It's not worth it."

"But—"

"But nothing. And you were wrong about me not finding anything useful. The bastard is tormenting you in your sleep."

"The nightmares," I whisper.

He frowns. "I'm sorry I brushed off the one you had with me. I should've known."

"You couldn't have."

He shrugs like he doesn't believe me. "Even so, if I'd have put any thought into it, I could've helped you already. You don't have to be awake to open your mind to me."

"What?"

He licks his lips. "I can break into your dreams if you let me."

"I don't think I can sleep here."

"I know. I think it's time we get you home."

"Babe, you don't have to do this," Kingston says, clutching my hand as I perch on the bed in Austin's lab. "I'll wait until next time. You've been through enough tonight."

I hold out my arm for Austin, and he quietly rubs a cool cotton ball over my skin. "I'm fine, Kingston. Chill out. I want to do this for you." Tilting my head up, I meet his gaze with a smile to assure him. Because really, the last thing I'm worried about is giving blood. Hell, if he gives me the same face he did earlier in the bathroom, I'll enjoy it too. Who knew I'd ever be excitedly anticipating feeding a vampire.

He chuckles, raising his eyebrows. "So that you know, this was *not* what I had in mind when I told you I'd devour you earlier."

"It wasn't?" I flutter my eyelashes. "I had no idea."

He smiles even wider, releasing a playful growl from his

throat. "The night might've been a disaster, but we can end it with a...bang."

I snort, covering my mouth at his innuendo. "Knock it off, Kingston."

I shouldn't expect anything less from Kingston than to take every opportunity to remind me of our body match. Or how hot making out with him earlier was. Or his sexy body peeking out from his half-unbuttoned shirt, clearly open to mess with me. He knows it. I know it. And eff is it working.

"Yeah, Kingston. Please do," Austin says, quickly and painlessly extracting a vial of blood. "Jewel's been traumatized enough. She doesn't need you to add to it."

I bat Austin's arm. "You knock it off too. You know Kingston wouldn't traumatize me. He doesn't even want to take my blood."

"He definitely didn't say he didn't *want* to take it, beautiful. Just that you didn't have to give him any." Diego appears in the door, already dressed for the day. I drink in the flexing muscles in his arms tightening the sleeves of his thin shirt. "And no one has to worry about our girl. She's with me today, and I'll take extremely great care of her."

I grin at Diego. "We're only going to be sleeping."

His smile widens even more. "And it'll be the best sleep of your life, beautiful."

Kingston and Austin share a silent look, frowning at each other, before Austin says, "Don't forget what the goal of this is. We're counting on you to help us find this guy. We can't have someone lurking around, claiming our girl has a blood debt to pay. It could ruin everything."

I jerk my attention to Austin. "What do you mean a blood debt? I don't owe anyone a blood debt."

The three of them all face me, something about Austin's words tickles a memory from last night. Tears burn my eyes at the weights of their stares, and without anyone having to say anything, I know that what they say is true—a vampire thinks I owe them a blood debt.

"I told your dad that," I say, recalling his interrogation. I was so confused by the night and supposedly being attacked that I had forgotten.

They nod.

Kingston takes my hand, sliding his fingers through mine. "Don't worry, babe. We'll get it figured out."

I turn my gaze back to Austin. "But what did you mean about it ruining everything?"

He twists his lips to the side. All three of the guys look like they don't want to tell me. Anger rushes over me as they do the whole mind communication with each other, which I don't actually know if they just know what one another is thinking or if they're actually in their heads.

"Stop it with that stupid silent mind talking you always do," I snap.

"We're not telepathic, babe." If Kingston's trying to change the subject it must be bad. "But you're right about us having a private conversation."

"How?" I scowl at my own question, because my curiosity won, and I relented to letting them avoid something obviously important.

"Whispering," Diego says. "We didn't think you noticed."

Austin takes my other hand. "But that's not important right now, and we're sorry for keeping you out of the conversation."

"Austin," Kingston warns. "You said she was already traumatized enough."

"I can handle it," I argue. "Someone just tell me. Don't make me bribe you with—"

"Jewel, if you do owe a blood debt, even if you're not aware of it, it must be paid," Austin says. "But the Blood Match nullifies it for you. No matter what the vampire thinks, he can't take you from us."

"Then how can it ruin everything?" I ask.

Diego cups my cheeks and looks into my eyes. "If negotiated right, a blood debt passes on to your next of kin."

Shadows edge my vision. "What? Are you kidding me? Our contract says that my family stays safe in Haven Springs. That's the benefit of Blood Matching."

"It's a loophole," Kingston says.

"Then I will pay. Ramona will not be a debtor."

"Jewel, you can't. Your matching pays for your family to be there."

A sob rips through me, stealing my breath. I don't know why I suddenly thought things might be different and that even if I breach my contract that maybe the guys liked me enough to still hold up their end of the deal, contract or not.

And now I feel stupid as hell about everything. They claim to like me. They claim that I'm their perfect match, but it doesn't feel like it right now.

"So that's how this is going to be," I say, my voice sharp. "To hell with my family as long as you get what you want from me. Who cares that it will destroy me, right?"

"We do care," Austin responds first.

"But the laws are strict," Diego adds.

"You break the rules!" I yell, throwing my hands up. "You ripped a man—"

Kingston's hand flies up to cut my words off. "Babe, please."

"You can't expect me to sit here and just accept that this is how things will be." I've never felt so hopeless in my life. How could this have possibly happened? I did this so Ramona would never have to find herself under the fang of a vampire. But now she will. If I break my contract, Dana and Fallon will be lost as well.

"Please," I whisper. "There has to be some other way. Ramona's smart and she will do good work. You guys can give her a job here. I just—I can't allow her to pay. I can't."

"Jewel, please trust us to take care of this," Diego says.

"But if it does come down to it, please don't punish my family and leave them for dead. Give them work or something. I can't live like this knowing Ramona is lost."

"Okay," Kingston says first. "If you feel you have to break our contract, I'll see to it that your next of kin still finds the life you want for them. But I assure you it won't come down to that. This is for your peace of mind only."

I swipe the tears from my eyes. "You have no idea how much this means to me."

Kingston leans in and kisses me. "I don't think you realize how much you already mean to us."

18

Haunting Dreams

"I NEED YOU TO REMEMBER that whatever happens in your dream is all in your mind. Nothing can hurt you. I'll only stay as long as necessary," Diego says, brushing my hair from my face. "Your first dream cycle is the shortest, so hopefully it's all the time I need."

I rub my lips together and nod. Curling toward him, resting my leg between his, I let him frame my face with his elbows. We stare at each other, his pretty gray eyes capturing me without him having to say anything.

"And whatever you dream stays between us, okay? I know

you can't control what your subconscious brings forward, and it's not necessary to tell my brothers. We're just trying to find the vampire messing with you, and I'm not going to judge you."

Ugh. I didn't even think about that. What if I dream up something humiliating?

"And if you happen to dream of either of my brothers, I can guarantee I'll never tell them," Diego adds.

My face flushes. "Diego, I—"

"Seriously, beautiful. Don't stress over it. If you want to know a secret, we're all actually surprised by how well this is working. You manage to make us all feel important to you."

"Because you are." My automatic admission lights up his whole face in the smile that gets to me every time, reminding me of the nickname I gave him before I knew his name.

Leaning forward, I surprise him with a kiss. I can't help it. Even with the dark thoughts lurking in the back of my mind, Diego helps me forget. He makes me feel safe and wanted and like I'm just as important to him as he is to me.

My fear and anxiety melt away the longer his lips explore mine as gently as the first time I kissed him. Except this time, I don't hold back. Running my fingers into his soft hair, I pull him closer, deepening our kiss. His tongue glides into my mouth, caressing my tongue before he sucks my bottom lip between his teeth.

My fingers trace down his neck to his muscular shoulders, and I continue to explore his chest through his shirt, slowly working my way down to the hem. He moans into my mouth, kissing me desperately with the same need rising in me. Flipping on top of me, he presses his body into mine without crushing me with his weight. One of his hands cradles my head while the other expertly traces my side to the hem of my own shirt.

I slide my hand from the waistband of his pants and up his stomach, dragging his shirt up in the process. It disappears so quickly that I release a small laugh against his lips and lean back to take in the view of him hovering over me. Arching forward, I brush my lips to his shoulder, trailing up toward his neck where I glide my tongue all the way up to his jawline.

"Jewel," he whispers. "I should stop."

I meet my lips to his again. If we stop, then I'll have to sleep, and I want nothing more than to stay awake. "You should take off my shirt. I give you permission."

He inhales a sharp breath, rolls with me still clinging to him, and lands with his back on the bed with me straddling him. His fingers play with the hem of my shirt, his breath coming as quickly as mine.

I bend over and kiss him again. "I don't feel like sleeping right now."

"I definitely don't feel like you sleeping either," he says. "But we need to do this."

"No, we need to do *this*. It's more fun." I hook my fingers around his wrists, tugging his hands up when he's not fast enough to take off my shirt for me. Desire warms my skin, sinking from me and into him, and he lets my shirt get halfway up my stomach before he sits up and wraps me in his arms.

Shuddering, he pants against my shoulder, trying to compose himself. "Do you really want to or are you trying to avoid sleep?"

I puff out my lip, getting my own breathing under control. "Um...both?"

He squeezes his eyes shut for a second. "Jewel, I'd usually gladly be your distraction, but the longer we wait—"

I groan and rub my hands into my eyes. "I know, and I'm sorry. I just—"

"Trust me, okay?" he asks, leaning forward to kiss me.

"I do."

Diego slowly tilts his head away and locks me in an intense gaze. "Will you let me help you?"

I nod. "Okay."

Closing the space, he rests his forehead against mine for a moment, blurring the world between us. My muscles relax under his touch as he kneads his fingers into my skin before he eases me out of his arms and onto the bed. I don't turn my gaze from his, letting him hold me with his eyes that seemingly peer right into my mind to caress my soul.

He props on his elbow, petting my hair out of my face, running his fingers along my jaw. "I'll be right here the whole time," he says, assuring me for the millionth time. "Now, sleep."

The long dining table stretches the length of the room with enough seating for twenty-two people. Along the wall, a few humans lean in strange chairs that force them to remain standing. Long tapestries cover the other walls, lit up by crystal chandeliers and silver candelabras with burning candles scenting the air.

Shadows dance against the wall, and I stroll along the length of the table with empty goblets and sparkling gold trays. Whispers drift around me in a melodious orchestra that draws me closer to where the humans await to serve the now empty room.

"Where is everyone?" I ask, reaching out to shake the closest man's arm.

His body falls forward onto the floor, his head rolling away from him without a drop of blood spilling.

Screaming, I scramble back into the table. I fall into it and knock off one of the burning candles. It lands on the floor under the tapestry, setting the old fabric ablaze. Smoke fills the room, stealing my breath. I rush toward the arched exit, but a figure darts in front of me and blocks my way.

Laurel yells incoherently at me, thrusting a pitcher of blood into my face. She shoves me back, her neck suddenly jerking toward the floor in an odd angle that sends bile into my throat. A black shadow grows behind her, and it wraps around Laurel. Her head snaps back to look at me, lolling in a circle, a wide smile on her face.

The shadow jerks Laurel forward like a puppet master, swinging her arms while dragging her feet across the blood-smeared floor. Laurel whips her head all the way back until she peers at me upside down with her head between her shoulder blades, her neck stretching longer than possible. The shadow jerks her arm up and slams it onto a giant red button I didn't notice on the wall.

A hissing sound erupts over the crackling fire, and the ceiling opens up to rain down red liquid on me. My white dress clings to me, stained with blood, and I slip and slide across the wood floor. The shadows move again and thrust me toward the long table. I slide across it, knocking everything off. The shadows grow larger, shifting and moving, yanking at my hair and dress, shredding my bloody clothes off my body to leave me naked and curled in on myself.

Laughter echoes through the room and freezing hands grip under my arms, yanking them over my head to drag me toward the head of the table. Fingers grab my chin, stretching my neck back until I peer into the vivid blue eyes of a familiar vampire. He flashes his white incisors, grinning at me from above.

"Hurry, lover," a feminine voice says from out of my view. "You promised me a taste."

The vampire sucks his lip between his teeth and bites down, making himself bleed. Leaning forward, he brushes his bloody lips to mine, kissing me hard enough that I can taste the bitterness of his blood in my throat, making me gag.

Heat washes over me, my body reacting to the sudden closeness of the vampire. He grins at me, touching my cheek, and then slides his fingers over my shoulder, making me squirm with a rush of desire. His finger trails down my arm, and he pinches my wrist, jerking my arm up.

"Lover," the feminine voice says again. "You promised."

"Whining isn't becoming of you," the vampire says to the face-

less woman. "But you're right. I did promise." He straightens my arm out, and I let him, not even moving from my place on the table, still pelted by the raining blood touching everything but the couple.

The blurry-faced woman leans closer, though I still can't distinguish her features. "Look how much she wants it. I don't know if I want to give her the satisfaction."

"Bite me." The words escape my lips out of my control.

The vampire man grins again. "I told you that you'd beg to be drained dry, my precious Jewel. You must wait a moment longer. Your father still pays his debt, though don't worry. It won't be for much longer."

"Jewel." The sharp voice cuts through me, dragging me across the table from the vampires. "Come on, beautiful. Listen to my voice."

I scramble to grab onto anything I can, my mind begging to escape while my body yearns to stay.

Diego stands in the opposite archway of the room, his arms open wide. "Jewel, come on. Come back to me."

I gasp, sitting up. Confusion washes over me as I blink a dozen times, my mind racing as the memory of my dream clings on, weirding me out. Diego scoops me from the bed to cradle me in his lap, just rubbing his hand up and down my back.

"Holy shit balls. Something is wrong with me," I say, suppressing the unbidden desire stirred inside me from my dream. "That was worse than before."

"That was because of me. I'm sorry it was terrible."

A knock sounds on the bedroom door a moment before it opens. Diego waves Kingston and Austin inside, and they cross the room together to sit on the edges of either side of the bed with us in the middle. I pull myself away from Diego and sit cross-legged facing them, running my fingers through my hair in an attempt to steady my racing heart.

"I know it's none of my business, but that sounded like one helluva dream," Kingston says.

"It was a horrible nightmare," I murmur, hugging my knees to my chest. "It felt so real. He's in my head. He—I think I drank his blood. My body—" I shiver at even the thought that I could react like that toward someone repulsive enough to torture me like this. To threaten my life. My sister.

Diego scoots closer to sit next to me again. Sliding his hand around my back, he shifts my legs to sprawl over his without tugging me back into his lap, but his closeness is enough to finally calm my out of control heart. "Do you remember what I told you?" he asks softly, his voice whispering in my ear. "It wasn't real. It was in your head. Everything you experienced came from your subconscious."

"And I'm pretty sure my subconscious liked it. How messed up is that? Blood raining from the ceiling and dead people propped on the wall, and there I was friggin' naked on a table, begging to be bitten..." I grimace and cover my face with my hands. "You all probably think that doesn't sound so—"

"That sounds fucking awful, babe." Kingston inches closer without touching me, though I see how much he wants to as his concern matches mine.

I hold my hand out for him to take. "What's awful is that I know it was a nightmare, but I'm—" I can't even muse the thoughts out loud. So embarrassing. "He gave me his blood."

Diego rubs his hand up and down my leg. "It wasn't real."

"It felt real."

"Do you know who it was, Diego?" Austin asks, speaking for the first time since coming in.

Diego groans and laces his fingers on the back of his head. "I've never seen him before. If he was ever on the estate, it wasn't by invitation from one of us."

"Shit," Kingston mutters. "Well, what else do we know?"

"Laurel made an appearance too, but I can't be certain if it means anything with Jewel's recent interactions with her. There was someone else as well, a woman, but Jewel was blocking her face," Diego says, glancing to me. "And the blood debt was inherited from her dad, or at least it will be. I think her dad is still alive."

I blink a few times. "I'm not so sure. It was a dream. We can't be certain."

"And there hasn't been any sign of him," Kingston says, looking at me. "I'm sorry, babe. We looked. But I'll make sure to do it again. Dark Terrace Ranch is quarantined, and smuggling unapproved donors out is an auto-death sentence. If your dad's alive, he'll still be in the city."

I clench my jaw to stop the tears from leaking onto my face. I can't even allow a blip of hope for my dad to be alive inside me, because even if he is, he still has the blood debt. It changes nothing. That can't be reversed until it's paid, and the price was steep enough that if he failed to pay, it falls on the rest of my family. And if this vampire is stalking me now, it nearly guarantees that my dad died by his hands.

"And what about Jewel's mind?" Austin says, seeing how much the subject of my dad upsets me.

Diego straightens his shoulders. "I've never felt anything like the mental manipulation this guy used on her, and I'm afraid to try to break it."

"So, he's just going to get away with being in our girl's head?" Kingston asks.

"It might damage her mind if I try. I couldn't live with myself if I messed up. Could you?" Diego asks Kingston.

I turn to Austin and touch his leg as he quietly listens to Diego and Kingston start to argue over the risks of getting into my head and if it would be worth it, which they both agree it wouldn't be.

"Is there something you can do to make sure it doesn't hurt me?" I ask Austin. Because I can't imagine living like this forever, constantly plagued by these weird dreams in my sleep.

He shares a silent look with his brothers for a moment, his jaw clenching as he considers if he's going to say what's on his mind. "I agree that we shouldn't try anything rash, but I do recommend we do something to prevent someone from getting into your head again. It might also help with the dreams."

I purse my lips. "Please tell me it's a medication and not

what I think it is."

Austin rests his hand on top of mine on his leg. "Not as much will be needed, so the side effects won't be so bad."

I groan. "You sure there's no other way? You guys already make me so...fuck me."

They all chuckle.

"Oh, stop it. You know I didn't mean it like that," I say, my cheeks warming.

"Don't worry, Jewel," Austin says. "I'll help you through this—"

"That's what I'm afraid of," I say, "because last time..."

Austin blushes now, though his smile pulls wider across his face. "Was interesting. I know. I still feel bad."

"Don't. You were trying to help."

"And I'll do better this time. I'll make sure you get just enough of our blood to be effective but not too much that it becomes overwhelming."

"*Our* as in all of your blood?"

"Not at once." Austin eyes his brothers. "The side effects can vary, and as the keeper of your health, I think it's best to see what happens with each of us first."

I release a breath. "I don't know."

Austin brings my hand up to his cheek, begging me with his vibrant green eyes. Obviously the no affection in the other's space rule is currently on hold since Kingston still grasps my other hand and Diego continues to knead circles into my back. "Will you at least try? Just one night. If it's unbearable, we'll figure something else out."

"We'll start with me this time," Diego adds.

I gulp, memories from earlier still fresh in my mind. "Fine, whatever. But don't expect me to suck your neck."

He gapes at me for a moment and then shakes his head and laughs. "Damn, that would start off my day right." Some other thought crossed his mind first, and I want to pry more to find out what the look was about, but he's teasing me for a reason.

Rolling my eyes, I let his comment slide and pull away from Austin and Kingston to hide my face. "Can I have something to eat first? The thought of drinking blood makes me…ew."

Silence.

I'm pretty sure my face will explode with fire at any second. If they were any other vampires, I'd have been slaughtered at least two or three times because of my lack of filter and vampire sensitivity. After the whole ocean-comment incident, all three have been careful with how they say things, even Kingston, and here I am offending the guys who currently make me feel like I'm more than the donor I grew up to be.

Diego nudges my shoulder until I drop my hands to see the smirk on his face. "No worries. We get it. Blood isn't normally part of your diet."

Kingston tips his chin forward, giving me what I can only describe as a cocky as hell smile, one side of his mouth higher than the other until he shows off his teeth. "I guess you wouldn't remember last time either, babe. Your reaction would be different. I wish it were my night with you."

I gawk at him.

Austin shoves his brother, making him laugh. Reaching out, he takes my hand. "I can pull him from the rotation if you want."

"Oh, um. It's fine. He's all talk."

That makes both Austin and Diego laugh. Kingston drops his gaze down my body and back up and winks. I snatch a pillow and toss it at his face. He purposely lets it hit him and continues to stare so intently, I squirm and force myself to look away.

"I'll ask you again when it's his turn," Austin says. "And to answer your question about food, sorry, no. It's better to drink on an empty stomach, but I'll go grab you something to eat for after."

"As much as I want to hang out, babe. I have a few things to take care of," Kingston says.

I blink a few times, realizing the whole blood drinking thing is in immediate effect. They both abandon me with Diego so quickly that I nearly miss them exiting. Diego shifts on the bed and reaches for an empty glass next to a pitcher of water for me on his night table. He smirks at me, licking his lips, and releases a breathless laugh.

"Why are you suddenly nervous?" I ask, highly aware of the shift in his demeanor. "Do I need to be concerned? Austin told me the side effects before, but I have a feeling you three are leaving something out. I'm not at risk to catch the plague or something, right?"

My words wipe the nervous smile right off his face, and I inwardly cringe, knowing I totally offended him. Again.

"Despite what your history says, we're not a deadly virus, and we're not contagious. If that were true, there would be a lot more of us who survive on blood," he says, rolling the cup between his hands.

"I'm sorry. I didn't mean to be rude. I just—you can create another vampire, can't you? You said your dad made you."

"He did. It was before the divisions of cities took place and Donor Life Corp put a stop to the slaughtering," he answers, turning his gaze from the glass and back up. "My transformation muddles a lot of my memories from that time, but Mitchell Divine chose us based on a checklist of sorts, which was the initial idea of the Blood Match Program. The three of us helped him with what it is today after the three stages of matches failed due to unforeseen circumstances. We realized a perfect Blood Match had to be on a completely new level above a donor to work successfully. The cost for a vampire to apply is high to dissuade constant re-matches and assure proper care for those who participate."

I bob my head, thinking about his words. I enjoy how open Diego is with me about the topics the others might not be as comfortable sharing. Like shedding light on the age thing I've been curious about. They most definitely don't look much older than me, but also don't act like the elderly people in The Boxes. Mature but young. Ageless.

"Oh."

"Just 'oh'? You can talk to me about anything, you know. Tell me what's on your mind, and I'll share as much as I'm allowed to since we're not officially matched."

"I'm not sure what to say. Kingston's going to be mad at you for such a revelation," I say, smirking. Because really, I'm not sure I want to know about the three stages of failed matches or to be reminded that there was a time worse than my own. Because growing up in Dark Terrace Ranch was still shitty compared to the back-world where everyone ate solids...and not each other. "I always suspected his nickname should be gramps since he enjoys my supposed back-world mouth."

The smile returns to Diego's face, his eyes darting toward the door. Without him having to say, I know Kingston heard me from wherever he is on the estate. Maybe now he won't listen in. "I'm never going to hear the end of this from him now. We're technically not supposed to divulge too much information to you until you make your decision. Whoever you pick will answer everything you can think of."

I groan.

"What is it?"

Shrugging, I force away the thoughts of having no idea how I will ever decide and say, "It's nothing. Just anxious. How about we get this over with so Kingston stops listening in on our night? I know he is."

He shifts again, still fidgeting with the cup. "You don't have to worry. He's not going to listen any more. That would be like if he—never mind. It's just me and you now."

I peek at the door. "All right then. Let's do this."

He nods, licking his lips. "Just need a sec."

Tilting my head at his words, I study him shift his legs off the edge of the bed under the weight of my stare. He clears his throat and smiles at me again. Things turn awkward quickly as we eye each other, his prolonging making me all sorts of nervous again.

Crawling closer, I sit next to him and hug him this time, sliding my fingers through his. I realize he might've been over-sharing things not only for my benefit but also his own. "Diego, what's wrong? Are you nervous because of me? I can turn around and not watch. I didn't realize this was weird for you. It slipped my mind because I'm used to giving my blood."

Releasing a small puff of air between his lips, he forces himself to hold my stare instead of gazing at the glass he treats like a bomb about to explode at any second. "It's not weird, beautiful. More personal than anything. I'm concerned it'll be unpleasant for you, and that's the last thing I want. I know this might gross you out, but it should be enjoyable for you."

"Oh," I whisper. "I'm less concerned about the unpleasantness of drinking it and more concerned about the pleasantness that comes after if that makes you feel better."

He chuckles. "It does actually, and I have an idea. Will you trust me and close your eyes?"

I raise an eyebrow but do what he asks and shut my eyes. Something warm and sweet drips onto my bottom lip, and I automatically lick it off, my tongue tingling for a moment as I swallow.

"Was that okay?" he asks.

I snap my eyes open and stare at the two circular wounds dripping blood on his arm. "That was your blood?"

He bobs his head, studying my face. I accidentally react and scrunch my nose, but not because it tasted bad. I'm freaked out by how delicious it was, almost like the fruity syrup I had with my waffle the other day.

Diego mis-reads me and my thumping heart, and his face falls into a frown for a split second before he turns serious. "I'm sorry. If it's that bad, maybe Austin can—"

I suck in a breath and lace my fingers around his wrist to pull his arm up to my mouth. I run my tongue over my lips and swallow. "That's not why I reacted like that. And please don't bring this up ever again or hold it over my head, because I never thought I'd ever say this, but you taste friggin' delicious."

His face lights up with a smile, followed by a laugh that sends my heart racing. "I can put it in a glass."

I freeze. I'm afraid that my need to want to hate this will overpower me, and I'll lose my nerve. "Oh, shit. I'm sorry. This is totally not cool, isn't it?"

Diego scoots closer and situates me on his lap, and I realize it's more than personal. Giving me his blood is a new level of intimate. "Drink how you want, beautiful. Whatever makes you comfortable."

I glide my tongue over the blood on his skin, just gingerly

tasting it a second time. Diego releases a low moan from his throat and digs his fingers into my hips, the slight pressure sending tingles through me.

I moan this time, bringing my lips to the blood dripping down his arm. "Tell me when to stop."

"Just a few mouthfuls."

Except it's so good, pulling out every amazing emotion inside me for Diego, breaking them free as I suck harder, his blood tasting better than anything I've had in my life. I moan so embarrassingly loud that Diego inhales a sharp breath, and I'm nearly certain everyone in the entire estate heard me.

"Okay, beautiful. Anymore and you'll—"

I suck harder, surprising him so much that he snaps his mouth shut and lets me continue.

Holy shit balls. I can't stop.

19

Different Life

IF I THOUGHT CLIMBING INTO Austin's lap during the Blood Match interview was the most embarrassing moment in my life it was only because I hadn't tasted Diego's blood yet. The fact that I was close to death when I first consumed vampire blood probably saved me from revealing the part of me I had no idea existed. Who even knew vampires could get hickies? Who knew *I* could give a vampire a hicky?

"Are you not hungry, Jewel?" Austin asks from across the table.

I tap my bare foot on his soft carpet, keeping my eyes

trained on the bowl of yogurt with chunks of fruit in it to go along with the French toast and scrambled eggs. Condensation drips down the glass of orange juice, and I take a sip, trying to suppress the never-ending blush burning across my face.

"It's just—" I can't even talk about it. For one, what I do with each of my Blood Matches is personal, even if everyone is well aware of the situation. But for two, Austin had to pry me away from Diego because he was having trouble wanting to let me go and I was having none of it.

"You don't have to be embarrassed," Austin says, getting up to come to me. He pulls out the chair next to me and sits, brushing his knees to mine. "This is new for all of us. It's one thing to possess the knowledge but actually using it doesn't always have the desired outcome."

I force myself to meet his green eyes as they bore into me. "So, Diego's never given anyone his blood before?"

"You'll have to ask him that. But I do know that you were my first, though I do wish it would have been under different circumstances."

"It will be next time," I say, covering my face with my hands.

"We will swap the schedule around, so you're not with whoever gave you their blood," he says, his face serious but the slight rise in his voice giving his utter amusement away.

Because not only did he have to peel me away from Diego, he also had to swap days with him. I drank so much of Diego's blood that I'm intoxicated around him, so now I get to hang out with Austin instead, which I don't mind. I just feel bad that any of the guys had to see me like this.

"Are you sure you want to deal with this?" I ask, waving a hand over myself.

He chuckles. "What kind of question is that?"

"Did you not see Diego's arm? It was awful."

"It was seriously impressive." Austin smiles at me, showing off his fangs. "Diego thinks so."

I scrunch my nose. "Still mortifying."

"I know I can tell you a hundred times not to be embarrassed, but I get it. So, how about instead of sitting around here and over-thinking everything, we get out for a bit?"

Pushing my bowl away, I stand from the table, pulling him up with me. Austin grabs one of my sweatshirts from his closet and tosses it to me to put over my dress. Since establishing that I'm not to be alone, the guys quickly scattered my stuff between all three of their rooms. I hadn't even realized it until I found one of the few photos of my family together, when Mom and Aunt Dottie were still alive, sitting on Diego's night table and now on Austin's.

Seeing the photo reminds me I haven't talked to Ramona since yesterday morning. Brayla's words swirl through my mind, along with what I know about the blood debt. "Would you mind if I called my sister before we go? It's still early enough that she should be awake."

Austin nods and guides me to where the phone sits at his desk. Unlike in my room with the projection on the wall, Austin's lights up on the giant screen in front of me with the only view behind me being his heavy curtain.

Austin taps the device a few times, switching it to the short list of contacts from my room and presses the digital button for me. Without me having to ask, he moves away and starts piling the plates on his table, moving them out into the hallway since the staff—especially Laurel—isn't allowed in anyone's rooms for now.

The call rings for an incredibly long time, but finally Ramona's face blinks onto the screen. I smile, so happy to see her after everything that has happened. "Hey, Ramona-Babona." I study my sister's serious face, trying not to let it get to me. "Look at your hair. It's so cute." I've never seen my sister with short hair before, and I almost don't recognize her under the bangs.

She smiles with her mouth closed. "Thanks, Jewel. You look good too. Are you wearing makeup?"

"Yeah," I lie. One of the side effects of drinking vampire blood is amazing skin. It probably doesn't help that my lips are swollen and my cheeks still flushed. "I'm going out in a bit."

"Oh, good. Then you won't mind that I can't really talk," she says.

I blink a few times, tears threatening to spill. Because I'd put off doing anything to talk with her for as long as possible. If the guys weren't so adamant about keeping the whole blood debt secret, I'd spill my heart out to warn her. To promise her that I won't let anything happen. I want so badly to bring up

Dad too.

"Where are Fallon and Dana? Can I talk to them?"

Ramona glances over her shoulder. "I'm sorry, Jewel. No. I don't think it's a good idea."

"What? Why?" And then I remember the looks of horror crossing their faces the last time and how they saw my stalker vampire. They probably hate me. I can feel the shift already in Ramona.

Screw it. I'm going to tell her. "Is this about the strange vampire in my room? I'm sorry. I had no idea—"

"Jewel," Austin says, materializing in front of the screen. He shakes his head at me.

"A strange vampire? What are you talking about? You're a Blood Match to three. It's kind of expected. And no, this isn't about vampires. It's about you."

"Me?"

Ramona turns her gaze away as to not look at me. "You're flaunting your new lifestyle like you actually enjoy it, and I'm afraid it's giving the girls the wrong impression."

Man, it's like she grew up overnight. And her words piss me the hell off.

"Flaunting? Are you kidding me? I did this for you!" My voice rises, nearly screeching.

"But you like it!" she yells right back. "I bet if the world exploded and things changed, you'd probably still stay there and continue to be—" She snaps her mouth shut, flaring her nostrils. "I hear the rumors around here. I know the possibility of what happens. The Blood Vows. They'll turn you against us."

"Ramona!"

She shakes her head. "I'm sorry, Jewel. I have to go."

"Wait! Don't hang up," I beg. "Please."

The call disconnects, leaving me heaving. I swing out my arm in frustration and grief, the shock of the conversation sinking deep into my bones. Austin catches his monitor before I knock the whole thing onto the floor. One second I'm smacking my hands on the desk, and in the next, I'm sitting on the edge of his bed, engulfed in his arms.

"I don't understand," I say, tears blurring my vision. "How could she say those things? What did she even mean by them? Blood Vows? And the vampire—" I scowl, jerking to face him. "Did someone get into her head? Brayla said the asshole scared the girls."

Austin presses his lips into a thin line. "My dad did what he thought was necessary to protect your family and to see if he could extract information from your cousins."

"He what?" Anger rushes through me, and all I can think about is how horrible being under his mind manipulation made me feel as he ripped answers from me without my permission. "How could he? They're fourteen. Kids are supposed to be safe. It's the law. My sister is protected too. What he did—"

"Was unacceptable, I know," he says.

"And you knew and didn't warn me?" I ask.

"Jewel, please."

I tug away from him, feeling like if I don't get space, I'll suffocate. "Did you all know?"

He doesn't respond. He'll take my anger on his brothers' behalf. The thing I'm most certain of with the Divines is that they're incredibly loyal.

"I can't believe this," I snap. "I think he damaged her. She'd have never talked to me like that before. She'd have never believed that I would ever turn against her because of whatever the hell a Blood Vow is."

"That wasn't my dad," he says. "Let me explain. Haven Springs is—"

I shake my head and get to my feet. "No. I don't want to hear it. You can't excuse this."

Swiping my hand over my face, I clear my vision the best I can and strut toward the door. I can't sit in here any longer. I need to be by myself. I need a moment to process and think. I need to figure out how to convince Ramona that no matter what happens, she'll always come first. She's my sister, my family. I gave up everything to see to it that she could live a different life from me.

I yank open the door and run right into Kingston's chest as he blocks my way. The second his hands touch my shoulders, I rip back and slide out of his way to head down the hallway in the direction I know I'll find the stairs.

"Babe, wait up," Kingston says. "Where are you going?"

"I need air."

"Come on, let me take you—"

Spinning around, I glare at him. "Away from you. All of

you. I need to be alone."

"Beautiful, we can't let you," Diego says, appearing on the other side of the hallway. "You know why."

I scream and cover my eyes with my hands for a moment. "Then just stay back. Just leave me alone."

Bowing my head, I rush past Diego, ignoring my body's urge to throw itself at him and run all the way to the stairs and down them. I don't stop at the door either. I push it open and race onto the terrace.

I lose myself to the hillside in the dead of night.

20

My Perfect Vampires

USUALLY I'D BE TERRIFIED KNOWING that three powerful vampires stalk me on my quiet descent down the winding road of the hillside, but now my mind, body, and blood battle it out in an earthquake of emotions that rattle me to the core. The feelings I have for Austin, Diego, and Kingston break away everything I thought I knew about myself to display the mess of chaos I'll never be capable of sorting through to rebuild who Jewel Jordan of Dark Terrace Ranch was before. That girl no longer exists as much as I want to deny it. Ramona was right. I have changed. Whether the change is good or bad is still yet to be determined.

"This is why you don't allow me to wear shoes, right?" I say to the black paved road in front of me. "So I can't comfortably run away and you guys can follow my blood trail." Because at this point, I'm pretty sure my feet are bleeding from scraping on the black pavement on the steep sections I had no choice but to run down.

No one responds to me, the quiet of the night only broken by the sounds of mysterious nearby animals I try not to freak out about. Surprise cows are on the top of my list of things I never want to experience again.

Craning my neck, I peek behind me, startled by the empty road. "Guys?"

My voice echoes through the air, sending goosebumps over my skin. What in the actual hell? They really abandoned me. And now that they're not here, a wave of fear rushes over me in an icy downpour that makes me freeze.

"Shit," I whisper. "Where are you?"

"Jewel."

I scream out at the sudden voice next to me. Tripping over my own feet, I fall off the paved road and into the cool arms of Austin. He scoops me up without setting me back on my feet. I bury my face into his chest, heaving another ragged breath, my nerves making it hard to calm my thrashing heart.

"You scared me," I say, digging my fingers into his back. "I was talking to you, you know, but you didn't respond. I thought maybe—"

"We didn't abandon you if that's what you think. You just made it clear that you needed space, so we were trying to give it to you to cool off." He hugs me tighter, accepting the fact that I obviously now think space from him is overrated.

"Yeah, well," I murmur. "I felt too alone."

He chuckles, leaning his face into mine to kiss my cheek. "I'm sorry if you feared we left you."

"And for everything else, babe," Kingston says, appearing from the trees. "Mitchell went against our wishes with your family, but you really shouldn't worry. They're fine. I promise." It's rare to hear Kingston call his dad Mitchell, and I wonder if it's because of what he did. There's something satisfying about knowing I'm not alone in my boiling fury every time I think of the man.

I huff. "You should've told me."

"We know, beautiful. We'll do better about keeping you involved," Diego says, coming up next to Austin. He holds up a pair of athletic shoes. "Also, I went back and got these like you asked. I wasn't sure which pair you preferred."

"Oh, now you give me shoes," I mutter. At this point as long as it's something I can walk in, I don't care. "Only took me nearly stubbing my toes to get some."

"Okay, babe. You're the one who stormed out without proper attire," Kingston says. "You can't hold that against us."

Diego dusts off my feet before quickly putting on my socks and shoes, making me feel like a child amid a tantrum. "Yeah, and what's up with the whole no shoe thing? You have more pairs than Kingston."

"I do not. There were none in my wardrobe."

The three of them look at each other, trying not to laugh.

"They were behind the rolling mirror," Diego says. "And now they've taken over all our closets."

They have to be joking. "Huh?"

"But no worries, babe. I'll always make room for you," Kingston says, grinning.

I frown. "You're shitting me. I thought it was because I was a donor and maybe it was part of my Blood Match contract. Like a status thing. Or that you were afraid I'd run away or something."

Austin brushes his lips to my cheek, and I grasp his chin to turn him to me, giving him a whisper of a kiss. "You're not a prisoner. You know that, right?" he asks against my mouth. "We were hoping you'd want to be here with us even after knowing why you chose to apply."

"I do want to be here," I say, my anger melting away the longer I stand under each of their gazes. "I love it here."

Kingston shuffles closer. "I never doubted that. I just thought you didn't like any of the shoes I picked out."

Diego takes my hand, and I automatically lean toward him, reacting to his blood. He touches my cheek, careful to keep a foot of space between us while Austin still holds me. "Or because you didn't like wearing any at all. Which is fine by me, beautiful. I'll carry you anywhere...tomorrow."

I meet Diego's gaze, my body lusting all over again at the

thought of being in his arms.

"And me tonight, I mean, if you forgive me and want to hang out still. Or if you still need space, we can follow you down to the beach." Austin breathes near my ear, turning me slightly away from Diego, more affectionate than I've ever seen him. I feel bad that I just stormed off on his night. But I was so mad. And I'm still angry. Just not so much at them.

"I didn't mean to get so pissed off. I love being around you—all of you—so much that...Ramona was right about me. And I'm sorry I took it out on you. It's just—damn it. I'm hurt. She's my sister. I did this for her, and she makes me feel like I'm the one in the wrong because I'm happier than I've been in a long time. It's like she thinks I should be suffering here."

Austin carefully sets me on my feet. "I don't think that's true. I think she's scared of losing you, so she's pushing you away. Those in Haven Springs see the world differently as they're all exempt from being donors. And honestly, Jewel, not all Blood Matches end up with the life we all yearn to create with you."

"Yeah, babe. I can attest that what we have is not the norm." Kingston rocks back on his heels and stares at the splatter of stars across the dark sky. "And not only because you matched with all three of us."

I groan. "Don't remind me. I don't even know how I will ever pick between any of you. You have all been amazing to me, and not once have you ever made me feel beneath you."

"Except for the supposed lack of shoes," Kingston says,

smirking.

I laugh. "Ugh, see. You always make me laugh. I don't think I've ever laughed so much in my life. I love that."

"And I love to hear it, babe. Especially the strangled, high-pitch, snorting giggle thing you do that literally sounds through the whole house when you watch one of the dumb movies Diego picks out for you."

"Not cool, Kingston. You just put down on something she likes," Diego says. "And those movies are awesome."

I touch Diego's shoulder, grinning. "And that's what I love about you. You get me and my obsession with back-world comedy. You always know exactly what to say to make me feel better. Like earlier with the whole dream thing."

"You forgot the blood thing," Kingston adds.

I groan.

Austin backhands his shoulder. "Knock it off, Kingston. She's already embarrassed."

"Hey, I thought it was hot. I'm jealous."

Diego nudges me. "He really is. Because I got your mark."

I close my eyes to stop my body from going out of whack under both their gazes. Austin wraps his arms around me, turning me away. "Ignore them. I'll make sure everything goes right next time. I promise."

Standing on my tiptoes, I brush my lips to his. "And this is what I love about you. You're in tune to everything I need, and you keep those two in check. You have no idea how thankful I am for you." I look at Kingston and Diego. "All of you. I feel so connected to each of you in different ways. And it gets more intense every night."

Austin kisses me again, smiling at me so widely that my whole body swells with happiness. I turn to Kingston and Diego next, and Diego motions for Kingston to accept my hug first. Our lips meet in the sweetest kiss, just long enough to make me crave more. He rests his forehead to mine for a second, nuzzling our noses together, and then motions for me to go to Diego.

My whole body hums in anticipation when Diego's gray eyes meet mine. He sucks in a breath, and I brace myself, suppressing the urge to fly at him. He closes the distance to me first so I don't have to move and envelops me in his arms. The second his hands slide around my waist, I release an unflattering, most definitely uncalled for, loud ass moan that makes Kingston bust up laughing behind me.

I flip him off and brush my lips to Diego's, skipping past sweet and practically consuming his lips while jumping up and wrapping my legs around his waist. He kisses me for not even half a minute before pulling back, beaming his brilliant smile, and hands me back to Austin.

"You know, babe," Kingston says, taking my hand to bring to his face. "I thought I wanted to devour you, but I'm pretty fucking sure I now want you to devour me."

OhmyeffingG. "Kingston," I warn.

He raises his hands. "Fine. I'm saving all my irresistible words of seduction for my night."

"You're probably safe to drink his blood on the same night

then, Jewel," Austin says. "Pretty sure that'll convince your body to control itself."

"Why can't my blood have that kind of effect of all of you?" I ask.

"It does," they all say at once.

"But you do as well," Diego says.

Kingston meets my gaze. "Just being close to you fills something inside me."

"Makes me feel out of control," Austin admits, blushing.

Hearing their admissions sparks something light inside me that pushes away the dark caused by Ramona hurting my feelings and the realization that I could contently live my life with each of them. "This is why I can't choose. Someone might as well do it for me."

"Jewel," Kingston says, his voice catching as his eyes shift from mine to his brothers. The use of my name sends my heart thudding, because whatever is on his mind must be serious.

They all look at each other with the intense mind reading faces that I now know means that they're whispering in a silent conversation in front of me.

I pull away from all three of them and wag both my index fingers. "No more doing that. You're making me feel left out." I try my best to hold a straight face, puffing out my bottom lip.

They continue to look at each other with quick glances at me.

"Now it's like I'm not even here," I tease, trying to lighten the intensity of the situation. "You know what? Keep doing that and I won't pick anyone. I'll just pick all of you. I'm pretty sure I'm obsessed wit—"

I realize they're all staring at me now, each of their beautiful eyes holding me hostage as I shift on my feet in front of them. Warmth blossoms up my chest and into my cheeks, this whole weird night getting even weirder, and I wonder if I've gone too far with my teasing.

"Um, I offended you all again, right?" I ask. "I'm sorry. I didn't mean to make the Blood Match not sound important. I just want you to know how much you mean to me. It hurts my heart that two of you will be disappointed."

"Beautiful, you talk a lot when you're nervous," Diego says.

I rotate on my feet, the pavement scraping the rubber soles of my shoes as I start to squirm. "Well, you are all making me nervous. None of you are saying anything. What is it? What are you whispering about?"

"Obviously you, babe," Kingston says, the moon reflecting in his eyes.

"And we're sorry," Austin adds. "But you keep saying things about your decision."

I frown. "About matching? I haven't made one. I just said that it'll be so hard."

They all close the distance to me, Austin hugging me from behind while Diego and Kingston link their fingers through mine. It seems all rules are off in this moment as they all want to tell me something together, and whatever it is freaks me out.

"Just spit out whatever you want to say," I whisper. "Have

you changed your mind about me? About you? You know the last thing I wanted was to come between you all. I love your loyalty to each other, and you all always stand up for one another. I just—I wish I had that."

Kingston leans into me. "Babe, you do."

Austin wets his lips, shifting. "We were going to wait to bring this up closer to the end of the thirty days, but every time someone talks about your decision, you stress out."

"And we don't want that. Especially with all the shit happening now," Diego says. "You remember when I told you that you managed to make us all feel incredibly important?"

I nod. "Because you all are."

The three of them smile.

Austin rests his chin in the crook of my neck. "And so are you."

"To all of us," Diego says.

I swallow, soaking in the heat radiating through me—the heat I share with each of them as they huddle close. "So, what are you saying?" There's no doubt in my mind that I know what they're getting at, but I need to hear the words out loud. I need to know it isn't in my head, and that my thoughts aren't ridiculous.

"Babe," Kingston says. "What we're getting at is that this works. For all of us. We want you to choose all of us and let us choose you."

His words sink in, filling my heart so much so that all my bottled up emotions spill over. Knowing that they don't want to put me in the position to choose between them—that I don't have to choose between them—leaves me a melted mess. Diego's my mind. Kingston's my body. Austin's my blood. Together they're my absolute perfect match, equal on all levels.

Except it isn't fair to them no matter if they agree that this can work. "I—" I can't even spit the words out because a sob bursts from me, startling all of them. They stand frozen around me while I cover my eyes.

"If this isn't what you want—"

I hold my hand up, cutting Austin off. "I do want this. So, so much. But the contract. I can't provide enough blood to sustain all of you."

Diego cups my face in his hands. "Hey, we'll figure it out."

"You don't call me Rule Breaker for nothing," Kingston says, bringing my hand to his lips to kiss the back of it.

Austin brushes his lips to my earlobe. "Things can change, Jewel. We'll change them for you."

"So you're really okay with this?" I ask.

They all nod.

"Then yes. I choose all of you."

21

Mind, Body, and Blood

THE MOON HANGS LOW IN the sky, sinking toward the ocean's horizon. White-capped waves crash on shore two dozen feet away, and I can't take my eyes off them. Something about the freezing sea spray misting my face, the hum of the tide rolling, the scent of burning wood makes my heart sing as much as the guys do—my guys. Saying it to myself doesn't feel weird. It's the most natural thing. *My guys.* My mind. My body. My blood.

Austin shifts me in his arms, hugging me closer. The bright fire pushes away the cold of the coming morning. If I could stay out here all day with Austin, Diego, and Kingston, I would. If only night could claim the sky a little longer.

"I think this is the calmest your heart's ever been while you've been awake," Austin whispers, brushing his lips to my cheek, begging me to meet his lips without having to ask.

So I do. Caressing my lips to his, I kiss him sweetly, just testing and tasting his eager mouth. His fingers play with my hair, tugging it gently off my neck. I shiver against the cold breeze, slowly breaking away to bury my face in the warmth my body created against his chest.

"I take it back," he whispers.

I tilt my head up and kiss the skin above the neckline of his T-shirt. "I can't help it."

He smiles, guiding my head to listen to his heart beating in fast thrums against my ear. "Me either."

I snuggle against him, turning my gaze back to the stretch of beach with gray water against the gradually lightening lavender sky. Kingston and Diego stand a few dozen feet down the beach talking and watching the waves, giving Austin privacy on his night while still being close to protect me.

"I just wish we could stay here all day. The water looked so pretty in the sunlight from my balcony," I say, half expecting for Austin to pick me up to race me back up the hill at any second.

"We might be able to arrange a short trip some other time," he says. "You didn't give us much time to prep—that doesn't matter. Some other time. Promise."

"Won't you like explode in the sunlight? I mean, I kind of enjoy you in one piece. Seeing the water in the sun isn't that important to me," I say.

He grins, brushing strands of my hair behind my ear. "Have you ever seen a vampire explode?"

I shake my head. "That's just..."

"Impossible. If we exploded in the sunlight, history might've been different. Repelled by silver, crosses? Garlic? We'd all be dead. Especially since you've eaten garlic bread twice this week."

I laugh. "Which obviously didn't repel any of you."

"We're not like the vampires from the old movies. We—as in vampires—just went with it because it was something the human race could understand."

They're like super humans. I knew this. Evolved. Alive. "Fear made it easier during The Division, right? That's what my history teacher said. People were easier to coax into supposed safe zones."

His jaw tightens. "And familiarity made it easier to compromise. The old entertainment business helped by glorifying and sexualizing vampires, which is why we use the name. People sought out vampires in droves, believing it was some sort of virus they could catch, making it easy to—" He sighs, licking his lips. Diego didn't get into this either. My dad always knew it was more than a supposed plague that only affected a small percentage of the world while allowing those evolved from it to decimate a huge percentage of humanity. Diego confirmed they aren't contagious. But it seems this is one of those truths that'll be kept from me, because Austin clears his throat and looks away.

"Slaughter everyone," I finish for him. I can't stop thinking about how easy it was for him to decapitate Master Caruthers.

He grimaces, surely noticing where my thoughts wander. "Unfortunately some believe they're above others. I, for one, don't believe that, which is why I did my best to establish new standards. Blood Life Corp put a stop to the massacres to bring civility into the new world. I was lucky to have been transitioned after the divisions, so I'm only familiar with the knowledge Mitchell has shared."

"The divisions," I say. "You mean corralling people into box cities, pretending we have any sort of—" I snap my mouth shut and suppress the rest of my sarcastic remark about keeping the food source in good condition, but one look at his pleading eyes makes me realize that it's more than that to him. He obviously doesn't consider me a blood supply like the shadow vampires. "I'm sorry."

"Don't be, Jewel." His Adam's apple bounces in his throat. "And so you know, I've never taken a human life. Not everyone agrees with The Divide, but it was there for a reason and not to control humans like you think. Quite the opposite. I just wish you never had to live like that."

A dozen memories flit through my mind. The funny thing is that I never really thought my life was awful until Mom and Aunt Dottie died. I had fun all the time with Ramona and

Brayla. I never felt without. I was happy. I didn't give blood donations or vampires much thought until the very first time Dad walked with me to the Blood Donation Center on my eighteenth birthday a few months ago.

I felt like an adult overnight. My dad sheltered me so much so that it was a shock. I just wish I could've stopped Ramona from ever knowing any different. But she's barely a year and a half younger, and she was my sounding board and hope when dad disappeared. All she knew was my fear. And she now assumes the worst. But this isn't Dark Terrace Ranch, and I'm not Jewel Jordan. I'm Jewel Divine.

"So, about the sun," I say, suddenly desperate to change the subject from things that remind me of my life before. "No exploding. You sure? I mean, have you tried?"

He chuckles. "If you insist, I'll show you, but think of it as a severe skin allergy. We have a slight mutation in some of our cells that while assisting in our constant regeneration—which is responsible for our lack of aging—also creates a chemical that causes extreme photosensitivity. It's incredibly unpleasant."

"Sounds like it," I say. "So I won't insist."

"You're going to pull every single secret from us, aren't you, babe?" Kingston says, appearing on the other side of the fire.

I stick my tongue out at him. "Without even trying, dude."

He tips his head back and laughs. "I'll remember that."

"I'm sure you will."

"I'll be hard to get to."

I swing my head back and forth, playfully pelting Austin with my dark tresses in the process. "Highly doubt it, but okay."

Diego appears on Kingston's right. "As much as I want to hang out here all day, we should get back. It's late enough that all the guests will be in their rooms now. If not, they probably will be when we arrive."

I stifle a yawn at the thought of returning to the comfort of a bed...and then I remember what comes along with it. Drinking their blood to help protect me from being manipulated shouldn't feel as intimate as sex, but after the last time with Diego, it definitely does.

"Come here, beautiful," Diego says, basically reading my thoughts. "Let's see if you need more blood before we return."

I hesitate, really wishing there was some other way to tell whether or not I'm still under Diego's vampire blood influence without closing the space between us. Because I already want to with his arms open and inviting me in.

Austin helps me to my feet, holding my hand until I have to let go because he doesn't move from his spot. I shuffle around the fire, my bare feet kicking up the sand, my shoes still where I left them on the old, cracked sidewalk. My heart thuds hard enough to worry me about trying to throw itself from my body and at Diego.

I hesitate and swallow my nerves. "I think it's still working."

Diego motions for me to close the distance. "I can't tell

with you way over there. Don't worry. I'm not afraid that you'll bite."

My cheeks burn.

He chuckles and ends up strolling closer, painfully slow and purposeful, almost cautious.

"You are totally scared I'll rush you," I murmur. "You're acting like I'm a wild animal."

"Just hurry up before I push you, Diego," Kingston says. "Morning's coming."

The thought of the sun rising with my guys right here on the beach, completely vulnerable, freaks me out enough that I dart forward to Diego. He straightens his shoulders, making it difficult to kiss him, which I want to, but not in the same way as before.

"It's nearly worn off," Austin says from behind me.

"But I still really want to kiss him," I muse from over my shoulder.

Kingston comes up next to me. "What about me, babe?"

I bat his shoulder. "Always."

"All right. I'll handle this. You guys go ahead," Diego says, turning to his brothers.

"You sure, Diego?" Austin says. "Last time—"

"I got it," he insists.

"We'll meet you halfway up." Kingston pats Diego on the back. Turning to me, he touches my cheek. "Please be easy on him. He doesn't have my restraint."

"Restraint?" I question. "I thought that might've been the

one thing you lacked."

He snaps his teeth at me, grinning. "We need to work on your memory, babe. If I recall, I—"

I cut his words off with my hand, glaring at him, knowing exactly what he's referring to on our first disastrous non-date to the Blood Match Center. When I know he's not going to tease me, I ease my hand away and replace it with my mouth, brushing my lips so softly to his that he meets my raised eyebrow with a playful glare of his own.

Austin shares a silent conversation with Diego for a moment, and I let him, noticing how nervous Diego is about this again. I'd be lying if my body wasn't trembling in nerves and anticipation.

"You'll both be fine," Austin assures. "I won't be far."

Austin and Kingston disappear, leaving me alone with Diego on the beach, our fire now extinguished with the trail of smoke disappearing into the wind.

I suck in a cold breath of the fresh ocean air and turn back to Diego. The second my gaze lands on the blood dripping from his wrist and into his hand, I take an automatic step closer. His muscular arm bulges as he flexes, the hicky I gave him earlier barely noticeable.

"I don't think this is a good idea," I say, my tongue licking my lips without my permission.

He smirks. "Don't worry, beautiful. Those sexy lips of yours will unfortunately not touch me. Just open your mouth."

I grimace, and then cringe, because disappointment washes

through me. My body reacts to my inner desire, and my head fully agrees that I want to experience Diego's closeness again, feel the rush that comes with his blood, and relish in an indescribable moment with him again no matter how mortified I was after the fact. Because there's nothing embarrassing about it now.

"Beautiful," Diego whispers.

I swallow and pull myself together.

Closing my eyes, I part my lips and tilt my head back, shivering with anticipation. I wonder what it would be like to do this with different intentions. To be this next level close for the sole reason of just experiencing the rush together without having to think about why we've agreed to be in this position, one I want to explore without restraint and control, one that allows us both to give in.

Diego's warm blood, quite the opposite of his cool body, coats my tongue, bursting with sweet flavor. A small moan escapes my mouth, and I swallow, licking my lips to wait for another taste that doesn't come.

"That's it," Diego says.

I slowly open my eyes, smiling at him. The rush of his blood isn't such a rush this time. It's like slowly soaking myself in the good emotions pouring from him to me as he offers me the brilliant smile I love.

Shuffling closer, I close the small amount of space between us and peer into his gray eyes. I stretch up to kiss him, just softly skimming my lips over his. He scoops me up, kissing me deeper but without the out-of-control desire that came last time. The world shifts, the wind whipping through my hair, but I don't pull away from Diego to see him running us back up the hill.

"You good?" Austin's voice calls out through the silent air.

Slowly pulling back, I try to glimpse him, but the world moves too fast.

"We're good." Diego kisses me once more, just a quick meeting of our lips, and says, "Brace yourself, beautiful. Time to go back to Austin."

I screech, Diego's arms suddenly disappearing. The world spins around me as I fly through the air for a split second not even long enough to take another breath before Austin catches me. I heave a gasp against his neck, feeling his skin vibrate with a soft hum.

"I'm not a friggin' doll!" I shout, still gasping. "You can't just toss me around like one."

Austin rests his head in the crook of my neck, letting me twine my legs around his torso to hide from the wind. "Sorry, Jewel. I told him he could wait until we got inside."

"But I was afraid I might not let you go," Diego says from somewhere to my right.

The world slows a moment later, and I pull my face from Austin's neck to see the grand staircase leading to the terrace. Austin jogs up the stairs behind Diego and sets me on my feet as dawn breaks, the rising sun lighting the world aglow.

"Come on, babe," Kingston says from behind me. "Getting

hot out here."

I turn away from the lightening ocean in the distance to meet the guys standing just inside the open side door out of the way of the warm sunlight cutting across the property. Peering back at the ocean once more, I make my way inside, sliding my fingers through Austin's.

He swings my arm with his, the two of us strolling ahead of Kingston and Diego until the long hallway ends with another door outside, an elevator, and a set of spiral stairs that go up a small tower to the floor with our bedrooms.

Austin freezes, pulling me closer to him. The elevator indicator lights up before we're even close enough to call it. Kingston appears in front of me, Diego staying behind. Soft footsteps come from the stone stairs. Their sudden tenseness sends my heart racing.

"No one should be here. Not even the staff," Kingston says out loud, probably for my benefit.

"It's Laurel," Austin says from beside me.

Kingston turns to look at his brothers. "Is that blo—"

The elevator door opens, and Austin spins me around so fast that dizziness rushes through me. I don't even have a chance to see who was in the elevator, and I'm glad for it. Because whoever—whatever—it is makes Kingston swear. Diego growls from deep in his throat, sending fear through me.

Austin hugs me closer. "Try not to freak out, but one of the staff has been deca—murdered."

"What?" I ask, panic rising in my chest. "Was it Lau—"

"Mr. Divines, welcome home." Laurel's sharp voice cuts through the quiet hall, startling me. "I've made your dinner."

"Get her out of here, Austin," Kingston says.

"Laurel's been manipul—"

"The only one to ever manipulate me, Mr. Divine, is you. But that's fine. I liked it. Feeling you in my head, holding me with your eyes." Laurel laughs from out of my view. "Getting us both disqualified from—"

"I said get Jewel out of here!" Kingston yells.

Austin hooks his arms around me, scooping me up to carry me in the opposite direction of Laurel. Her voice continues to cut through the hallway. Something explodes in front of us, glass cascading through the air, causing Austin to spin back around again. I gape in horror, catching sight of Laurel bleeding outside the open elevator covered in blood with something strewn across the floor—not something—someone.

"Austin!" Diego yells.

An alarm rings through the air, startling all three vampires. The high-pitched warning mutes all other noises, piercing my ears. Austin shakes his head in disorientation, stumbling with me in his arms toward the door in which we entered. A shadow crosses my vision, cool fingers grazing my back. The door leading outside flings open off its hinges to crash into the ground.

Two figures stand in a halo of bright sunshine, setting the small foyer aglow. Everything happens so fast that I don't have time to react. One second I'm inside and then the next I'm on the ground, my cheek pressing into the warm pavement. A river of blood pools against my arm, and I screech, seeing the open, lifeless eyes of one of the groundskeepers.

Austin yells, the pain radiating in his voice stabbing right through me. I push up on my hands to get back to my feet, my knees burning and bleeding with scrapes from rolling across the pavement. Spinning around, I catch sight of Austin on the ground, covering his head with his shirt, his hands burning along with the sliver of skin on his back, but even the shirt starts to smoke.

"Jewel, run! Stay out of the shadows!" Diego shouts from the open door. "Keep to the path and run. Run and hide. We'll find you."

Fear freezes me in place as I search around for vampires in the shadows. But it's not the vampires I need to worry about.

"Behind you!" Kingston yells. "Run!"

But I don't get the chance. Pain bursts in the back of my head, hazing my vision. I fall forward on my hands and knees. Someone stomps their foot into my back, winding me, and I gasp and spit, trying to stumble forward.

The last thing I see is Kingston and Diego braving the sunlight, trying to get to me. The sun disappears with my vision, and I curl in on myself, falling unconscious to the sound of my guys shouting my name.

22

Mercy

BLOOD RAINS DOWN FROM THE ceiling, soaking into my white dress. Strong hands latch onto my wrists and pull me across the long, sturdy wooden table. I struggle to free myself, slipping and sliding on the sticky blood. Shadows shift from the wall, pinching and ripping at my dress, leaving me exposed.

"My precious Jewel," a familiar voice whispers. "It won't be long."

The familiar vampire with the startling blue eyes materializes above me. I try to scramble away, fear blossoming through me. But he's too fast. All I can do is scream as he drags me off the table to hold me in front of him. He bites hard on his lower lip, coating it in blood. Closing the distance, he kisses me, sliding his bloody tongue across mine, sending a wave of desire through me. My body ignites, and I arch toward him against my mind's consent.

He laughs, shifting his hand to slide over my shoulder and down the length of my back, making me squirm in uncontrollable desire. "I can't wait to hear you beg."

I gasp, bolting upright. An uncontrollable moan escapes my mouth the second before someone slaps me across the face, sending pain bursting in my cheek. Fingers dig into my hair, stopping me from recoiling. Tears burn my eyes, blurring the room around me.

"You're disgusting," Laurel says, shaking me a few times until my vision clears and she comes into focus. "A complete embarrassment to the Divine name. I mean, look at you. So full of yourself that you string all three of them along when they could already apply to be re-matched with those of us who actually want to be someone's perfect pair."

I frown at her words, trying my best not to react. "I didn't write the contract."

She scowls at me. "But you signed it."

Arguing with someone who clearly has a vendetta against me is pointless. Instead of giving Laurel another moment of my attention, I peer around the plain bedroom with white walls, a single bed with tan linens, and a small dresser. A window provides a view of tall trees that remind me of the forest growing up the hillside. Spotting the familiar vegetation is the only thing keeping my panic from consuming me.

"It doesn't matter anymore," Laurel says. "You're not going to be alive long enough to fulfill it."

Anger rushes over me at her words. "Neither will you once the sun sets."

She only laughs and rolls her eyes. "I'll be gone by then, which is kind of a shame. Seeing Kingston's face earlier was more satisfying than I expected."

"Are you in love with him or something?" I can't stop the words from coming from my mouth. This is more than her thinking I'm not worthy to be matched to Kingston, Austin, and Diego.

Laurel rolls her eyes again. "Would you like me to say yes? Give you an excuse to why I helped separate you long enough to—"

The door swings open, and an old woman knocks her cane on the doorframe, pulling Laurel's attention from me. Without having to ask, I can tell the woman is related to Laurel, possibly being her mom.

"It's time to go, dear," the woman says. "Our transport arrived."

Laurel nods at the woman and gets to her feet. I get up to follow her, to scream at her, to beg her to let me go, but my foot catches on a metal chain. Falling flat on my stomach, I heave a breath. Both Laurel and the old woman look at me, and for the first time, I think I spot pity in Laurel's eyes.

"Please," I manage to spit out. "Let me go. I'll make sure

the Divines don't hurt you. Please, we can work something out."

Laurel hesitates, opening and closing her mouth, but turns away without answering me. The old woman hesitates in the doorway, trailing her eyes over the room before focusing on me. She reaches into the pocket of her long dress and tugs out a small red and silver oval-shaped object and tosses it on the floor in front of me.

"I'm sorry things have ended this way for you, Jewel. Unlike what my Laurel thinks, you'd have made a wonderful Divine. But please, try not to blame us. You know we humans have to do what we have to in this world, and you should blame your misters for the position you're in. They've left a lot of enemies in their wake. Just like your father. There are those who seek revenge and those who seek to collect. It's unfortunate you have to pay for everyone else's mistakes, but I find this arrangement more merciful. In the end, the choice is yours. We humans must do what we can."

The old woman purses her lips and leaves the room, shutting the door on my screams. Her words spin through my mind as I try to make sense of things. I knew that Austin, Diego, and Kingston worried about my safety, and I knew they had a ton of security for a reason, but I never expected to find myself in the middle of what feels like a blood feud.

As for showing me mercy? I'm afraid to find out. It sounded like the old woman knew about the blood debt that my dad owed the asshole vampire haunting my dreams, but I don't think that is why I'm chained in a room in what looks like a human house in the middle of the forest not far from the estate.

I sit up and cross my legs to inspect the shackle on my ankle. Tugging at the chain, I attempt to yank it free from where its end hides under the bed, but it doesn't budge. All the force does is turns my hands red in the process.

Fucking shit balls. I hate to think it, but this is how I imagined a Blood Match to be—me chained to the wall in a tiny room constantly waiting for a vampire to come in and drink my blood. And surely that's what's going to happen to me now.

My gaze falls on the small red and silver object the woman tossed on the floor with her mercy speech, and I scoop it into my hands. It's a pocket knife. Dad carried one similar to it, and I can't help but wonder if this is the small mercy the woman referred to.

Prying it open with my nail, I stare at my fuzzy reflection in the blade for a moment. Whatever happens now is up to me. She said it was my choice in the end. But there's no way I'm going to act like this knife is a gift of mercy from people not much different than me. The old woman was right. We do what we have to.

I'm not leaving Ramona to face the aftermath if I succumb to fear. I'm not giving up on a life of my making with three amazing guys who helped unveil parts of myself that I didn't even know existed.

I might not be brave or powerful. I might jump at every little thing that startles me. But even if the world comes after me, snapping its teeth, threatening to rip me apart piece by piece, I'll face what I have to for my family. For my guys. They're the ones who give me the courage to get off the floor. To not let the cruelty in the world deprive me of dignity. Because I'm more than what my vein offers, and I see it more clearly than ever.

After unsuccessfully trying to cut off the shackle with the knife, I pace the room, attempting to recall the few self-defense moves Diego taught me what feels like forever ago. When I realize fighting a vampire is probably the worst idea ever, I follow my chain to the wall and under the bed. The bed shifts after a few good pushes, and I spot the anchor screwed into a thick piece of wood on the wall.

"Fuck yeah!" I yell, studying the chain hooked to the anchor. This is something I can handle. I worked with my dad on repairs throughout many of the apartments in The Boxes during my short apprenticeship before he left. Every adult human is required to learn a trade regardless of their donor status, and I was following in Dad's footsteps. The first thing he did was teach me about tools and hardware. This pocket knife should work with some effort to loosen the blissfully shoddy install job hidden by the bed. I might actually manage to free myself and leave.

Before I start, I lug the mattress as far as I can across the room, shoving it against the door. By the time I drop the box spring and frame on top of it and lean the tiny empty dresser against the pile, I'm pouring sweat and out of breath. But I need to make sure I have time to react if I can't get the screws undone in time. I need a moment to brace myself to fight.

The sun blazes streams of light across the room as it trails through the sky. My fingers ache from twisting and turning the knife into the obnoxiously long screws to loosen them from the wood plank. A thud sounds from outside the room, and I rush as fast as I can to unscrew the anchor. I break four nails in the process, and my palm bleeds from being rubbed raw.

More noise sounds out on the other side of the door, and I end up kicking the last screw with my bare heel until it pops free, releasing the anchor. Scrambling to my feet, I wind up the short chain around my good hand and head to the window. If the old woman wasn't responsible for my being here, I'd thank her for the unintentional direction her act of mercy led me by giving me the knife. Now, I'll just remember that if the guys go after her and Laurel, so I can return the favor.

I mess with the window lock, my fingers begging me to just stop using them. They're useless at this point. Instead of hurting my hands even more, I yank down the heavy curtain from the rod, hold it under my arm, and use the chain to smash through the non-tinted window of the obviously human home. A screeching alarm goes off, surprising me. Someone bangs on the door, shoving at the haphazard furniture I piled in front of it. I use the curtain to swipe away the remaining glass and drop it over the pieces to protect my bare feet the best I can as I swing each of my legs over to drop only a few feet to the ground.

Voices yell through the air, and something crashes inside. I don't stop to look behind me, running the best I can through the dry vegetation outside the small house surrounded by the tall trees of the Divinity Estate hillside.

The heavy chain around my ankle makes it hard to move, but I force myself to keep going, running up the hill instead of down in fear of losing my way in the wilderness. With the voices still yelling out, I don't want to risk circling the property in search of the road that'll take me down to the beach if that's even the side I'm on. I'd rather trek back up to where I know I'll eventually come to the estate. My guys can find me faster that way, even if I don't make it to the top by the time the sun sets.

I lose track of time, my body complaining the harder I push myself. My bleeding legs burn worse than ever, and I now hate the dresses I've grown fond of. Gasping, I lean against a tall tree, using the trunk to stop from giving into my body's need to plop down and rest. Sweat drips down my face, my legs covered in dirt and scratches. My dry mouth craves something to drink, my throat burning along with my skin from staying in the sunlight cutting through the trees like Diego instructed instead of the shade.

I try my best not to think of my guys—about Austin. He looked so defenseless cowering and yelling in the sun. I pray Kingston and Diego managed to get to him even if they couldn't get to me. The one thing that stops me from breaking down is my last conversation with Austin about sunlight and how vampires don't explode. But I still can't imagine too much exposure to be good. What if they're too injured come nightfall? What if they can't regenerate?

A whistle sounds through the air. "Over here!"

Panic twists my stomach, and I practically throw myself from the tree to run again. A heavy body crashes into me, knocking me into the dirt. I scream, swinging my hand with the chain out, clocking the unfamiliar man in the side of the head. He roars, falling off me, and I scramble away from him.

My feet fly out from under me, and I land hard on my stomach. Dirt fills my mouth, my skin screaming as I'm ripped back by the chain around my ankle. The man drags me toward him with blood pouring from his nose and mouth. He bares his teeth at me, one chipped.

"Fucking bitch!" he screams, sinking his callused fingers into my shoulders. "I'm going to mess you up."

I squeeze my eyes shut, bracing for his heavy fist to collide with my face.

"Rich, watch it. Katherine will rip your neck open. We have to be discreet. No blood. The girl's left a trail already, and we can't have this landing back on Katherine. It's gotta stay directed at Orlando."

Katherine? The name tickles my memory, and the beautiful vampire from the Blood Match Center comes to my mind. Did I offend her so much by accidentally calling her a beast that she's gone out of her way to torment me? But who the hell is Orlando and why do they intend to blame him?

I don't stop to ask.

Jerking my fist up, I punch the man on top of me in the throat. His weight falls off me, and I rip the chain as hard as I can away from the new guy, scrambling to close the space to me. He shoves his fingers into his mouth, releasing a whistle. But I don't stop crab-walking. I get as much space as I can until I manage to rip my chain from his hands to pull it the rest of the way to me.

The other guy, the one New Guy called Rich, stumbles to his feet. They each focus their attention on me, and New Guy whistles again. I half expect an army of humans to get to me, but the only noise I can hear comes from the vegetation crunching and cracking from the two men not doing much better than I am trying to ascend the steep terrain.

"Come on, girl," New Guy calls out. "Give up already. Sundown's coming and your keepers will never get to you before Ms. Katherine does. You're only gonna wear yourself out and make us carry you all the way back."

"Fuck off, assholes," I say, grabbing at the tree trunks, pulling myself up the sections of untouched hillside.

Sweat pours down my face, soaking my hoodie. The heavy fabric clings to me over my dress, being my only saving grace from the cuts and bruises my hands, legs, and feet suffer from. I push on, my body screaming to give up while my brain demands that I better get my shit together and hustle or I'll die.

The top of the steep incline disappears. Using my hands to pull me the rest of the way, I make it to the top, nearly eating shit on the black paved road I land on. Pain swallows me, stealing my breath away. It's like the moment I hit the ground, I can't get back up again. My body's had enough. My arms shake, trying to summon the last bit of strength to get back to my feet, but someone grabs my ankle, yanking me back down.

"All right, bitch," Rich says, scowling at me. "I don't care about a fucking blood trail. Get over here. I'm going to knock all your damn teeth out. Katherine doesn't need you pretty for what she wants."

He drags me toward him by my legs and flips me over, spitting in my face. His fingers clench the front of my sweatshirt, holding me still. Raising his other arm, he balls his hand into a fist and aims it at my face.

The pure evil of his stare snaps something inside me. I refuse to close my eyes and look away. I refuse to let him see me cower in fear. Because I'm not afraid of him. I'm pissed off. Clawing at the dirt off the side of the road, I scoop up a handful and throw it in his eyes. He hollers, ramming his fist down, but it misses me by inches and collides into the edge of the pavement.

An ear piercing holler rings out through the air, and it takes me a second to realize it doesn't belong to Rich. It belongs to New Guy, who hasn't made it all the way up the steep terrain. Rich swears, shaking his hand out, swiveling to look behind him. In that moment, I reach for my pocket knife and shove it into his stomach and push him back. He topples down the hillside, his body slamming into a tree, his screams cutting off at the force.

I gasp deep breaths, my head spinning, my mind trying to process what I did. How I stabbed a man and pushed him down the hill. How I'm not even sorry about it. Rustling noises from below draw my attention from trying to stop myself from throwing up and to the shadow moving in the tree. Rich groans, attempting to get to his knees.

But he doesn't make it far. I watch in shock as his body is dragged from the ground and hoisted into the air. His screams cut off as his body falls to the dry vegetation, his head dripping blood while hovering midair.

"Holy shit balls. Fuck," I say, my body relenting to my brain's command to keep moving.

Within the shade of a tree stands the familiar vampire from my dreams with the intense blue eyes, now flashing silver at me, waiting for the last sliver of sunshine to disappear into the horizon. He flips Rich's head over, running his tongue over the man's severed neck, and then smiles at me.

I screech and get to my feet, rushing up the road and away from the familiar vampire—the one I'm pretty sure is named Orlando—staying in the sun where it's safe. If only it didn't sink so quickly into the horizon.

In a few minutes, he'll come for me, and there won't be anything I can do.

23

Loyal

I CLUTCH THE POCKET KNIFE in one hand and the chain in the other, hobbling as fast as I can up the road. The closer I get to the estate, the higher my chances of my guys getting to me first. It's all I can hope for at this point.

"I'm on the road!" I shout, risking the whole hillside hearing me. But I don't have a choice. There's nowhere to hide, and I hope if I yell loud enough, my guys will know where I am. "Orlando is after me. He's here. He's going to take me the moment the sun—"

A hard body collides into me, knocking me off the road

and into the scratchy dead grass off the hillside. I realize my mistake the second the air whooshes out of me and the pretty vampire with sparkling earrings and ruby lips flashes her fangs at me. I was too busy trying to get up the hillside that I didn't pay enough attention to the shadows crossing the road from the trees.

I shove my hand up and press it against the chest of the woman I recognize to be Katherine, stopping her from sinking her teeth into me. She reacts to my fighting, snatching my arm by the wrist and twisting it so quickly that I don't have a chance to fight before pain explodes in my arm. I scream, tears bursting in my eyes from a pain so intense I can't even manage to see clearly.

Katherine shoves her hand to my mouth, stifling the shrieking noise ringing through the air loud enough that I'm sure even the shadow vampires in Dark Terrace Ranch heard. Her head jerks to the side, and she listens to something I can't hear.

Yanking me up, her quick movements blur the world. I can't gather any sense of direction. I can barely hold onto my consciousness as my body slackens in her grip, her sharp nails puncturing my back hard enough to draw my focus from the pain in my wrist for a split second to take a gulping breath.

"Orlando wants to hear you beg him to bite you, but I can't wait to hear you scream and beg for me not to," Katherine says, humming in my ear.

I groan, unable to get my tongue to do anything other than

lick my dry lips, cracked from the chill of the air and the direct sunlight I've been trudging through all day. I might've been better off staying with the hillside assholes. At least then I'd have the strength to fight. To do something more than cry and scream.

My back slams into the dirt so hard that I can't even manage to make a sound. I must black out for a moment because when I open my eyes, I'm sheltered under an open barn surrounded by the black and brown cows not even moving from their spots. Twilight descends and the last rays of light disappear from the sky. If I can hang on for another minute, I know my guys will find me. They'll rip Katherine apart piece by piece on my behalf. I just have to make noise. Do something they can hear.

I open my mouth to try to scream, but Katherine shoves the sleeve of my sweatshirt in my mouth. I can't recall her taking it off me, but now I gag on the filthy fabric as she stops me from doing the only thing I can to save myself.

She leans into me, inhaling a long breath near my ear. "Make a sound again, and I'll bite your tongue off. Struggle, and I'll break your legs. But if you're a good little bitch, I might let you enjoy it as I tear you apart like your masters did my brother. To think I almost matched with you, but he begged me to retract my application after he sipped your blood. I never did get a taste."

Her admission only has seconds to swirl through my mind before her teeth graze my throat, stinging my skin as they scratch from my earlobe to my collarbone. I can't stop the uncontrollable whimper from escaping my lips.

Latching her fingers to my chin, she grips my face and tugs the hoodie from my mouth. She uses her free hand to pry my jaw apart, using her nails to pinch my tongue. Panic crashes through me in a wave. I thrash beneath her, trying to shove her off, but she overpowers me. I feel around the ground for anything I can use to protect myself, my fingers grazing over the cool metal of the pocket knife that must've fallen from my sweatshirt. I knick myself on the blade, causing Katherine to freeze, her nostril's flaring.

I jerk my hand up in desperation, attempting to stab her, but she snakes her fingers around my hand, closing her hand so tightly that my whole body screams in pain. She slowly crushes the bones in my fingers, a sadistic smile lighting her face. She soaks up my pain, not even trying to muffle my screams anymore.

I see the shadow before she does. One second she's on top of me and in the next, she dangles off the ground, flailing and swiping her nails, attempting to attack the force holding her back.

I don't even know how I manage, but I roll on my stomach and pull myself to my feet with my aching hand, thankfully the opposite of my screaming wrist. I wobble on my feet, meeting the blue eyes of Orlando shining from over Katherine's shoulder.

"My lover, you knew she was soon-to-be mine," the vampire says, kissing her throat. "I told you I'd let you have a taste."

She screeches, kicking her legs. "Those bastards killed Roger for her. I want her to suffer. I need more than a taste. I need her dead."

"He deserved it!" I yell, stumbling forward, clutching the pocket knife in my hand.

Orlando only laughs, holding Katherine away from him. I jerk my hand forward, sinking the pocket knife into her stomach. And I don't stop. I can't stop. I shove it in over and over again, feeling her warm blood coat my hand as something dark comes over me, all the pain and anguish I've felt over my entire life exploding from me at once.

Katherine shrieks, her voice ripping through the air. Orlando continues to laugh until I stagger away, smearing blood across everything I touch. A thud sounds out from behind me, and Orlando drops Katherine to the dirt. I scream out, holding my good hand up, knowing that he's going to take me away.

He grips my face in his hands, kissing me softly to stifle my screams. "My precious Jewel. You're better than I could hope for. Your debt very well could lead to a vow if you continue to surprise me."

Tears burn my eyes. "Please, the Divines will pay for my debt. There has to be something."

He purrs from deep in his throat. "How nice of you to remember so I don't have to explain. I must be wearing on you, my lovely. And I truly did want you. But there's still time to consider your offer, I suppose. I see where you inherited your fight from. We can talk more about that later. Your keepers are getting closer, and I want you to forget about me except in your dreams. And thank you for helping me with Katherine. Those not loyal deserve such a fate."

He disappears, leaving me in the open barn with Katherine squirming on the floor, attempting to get to her feet. I yelp, scrambling back as she continues to crawl her way toward me, silver flashing in her eyes, her fangs extended. The beauty she encapsulated before now gone with the evil scrunching her face, her ashen skin sinking in around her eyes.

I hobble away, the edges of my vision darkening.

And then Katherine's up, lumbering toward me still faster than I can move.

Raising my hands to protect myself, I scream out with the movement of my arm, jostling my bent wrist. Katherine throws herself at me, knocking me back, her fangs sinking into my shoulder.

"No!" a masculine voice yells.

Blood splatters across my face, and I lie frozen as my mind, body, and blood come together to rip Katherine apart. Austin's at my side first, his still-blistered hands grazing over my face and trailing to my shoulder. He doesn't touch me while inspecting every inch of my bruised and broken body, his chest heaving, his eyes darting wildly around. His fangs extend in fury that doesn't scare me. It makes me feel safe if anything.

"Jewel, hang on," he whispers. "We're going to get you home."

I close my eyes, my head pounding. If I could gather my strength to lift my arm to touch Austin's face I would. But my body denies me the comfort and refuses even to try. Everything hurts. I just want to sleep, but I'm afraid. If I sleep, I'll dream of him—of Orlando. His manipulation failed to erase my mind. He underestimated me. He underestimated my guys.

Cool hands touch my face. "Babe? Babe, you gotta keep your eyes open. Please try for me."

No matter how hard I try to look, I can't.

"Give her here," Diego says. He intakes a sharp breath, and I think he holds me. I can't be sure. I can't feel anything, tingles running through my limbs and to my torso. "She bit her. Do you think—?"

"I can't be sure yet," Austin says, cutting him off. "We're lucky she's alive."

"We've failed her," Kingston whispers. "We're fucking useless. How could we let this happen? Half the staff against us. Fuck. We breached the contract. You know what—"

"There might not be a contract to breach," Diego says. "If Katherine—"

I groan, begging my mouth to open up to talk. My heart aches worse than my body hearing their hushed conversation. I want so badly to tell them that this wasn't their fault, and they didn't fail me. This act of revenge was unwarranted. I don't care if my guys ripped Master Caruthers apart. The gross vampire deserved it trying to match me out from under my three perfect vampires. For threatening me. Treating me like I was property and not a person.

And Katherine... Shit balls. Orlando saved me. But not only did he save me, he also confirmed my dad is alive.

"Hey, beautiful. I know this is hard, but can you try to open your mouth. I'm going to give you more blood."

I don't have to see Diego to recognize his touch. His finger gently touches my bottom lip and sweet, warm liquid drips down my throat, combating the numbness taking over me in a wave of new tingles that make it easier for me to breathe.

Kingston carefully grasps my fingers, his hands softer than both his brothers', and his lips caress my knuckles. "Babe, I know I haven't had time to get you all warmed up and prepared, but I need to give you some of my blood too."

I smile, my lips aching at the gesture, but despite the pain, my heavy heart lightens. "Dude," I whisper.

He chuckles a moment before sucking in a deep breath. Warm liquid dribbles into my mouth bursting with a spicier flavor—like cinnamon sweetened with sugar—than Diego's fruit syrup tasting blood. A moan escapes my mouth as I swallow, the pounding in my head easing. I finally open my eyes, the edges of my vision dark and my focus blurry, but I manage to make out Kingston's form hovering over me. His lips press against my forehead, and I squeeze his hand.

Another hand touches my cheek, drawing my gaze from Kingston. Austin's fuzzy form clears, and I meet his glassy green eyes. A tear lands on Austin's cheek before trailing off to splash against mine, and he quickly smears it, using his shoulder to dry his own eyes without taking his hands from me.

I reach up and glide my finger across his damp cheek, the pain in my wrist so much better already. “I’m so happy you’re okay.” My hoarse voice barely sounds a whisper, but his lips pull from a frown and into a smile that gives me the hope to know that things will be okay.

He nods and cups my hand to his face, feeling my fingers sink into his cheek. “You have no idea how happy I am we found you. The staff—I’m so sorry, Jewel. This should’ve never happened. I just wish we could’ve got to you sooner.”

“You’re here now,” I say.

He nods. “Always, okay. This will never happen again, even if it means...” His words trail off. “Let’s not worry about it now. I need to give you a little more blood, if that’s okay. I know it’s not how I had planned, and the side effects are—”

“I trust you,” I say, cutting off his words.

Austin doesn’t even hesitate to sink his fangs into his arm. He helps me lift my head, cradling against him, and I drink right from his arm, my body remembering exactly what it likes about Austin as his tangy, almost citrusy tasting blood coats my palette to travel down my throat.

Before my mouth gets carried away, he gently pulls back and replaces his arm with his lips, kissing me softly, so tenderly like his lips will heal every inch of me if I allow them to explore. I sink against him, hugging him close. I already feel so much better, the throbbing in my wrist now a dull ache.

“I’m sorry. I should’ve asked,” he whispers.

I shake my head, rubbing my nose to his. "I'm tired of that rule."

He chuckles and kisses me again. "Me too."

"Damn straight," Kingston says, taking me from Austin to allow him to get up without jostling me. "I mean, if it applies to me as well."

I barely get a nod in before he presses his lips to mine, sending a wave of everything good he summons in my body to the surface. He gently touches my face, kissing me long enough to crave more without setting me off on a wave of blood-induced lust, all three of my guys' blood humming through me but not making me feel completely out of control.

"What? No dry humping?" Kingston asks.

I laugh and smack his shoulders. "Some other time."

He exhales an exaggerated breath. "Of course you wouldn't get my favorite side effect with my blood. It's a good thing you don't need it for me to drive you wild."

Kingston hands me to Diego, who studies my face for a long moment in anticipation, waiting for me to react like the other times before. I reach up and glide my finger over his lips until he gives me the smile I love seeing on his handsome face.

"What? No kisses?" I tease.

He bows his head to meet my lips, gently kissing me like he did on our first night together. "I think our blood balances out the side effects."

"Makes sense," Austin says. "I just wasn't sure and didn't want to risk it."

"Thank God you did now," I say, my voice growing stronger by the second. "Because I thought I was going to die. I was so scared I would never see you guys again. Katherine set it up to take me not only from you but from Orlando. I think she was using him to get close because of the blood debt."

Kingston holds my hand. "You got his name? I knew you were awesome, babe. But you are fucking badass. I also can't believe you managed to stab Katherine."

Diego nods. "Over forty-two times."

"Her intestines—" Austin snaps his mouth shut. "Doesn't matter. How about we get you home and finish talking there? You're still healing."

"I've never wanted anything more in my life than to take care of you, babe," Kingston says.

Diego smirks. "And cuddle you."

"Feed you too," Austin adds.

Kingston bumps Diego's shoulder. "Dibs on the bathing with you, babe."

I raise an eyebrow. "Eating first and then cuddles."

Kingston sighs.

"And then the bath. But only because I've never had one. I expect tons of bubbles like the old movies." I laugh as I say it, but heat crawls up my neck at the thought.

"You'll get the candles and banging music, too."

I groan. "Fuck. Me."

"Whatever you want, babe."

24

Breach in Contract

KINGSTON PLAYS WITH MY DAMP hair, gently combing his fingers through my tresses over and over again. I lean against his chest, propping up the biggest bowl of ice cream in the existence of the entire universe. I don't know how Austin manages to pull things off, but it's like he knows exactly what I need, and this sweet caramel-drenched vanilla ice cream makes me feel better.

"You're positive?" Diego asks Austin in the hallway. "They're taking longer than anything else to heal."

"Her blood work looks normal, even with the amount of

our blood she consumed. If Katherine did inject her with her venom, she either wasn't compatible, our blood worked as an anti-venom, or Jewel's immune."

"Immune? No one's immune," Kingston says from behind me.

I shift in his arms and frown at him. "If you're going to discuss my health, at least talk to me and not about me while I'm sitting right here."

The door to Kingston's room flies open, and Austin appears by my side before I can even set my bowl of ice cream down. He searches my face without a word, tilting his head, narrowing his eyes.

"Kingston, did she hear you?" Austin asks, his intense gaze turning to his brother behind me.

"There's no way," he says.

"Guys," Diego says, drawing their attention from each other. I follow their gaze to Diego strolling closer. "She didn't hear only you, Kingston. She heard all of us, right beautiful?"

"Well, yeah. You're not exactly being quiet," I say.

"Jewel, look at me," Austin says.

I turn my gaze to him. "What?"

He leans closer. "Watch my lips."

"Okay."

"You shouldn't be able to hear us right now."

I gasp, covering my mouth. "Holy shit balls! Your mouth wasn't even moving. You were doing that stupid whisper thing I can't hear." I twist and backhand Kingston's arm because he's closest. "You said you wouldn't do that anymore."

"Looks like we might not be able to," Austin says.

He sits on one side of the bed, and Diego perches on the other, the mattress not even moving under their weight. I absently grab my mixing bowl sized amount of ice cream and start shoveling it in my mouth. Something about the weight of their gazes makes me nervous, and all I want to do is consume every last bit of way too much ice cream so I don't have to talk.

"I need you to think back today," Austin says. "I know you already told us, and I know you don't want to go over things again, but I think it'll help to repeat it to make sure you didn't miss anything. Did Orlando do anything weird when he helped you? Give you his blood too? What about Katherine? You were gone all day."

I sigh. "I didn't forget anything. Laurel had some sort of grudge against Kingston, so she agreed to help Katherine. She offered her something that was apparently worth it."

"It's a long story, babe," Kinston says. "I had no idea that Laurel would resent me so much."

"You applied to match with her," I say curtly, surprised by the mixture of jealousy and annoyance coursing through me the more I think about it. "And then you thought it was a good idea to allow her into our rooms. If I had known, I would've told you that she was purposely hostile to me. I thought she was mad because you all went off on the staff when I didn't alert security of my whereabouts."

Austin whacks Kingston. "See, I told you the blood spill

wasn't an accident."

"Who knew someone could hate me for saving her life. I tried to match with her only because I saw the lineup who applied."

"And you purposely got both of you disqualified," Diego says. "She wanted to try to match with Giorgio."

"Which was impossible. She'd have matched with—"

I shove a spoonful of ice cream into Kingston's mouth, cutting off his words before he and Diego get into it. I regret bringing it up, because with the way Laurel acted, I thought she might've liked Kingston. And maybe she did. I'll never know. As much as I'm pissed off she did what she did, I'm grateful for the old woman, who Austin said was definitely her mother, and her act of mercy that helped me save my life.

Kingston puffs out his cheeks and spits the ice cream into his hand. He disappears from behind me for a second and returns with a glass of blood. He dares me to watch him. I accept his challenge, and he watches me watch him tip the glass and down it in one long swallow.

"So, you don't like ice cream?" I ask.

He sucks in his bottom lip, hiding all evidence of the blood coating his mouth. "How would you like it if I stuck a spoonful of this rather bland gen. pop. blood into your pretty little mouth?"

"It probably tastes better than the food in Dark Terrace Ranch," I say, pursing my lips.

"I swear, Kingston, if this little play fight turns into Jewel ripping your clothes off—"

I whip my head to glare at Diego. "Seriously?"

He palms his forehead. "Shit. I forgot you could hear me."

Scooping up a pillow, I toss it at his head. He lets it hit him and then hugs it to his chest. The guys stare at each other, this time really only conversing with their eyes. Worry lines steal away the smiles I need, so I do the only thing I can think of.

Snatching the glass away from Kingston, I bring it up to my lips and sniff. "What does it even mean? What do you think is wrong with me?"

The guys freeze, all their gazes locking onto me and the glass with less than a mouthful of liquid in it.

I sniff it again, trying not to laugh when I say, "Bland? It smells delicious. Damn. You must have incredibly high standards. I bet it tastes better than all of your bloods."

Austin swears.

Diego's eyes widen.

Kingston pales.

Tipping my head back, I release a loud laugh, tossing the glass back to Kingston. Silence greets my laughter, and I meet three serious gazes. I think I might've gone too far with the joking. I was trying to make them laugh.

"I was kidding, jeez. That weird smelling gen. pop. blood could never taste as good as any of you." I frown. "That sounds terrible saying the words out loud."

"Babe." Kingston tightens his lips, narrowing his eyes.

"Not cool."

"Sorry, Kingston. If I can't laugh about this whole messed up day then I'm going to break down and cry." The second the words flee my mouth tears escape my eyes. I thought I was okay. I thought that being home in the safety of my three vampire matches would distract me from the fact that I guaranteed one man's death today while ensuring the end of one of five female vampires in the area. Not to mention that I have a looming blood debt. Or that my dad is still alive and Orlando is using every opportunity he gets to torture me for a reason I don't understand. Maybe because he just likes to, maybe because of my guys, either way, I'm afraid I'll soon find out.

"Come here, beautiful," Diego says, holding open his arms. "I know today was hell, but it's over, and we're going to do what we can to make sure you're always safe."

Kingston grabs my hand. "Yeah, babe. I'm sorry. I didn't mean to snap at you. I just—forgive me."

Austin holds my other hand. "And I don't want you to worry about your health. You're fine. Your blood work is normal. We're just trying to figure out—"

"If I'm turning into a vampire?"

He tightens his jaw. "Yeah."

"I thought you weren't contagious," I say. "I've seen someone survive a bite before. And Kingston sort of bit me the first day we met."

"Bites are usually fine, but the one Katherine gave you is taking longer to heal than it should. We think she might have released her venom. It's why humans called our evolution a plague. The first new vampires didn't realize they could control the venom. People who weren't killed, changed."

I blink at his revelation. "Shit." I don't know what else to say. "What does that mean for me?"

"It's a breach in the Blood Match contract if you're sired by someone else. Your family loses their benefits. You..."

"End up in the shadows, right? Because I have nothing."

Diego hugs me tighter. "We'd never let that happen. Ever. We weren't kidding about wanting to be with you. If it comes down to it, we'll—"

"It's not going to come down to it," Austin says. "I think this will pass in a few days."

I nod. "A few days. I can manage."

"And when it does." Kingston's soft voice draws my attention. "You should know that we were the ones who actually breached your contract. We didn't protect you."

I frown. "You saved me, though."

They all look at each other with sullen faces, their sadness stealing the breath out of me. I can't stand it that they blame themselves. I don't care if a monster like Katherine feels her decision was justified or that Laurel held a grudge because she couldn't see that her life was in danger. My guys did all that they could to see to it I was safe. I won't let them carry the blame.

"You protected me to your best abilities. None of us could have known that some disgruntled beast managed to get through to the staff," I say.

"Jewel," Kingston says. "You don't have to worry about what a breach on our part means for you."

"But my family—"

"Can't have their benefits revoked. And you..." Kingston brings my hand to his cheek. "You can walk away from the Blood Match Program and join them in Haven Springs. You can have a life with your family."

"What?" I say, my heart racing, my eyes blurring with tears. "I don't understand."

"You can file the paperwork that we breached your contract by not providing an environment that kept you away from other vampires not on the contract," Austin says. "You can reunite with your family by the end of the week."

I sit in shock, the information circling through my mind, replaying over and over again. All it takes is filing one little form, and I get to live in Haven Springs. No more blood draws. No more worrying about whether or not they're okay.

But that would mean...

"What about you?" I ask, looking each of them in the eyes.

"We lose the right to re-match," Kingston says. "Not that I'd ever want to. You're my perfect match, babe."

"All of ours," Austin says.

Diego rests his chin on my neck. "That won't change."

I swallow the burning in my throat, a million thoughts rushing through my mind. Could I do it? Should I do it? The thought of leaving Diego, Austin, and Kingston opens up a hole in my heart that screams at me not to put it through such agony. Because they're right. They're my perfect matches, and without them, I don't know if I could ever feel like myself again. Like Jewel Divine. Because Jewel Jordan, the scared girl from Dark Terrace Ranch disappeared. She's long gone. She never even looked back.

And I can't now.

"And this won't either," I say. "I'm not leaving."

"You have no idea how much that means to me," Austin says. "Because you're everything to me."

"To all of us," Kingston and Diego say together.

"You're my mind, Diego," I say, turning to meet his gray eyes. I hug him, just soaking in everything he ignites in me for a long moment. Scooting to Kingston, I relish his closeness as he envelops me in his arms. "And you're my damn sexy body, dude."

He chuckles and tucks my hair behind my ear, "And your damn sexy body is mine."

I laugh, touching his shoulder and then meet Austin's beautiful green eyes. "And you're more than just my blood. You're what gives me life. I can't—no, I won't—imagine a life without you three."

"Good, because we don't want that, beautiful. Ever," Diego says. "We will figure all this out. Promise."

Kingston glances at his brothers. "And we'll never fail you again, babe."

"We'll take care of the blood debt stalker and negotiate

how to pay your dad's debt so you never have to worry," Austin adds.

I nod. "Together, right? No more whispering or plotting without me."

They nod, and Diego says, "Together. All of us."

Hugging my arms around the three of them, I relish in how safe and perfect it feels, knowing that they were right. That this can work. "Exactly how it should be."

Epilogue

Perfect Match

A DEEP MOAN STARTLES ME awake. I gasp, scrambling to sit up to make sense of where I am. Austin slides his arms around me, snuggling me close. He rubs my back until I shudder, my whole body humming from the memory of my dream.

"Damn, babe. That sounded like some nightmare," Kingston says, drawing my attention to his dark eyes only lit by the city lights around us. "If only you'd let me figure out how to recreate a moan like that when you're awake."

My cheeks burn at the thought.

Diego knocks his fist into Kingston's arm, making him

swerve the car a little. Turning in the front passenger's seat, he meets my gaze. "You okay, beautiful? I can try to help you again."

I reach out my hand and squeeze his shoulder. "Nope, I'm good. It wasn't a nightmare. It was a pretty great dream actually."

"About me, right?" Kingston asks, shifting to peek at me.

I smirk at him. "Nice try, dude."

Austin chuckles. "We won't blame you, Jewel. At least in your dreams he doesn't have to actually be involved."

Kingston jerks the wheel, sending Austin sliding into the other door while I remain strapped in place. Austin laughs again, buckling himself in the middle and leans over to kiss me. I run my fingers through his blond hair, pulling him closer, letting him taste the sweetness of my lips from the chocolates he surprised me with when we got in the car.

Diego clears his throat. "We'll be there in five. Do you remember what we told you, beautiful?"

I slowly ease away from Austin to lean toward the middle to meet his gaze. The last few days have been nothing short of amazing not having to leave the comfort of the Divinity Estate, but all three of them have been called to the Blood Match Center to process this week's matching applications.

"Don't call anyone a beast," I say, laughing at my own joke. Because if I can't laugh about Katherine or what she put me through, I start bawling my eyes out.

Kingston reaches back without looking away from the road

and rests his hand on my knee. "Definitely not. What else?"

I appreciate that none of them point out how awful my joke is. "If Mitchell tries to break into my mind, go with it."

"That goes for anyone," Diego says. "It's important you tell them what they want to hear. We don't want anyone to know that you can't be manipulated."

"Or that you can hear their conversations across the room," Austin adds. "If someone finds out you've been bitten and injected with venom, they'll try to void our contract and take you from us, especially since you haven't and won't completely change."

"You hope," Kingston says.

Diego licks his lips. "We all hope."

I swallow, my anxiety tightening my chest, making it hard to breathe. All three of their heartbeats pick up speed with mine, and I wish I couldn't hear them. I wish that the puncture marks on my shoulder would finish healing already, and that my body would return to what it used to be. But what I'm really afraid of is that it won't. According to Austin's daily blood work, I'm still human despite the weird side effects of my now perfect skin, excellent hearing, and what all three declared a sudden shift in my already delicious blood.

"I should've just stayed home," I say like it was even an option. If I'd let them, they'd probably follow me into the damn bathroom at this point. But I don't mind much. Privacy isn't a thing even though we pretend it is. They also lost their privacy with my super hearing.

"It's going to be fine, beautiful. You're going to shadow Kingston, and he'll take good care of you."

"The best care," Kingston says, maneuvering the car onto the sidewalk and right next to the steps of the Blood Match Center.

I peer around at the glittering towers of Dark Terrace Ranch, a small, super tiny part of me missing living here with my family. I manage to suppress all the bad things that came with living in The Boxes as to not ruin the memories I struggle to hold onto of the girl I was before.

"Keep your head up, meet everyone's eyes who look at you, and show them what a badass perfect Blood Match you are, babe," Kingston says.

I nod and let him pull me from the car. "Let's just get this over with. All I want is to go home and see if my dream might come true."

All three of them laugh, surrounding me with their muscular bodies so none of the shadow dwellers even get a chance to glimpse me. I never thought I'd feel like royalty, but the three heirs of the Divine legacy sure feel like my princes.

We enter the lobby, and I do what Kingston instructed and keep my head high. He holds me by my waist, putting pressure on the curve of my hip with his fingers, making me wish we could run to the elevator and hide in his office.

Ms. Sybil sits behind the counter, tapping away at her digital keyboard until Kingston leans over to glance at her computer screen. She tips her head back and smiles at him and then offers me one just as big.

"Oh, Ms. Divine, what a nice surprise," she says. "I was hoping the misters would bring you back."

I glance at Kingston in my peripheral vision. He bares his bottom teeth at me in an awkward smile. I know he or one of his brothers manipulated her mind to be nice to me. She was pretty rude on the day of my matching until the end.

"I try not to let them make a habit out of it," I say, keeping my eyes on Kingston.

She chuckles. "Oh, but everyone loves you. Did you know our client applications have tripled over the last week? I think the community finally understands what we've been trying to accomplish with our Blood Match Program. Your old companion had sixteen applicants."

I blanch, frowning. "Wait, Brayla matched already?"

"Yes, Ms. Divine. Today. She's still in the building, actually. Mr. Ortega arranged some accommodations for the night until he could retrieve her."

"Why didn't you tell me?" I ask Kingston. "I wanted to be here for it."

His jaw tightens, and he glances over his shoulder. "She wasn't scheduled until tomorrow."

"One of the applicants insisted we move her appointment. He paid extra to try. Which worked out lovely for him since he was an astounding eighty-nine percent match. Nearly as good as you, Ms. Divine."

"I need to see her," I tell Ms. Sybil. "What room?"

She pouts her bottom lip. "I'm sorry, Ms. Divine. That information is classified and can only be given with permission from Ms. Ortega's Blood Match."

Kingston releases a low growl from his throat, getting into Ms. Sybil's face. His eyes flash silver as he captures her in his gaze. "Tell me what room, please."

"Pardon me," a familiar voice says from my right, nearly making me jump out of my skin. "I'm here to pick up my beautiful match. Brayla Ortega."

Kingston tightens his hold on me, slightly tugging me away from the man at the counter next to me. It takes everything in me not to react to the sight of my stalker vampire leaning his elbows on the counter, smiling at Ms. Sybil without even looking at us.

Austin and Diego come up to me and Kingston, flanking our sides. I swallow, my heart betraying me by picking up speed. As the man turns around, I take an automatic step away but hit my back against Austin. The elevator dings, the sound startling me.

"Jewel!" Brayla practically screeches the second she sees me.

The whole room of vampires turns in our direction, and I cringe under their unwanted scrutiny. She rushes across the lobby, her face beaming. I half expect her to tackle me with a hug, but she shifts her attention from me to my stalker vampire, now standing a foot away, opening his arms.

"Orlando!" she squeals, throwing her arms around the vampire who's been plaguing my nightmares. "You said you were going to be late, but I'm so happy you're not. Do you know the Divines?"

Orlando slowly turns his attention toward us, his eyes capturing mine in their startling blue gaze. My heart sinks into my stomach, fear stealing my breath. If Kingston wasn't holding me up, I'd have already landed on my knees.

Orlando extends his hand to Kingston first. "I haven't, but I've always heard great things." His words dig into me, laced with something dark and dangerous despite their nicety.

Kingston remains as expressionless as Austin and Diego. "Pleasure. Congratulations on finding your perfect match."

"Looks like your luck rubbed off on me, Jewel," Brayla says, grinning at the vampire, though his gaze doesn't avert from mine.

"Precious Jewel," Orlando says, parting his lips in a smile. "What a lovely name."

I drop my gaze to the tile. "Thank you, sir."

"It's my honor. Now, if you'll excuse us, we must be going. Brayla's such a delight. I just can't wait to get her home. She'll be cared for well. I promise."

Brayla engulfs me in a hug, kissing both my cheeks, looking so beautiful in her white dress. I stand frozen in shock, blinking my eyes to stop them from crying. I don't even get to muster a goodbye as Orlando twines his fingers with my best friend's, gives all three of my matches handshakes, and disappears out the front door.

I suck in a shuddering breath. "We have to—"

Kingston cuts my words off with a kiss, the world blurring around me. I don't even have a chance to react before I find myself sitting on a leather couch in a sleek, expensive looking office. Austin and Diego kneel in front of me while Kingston cradles me in his lap, kissing the tears spilling from my eyes, doing his best to rub away the convulsions pulsing through me.

"Why didn't you do anything?" I ask, burying my face into Kingston's chest to muffle my sob. "He's going to kill her."

"We couldn't react," Kingston says. "He doesn't know we know and the room was watching."

"I don't care!" I scream.

Pushing away from him, I get to my feet and pad across the room and to his office door. Austin blocks my way, opening his arms to beg me to fall into them. I don't. I try to push past him to hook my fingers on the handle, but it doesn't open. I have to activate the lock, and I'm pretty sure my handprint won't cut it.

"Let me out," I demand. "If you won't do anything, I will."

Austin stands close without touching me. "Jewel, please. You can't just go storming out of here. This isn't the estate."

"You remember what happened last time," Diego adds.

"How could I forget?" I shout, hugging myself to turn away from them. "But that was just one day. Orlando has her for the rest of her life. I can't do nothing."

"And you won't," Kingston says. "We won't. But we have to think things through. We have to plan. I'm not allowing you to thrust yourself into danger."

"*Allowing* me?"

He sighs, closes the distance, and picks me off my feet. I automatically wrap my legs around his waist to support myself as he spins me back toward the couch to sit with me on his lap. Leaning forward, Kingston rests his head to mine, just breathing quick breaths until they slow along with his racing heart.

"I'm sorry. That came out wrong, babe," he whispers. "Forgive me?"

Slowly, I nod my head and give into his pouty lips, kissing him a few times. "I hate this."

"I know, beautiful," Diego says from next to me. "We'll fix this. Brayla will be okay. It might feel like the world is ending, but this might be a good thing."

"A good thing? Are you shitting me?" I ask.

"He's gotten bold. We can now find out his address," he says.

I crinkle my brows. "I thought all that was confidential."

"It is," Austin says, taking my hand. "But when have the rules stopped us?"

"Seriously, babe? It's like you don't even know me," Kingston says, teasing me.

"Oh, I know you, Rule Breaker," I say, giving into his smirk to smile at him. "And I'm sorry for overreacting. It's just been—"

Kingston cuts me off with another kiss. "It'll get better."

"This will help us find your dad and take care of the debt. And Brayla will be okay," Diego says, resting his chin on my shoulder when I pull away from Kingston.

Austin nods. "We're going to get this asshole."

I bob my head, sliding off Kingston's lap to meet each of their gazes. "We're going to get this asshole," I repeat. "And when we do, you're going to let me do the honors of ripping him apart."

TO BE CONTINUED...

Loved *Blood Match*? Make sure to let fellow readers know by kindly leaving a review. To stay up-to-date on new and future releases, including *Blood Rebel, The Divine Vampire Heirs,* Book 2, sign up for Ginna Moran's newsletter or follow her on Amazon and BookBub. Join her Facebook Group for sneak peeks, bonus content, and fun!

Other Young Adult Series by Ginna Moran

PARANORMAL

Call of the Ocean Series

Demon Watcher Series

Demon Within Series

Destined for Dreams Series

Finding Nate Series

Going Ghostly Series

Spark of Life Series

When Souls Collide Series

REVERSE HAREM

The Divine Vampire Heirs Series

CONTEMPORARY

Falling into Fame Series

Life After Lila

Acknowledgments

THANK YOU SO MUCH TO my amazing team! Sarah and Katie, you two are invaluable, incredible, and forgive me for my back-world mouth—amazeballs and Da Bomb. Without you, this writing journey would be shit balls. ☺

A special thanks to the fabulously helpful authors from the Blurb Exchange for helping me survive blurb writing hell. And to those in AAYAA, for your endless support and feedback and advice.

Lastly a special thanks to my readers—old and new—without you, none of this would be possible. You all rock!

About Ginna Moran

GINNA MORAN IS a writer from sunny Southern California. She started writing poetry as a teenager in a spiral notebook that she still has tucked away on her desk today. Her love of writing grew after she graduated high school, and she completed her first unpublished manuscript at age eighteen.

When she realized her love of writing was her life's passion, she studied literature at Mira Costa College in Northern San Diego. Besides writing novels, she was senior editor, content manager, and image coordinator for Crescent House Publishing Inc. for four years.

Aside from Ginna's professional life, she enjoys binge watching television shows, playing pretend with her daughter, and cuddling with her dogs. Some of her favorite things include chocolate, anything that glitters, cheesy jokes, and organizing her bookshelf.

Ginna Moran loves to hear from her readers so visit her online at www.GinnaMoran.com. You can also find her on Facebook, Twitter, Instagram, and Snapchat. To stay up-to-date on new releases, sign up to her newsletter. You'll not only get exclusive access to extra stories, but you'll be able to participate in monthly giveaways!

Ginna Moran is currently hard at work on her next novel.

16642459R00201

Printed in Great Britain
by Amazon